Readings in
Social Psychology
Today

Contributing Editor, James V. McConnell
PROFESSOR OF PSYCHOLOGY, UNIVERSITY OF MICHIGAN

Readings in
Social Psychology
Today

CRM BOOKS
Del Mar, California

Contents

Introduction

A decade ago, any book of readings in the field of social psychology would surely have been oriented around psychological and sociological principles, for, in general, the late 1950s and early 1960s were the era of social *science*. That is, courses and textbooks tended to emphasize theory, to answer the question "Why?" One explained human behavior in certain theoretical terms, one drew predictive equations on the blackboard or the printed page, and for the most part, that was what social psychology was all about. The thought that some of the data gathered so painstakingly in social psychological laboratories would somehow be put to *use* in real-world situations would probably have been rejected by most textbook authors. Pure science, after all, could not sully itself with applications.

Yet the history of all scientific disciplines teaches us that applications almost always follow hard on the heels of discovery. And just as the ultimate end of knowledge about physics lies in its application to the control of the physical world, so the ultimate end of knowledge about social psychology is in its application to the influencing of human behavior.

By the beginning of the 1970s, the emphasis had switched to *social* science, that is, the gathering of information that can be of use to people in solving the often staggering problems that face them in the real world. Today, the question "How?" is as important as "Why?" This book of readings, then, taken from past issues of *Psychology Today*, is action-oriented, as the field of social psychology itself is action-oriented. True, you will find much laboratory data in these pages, but almost always the data points are aimed at real-life targets. The world is too much with us today; the ivory towers of academic life have been invaded by student activists demanding that social scientists become involved in life outside.

Of the many issues that occupy the thoughts and activities of social scientists today, four seem particularly pertinent. The first concerns the cities, the sprawling metropolises that grow larger every day. What can social psychology tell us about how to make city living more humane and less frightening? The second great issue is that of race. What have we learned about human behavior that will help us bring white and black together, that will help us change prejudice and misperception into cooperation and admiration? The third problem involves hate turned to aggression. What is to be done about riots, wars, murders, and mayhem? How close is our society to open rebellion? Who are the rebels, and what do they want? Can man's aggressive behaviors, learned or instinctual, be directed into productive rather than destructive channels? And last, but certainly not least, what about the seeming rise in deviant behavior in our society? Are we becoming a nation of drug takers who escape from the harsh realities of the outer world by plunging into the molecular mazes of inward-directed perception? Is the sexual revolution we see all about us a sign of increasing sophistication or merely a harbinger of ultimate moral decay? Have the magnificent machines man has built freed him to be creative or enslaved and dehumanized him?

"How?" questions, all of them. This book contains a great many such pointed questions, and but a few, a very few of the answers. But to ask the questions is to realize that answers can be sought. And that is what social psychology today is all about.

I
Cities, Ghettos, and Politics

When Will People Help in a Crisis?

John M. Darley and Bibb Latané

Most of America lives in cities, and it is one of the major tragedies of these times that our cities are in deep trouble. In small towns throughout the country, people still leave their houses unlocked and the keys in their cars when they park. No one living in a rural community would dream of stealing from someone else, because everyone knows everyone. Who wants to steal from people he knows? And if you stole a friend's car, where could you drive it in a small community that it wouldn't instantly be recognized? When everyone knows everyone, complex social systems are not needed to help alleviate those disasters that strike—the fire and police departments are staffed chiefly by volunteers (who never go on strike), and the welfare department consists of charitable neighbors rather than squads of social workers.

Cities are supposed to be collections of small towns, but in at least one important sense, they are not: in a rural community, everyone sees the (often rather crude) machinery of government and feels that it is available to him. In large cities, this machinery is mostly invisible, hidden away in inaccessible Kafkaesque corners. Involvement in local affairs is almost forced on the small-town citizen; the apartment dweller in New York withdraws into his own little world not so much because he wants to as because he has no ready means of participating actively in the life of his city even if he wants to. And, as John M. Darley and Bibb Latané point out, withdrawal from and lack of concern about one's fellow citizens can become a terrible habit.

Kitty Genovese is set upon by a maniac as she returns home from work at 3 A.M. Thirty-eight of her neighbors in Kew Gardens come to their windows when she cries out in terror; none comes to her assistance even though her stalker takes over half an hour to murder her. No one even so much as calls the police. She dies.

Andrew Mormille is stabbed in the stomach as he rides the A train home to Manhattan. Eleven other riders watch the seventeen-year-old boy as he bleeds to death; none comes to his assistance even though his attackers have left the car. He dies.

An eighteen-year-old switchboard operator, alone in her office in the Bronx, is raped and beaten. Escaping momentarily, she runs naked and bleeding to the street, screaming for help. A crowd of forty passersby gathers and watches as, in broad daylight, the rapist tries to drag her back upstairs; no one interferes. Finally two policemen happen by and arrest her assailant.

Eleanor Bradley trips and breaks her leg while shopping on Fifth Avenue. Dazed and in shock, she calls for help, but the hurrying stream of executives and shoppers simply parts and flows past. After forty minutes a taxi driver helps her to a doctor.

The shocking thing about these cases is that so many people failed to respond. If only one or two had ignored the victim, we might be able to understand their inaction. But when thirty-eight people, or eleven people, or hundreds of people fail to help, we become disturbed. Actually, this fact that shocks us so much is itself the clue to understanding these cases. Although it seems obvious that the more people who watch a victim in distress, the more likely someone will help, what really happens is exactly the opposite. If each member of a group of bystanders is aware that other people are also present, he will be less likely to notice the emergency, less likely to decide that it is an emergency, and less likely to act even if he thinks there is an emergency.

This is a surprising assertion—what we are saying is that the victim may actually be less likely to get help, the more people who watch his distress and are available to help. We shall discuss in detail the process through which an individual bystander must go in order to intervene, and we shall present the results of some experiments designed to show the effects of the number of onlookers on the likelihood of intervention.

Since we started research on bystander responses to emergencies, we have heard many explanations for the lack of intervention. "I would assign this to the effect of the megapolis in which we live, which makes closeness very difficult and leads to the alienation of the individual from the group," contributed a psychoanalyst. "A disaster syndrome," explained a sociologist, "that shook the sense of safety and sureness of the individuals involved and caused psychological withdrawal from the event by ignoring it." "Apathy," claimed others. "Indifference." "The gratification of unconscious sadistic impulses." "Lack of concern for our fellow men." "The Cold Society." All of these analyses of the person who fails to help share one characteristic; they set the indifferent witness apart from the rest of us as a different kind of person. Certainly not one of us who reads about these incidents in horror is apathetic, alienated, or depersonalized. Certainly not one of us enjoys gratifying his sadistic impulses by watching others suffer. These terrifying cases in which people fail to help others certainly have no personal implications for us. That is, we might decide not to ride subways anymore, or that New York isn't even "a nice place to visit," or "there ought to be a law" against apathy, but we need not feel guilty, or reexamine ourselves.

Looking more closely at published descriptions of the behavior of witnesses to these incidents, the people involved begin to look a little less inhuman and a lot more like the rest of us. Although it is unquestionably true that the witnesses in the incidents above did nothing to save the victims, apathy, indifference, and unconcern are not entirely accurate descriptions of their reactions. The thirty-eight witnesses of Kitty Genovese's murder did not merely look at the scene once and then ignore it. They continued to stare out of their windows at what was going on. Caught, fascinated, distressed, unwilling to act but unable to turn away, their behavior was neither helpful nor heroic; but it was not indifferent or apathetic.

Actually, it was like crowd behavior in many other emergency situations. Car accidents, drownings, fires, and attempted suicides all attract substantial numbers of people who watch the drama in helpless fascination without getting directly involved in the action. Are these people alienated and indifferent? Are the rest of us? Obviously not. Why, then, don't we act?

The bystander to an emergency has to make a series of decisions about what is happening and what he will do about it. The consequences of these decisions will determine his actions. There are three things he must do if he is to intervene: *notice* that something is happening, *interpret* that event as an emergency, and decide that he has *personal responsibility* for intervention. If he fails to notice the event, if he decides that it is not an emergency, or if he concludes that he is not personally responsible for acting, he will leave the victim unhelped. This state of affairs is shown graphically as a

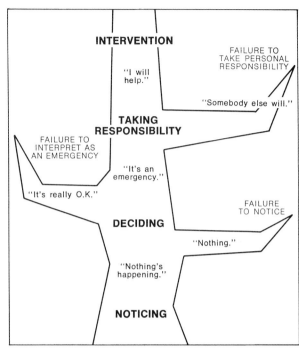

Figure 1. The decision tree; note that only one set of decisions leads to intervention.

"decision tree" (see Figure 1). Only one path through this decision tree leads to intervention; all others lead to a failure to help. As we shall show, at each fork of the path in the decision tree, the presence of other bystanders may lead a person down the branch of not helping.

Noticing: The First Step

Suppose that an emergency is actually taking place; a middle-aged man has a heart attack. He stops short, clutches his chest, and staggers to the nearest building wall, where he slowly slumps to the sidewalk in a sitting position. What is the likelihood that a passerby will come to his assistance? First, the bystander has to *notice* that something is happening. The external event has to break into his thinking and intrude itself on his conscious mind. He must tear himself away from his private thoughts and pay attention to this unusual event.

But Americans consider it bad manners to look too closely at other people in public. We are taught to respect the privacy of others, and when among strangers, we do this by closing our ears and avoiding staring at others—we are embarrassed if caught doing otherwise. In a crowd, then, each person is less likely to notice the first sign of a potential emergency than when alone.

Experimental evidence corroborates this everyday observation. Darley and Latané asked college students to an interview about their reactions to urban living. As the students waited to see the interviewer, either by themselves or with two other students, they filled out a preliminary questionnaire. Solitary students often glanced idly about the room while filling out their questionnaires; those in groups, to avoid seeming rudely inquisitive, kept their eyes on their own papers.

As part of the study, we staged an emergency: smoke was released into the waiting room through a vent. Two-thirds of the subjects who were alone when the smoke appeared noticed it immediately, but only a quarter of the subjects waiting in groups saw it as quickly. Even after the room had completely filled with smoke one subject from a group of three finally looked up and exclaimed, "God! I must be smoking too much!" Although eventually all the subjects did become aware of the smoke, this study indicates that the more people present, the slower an individual may be to perceive that an emergency does exist and the more likely he is not to see it at all.

Once an event is noticed, an onlooker must decide whether or not it is truly an emergency. Emergencies are not always clearly labeled as such; smoke pouring from a building or into a waiting room may be caused by a fire, or it may merely indicate a leak in a steam pipe. Screams in the street may signal an assault or a family quarrel. A man lying in a doorway may be having a coronary or be suffering from diabetic coma—he may simply be sleeping off a drunk. And in any unusual situation, Candid Camera may be watching.

A person trying to decide whether or not a given situation is an emergency often refers to the reactions of those around him; he looks at them to see how he should react himself. If everyone else is calm and indifferent, he will tend to remain calm and indifferent; if everyone else is reacting strongly, he will become aroused. This tendency is not merely slavish conformity; ordinarily we derive much valuable information about new situations from how others around us behave. It's a rare traveler who, in picking a roadside restaurant, chooses to stop at one with no cars in the parking lot.

But occasionally the reactions of others provide false information. The studied nonchalance of patients in a dentist's waiting room is a poor indication of the pain awaiting them. In general, it is considered embarrassing to look overly concerned, to seem flustered, to "lose your cool" in public. When we are not alone, most of us try to seem less anxious than we really are.

In a potentially dangerous situation, then, everyone present will appear more unconcerned than he is in fact. Looking at the *apparent* impassivity and lack of reaction of the others, each person is led to believe that nothing really is wrong. Meanwhile the danger may be mounting, to the point where a single person, uninfluenced by the seeming calm of others, would react.

A crowd can thus force inaction on its members by implying, through its passivity and apparent indifference, that an event is not an emergency. Any individual in such a crowd is uncomfortably aware that he'll look like a fool if he behaves as though it were—and in these circumstances, until someone acts, no one acts.

In the smoke-filled-room study, the smoke trickling from the wall constituted an ambiguous but potentially dangerous situation. How did the presence of other people affect a person's response to the situation? Typically, those who were in the waiting room by themselves noticed the smoke at once, gave a slight startle reaction, hesitated, got up and went over to investigate the smoke, hesitated again, and then left the room to find somebody to tell about the smoke. No one showed any signs of panic, but over three-quarters of these people were concerned enough to report the smoke.

Others went through an identical experience but in groups of three strangers. Their behavior was radically different. Typically, once someone noticed the smoke, he would look at the other people, see them doing nothing, shrug his shoulders, and then go back to his questionnaire, casting covert glances first at the smoke and then at the others. From these three-person groups, only three out of twenty-four people reported the smoke. The inhibiting effect of the group was so strong that the other twenty-one were willing to sit in a room filled with smoke rather than make themselves conspicuous by reacting with alarm and concern—this despite the fact that after three or four minutes the atmosphere in the waiting room grew most unpleasant. Even though they coughed, rubbed their eyes, tried to wave the smoke away, and opened the window, they apparently were unable to bring themselves to leave.

These dramatic differences between the behavior of people alone and those in a group indicate that the group imposed a definition of the situation upon its members that inhibited action.

"A leak in the air conditioning," said one person when we asked him what he thought caused the smoke. "Must be chemistry labs in the building." "Steam pipes." "Truth gas to make us give true answers on the questionnaire," reported the more imaginative. There were many explanations for the smoke, but they all had one thing in common: they did not mention the word fire. In defining the situation as a nonemergency, people explained to themselves why the other observers did not leave the room; they also removed any reason for action themselves. The other members of the group acted as nonresponsive models for each person—and as an audience for any "inappropriate" action he might consider. In such a situation it is all too easy to do nothing.

The results of this study clearly and strongly support the predictions. But are they general? Would the same effect show up with other emergencies, or is it limited to situations like the smoke study involving danger to the self as well as to others—or to situations in which there's no clearly defined "victim"? It may be that our college-age male subjects played "chicken" with one another to see who would lose face by first fleeing the room. It may be that groups were less likely to respond because no particular person was in danger. To see how generalizable these results were, Latané and Judith Rodin set up a second experiment, in which the emergency would cause no danger for the bystander, and in which a specific person was in trouble.

Subjects were paid $2 to participate in a survey of game and puzzle preferences conducted at Columbia by the Consumer Testing Bureau (CTB). An attractive young woman, the market-research representative, met them at the door and took them to the testing room. On the way, they passed the CTB office and through its open door they could see filing cabinets and a desk and bookcases piled high with papers. They entered the adjacent testing room, which contained a table and chairs and a variety of games, where they were given a preliminary background information and game preference questionnaire to fill out. The representative told subjects that she would be working next door in her office for about ten minutes while they completed the questionnaires, and left by opening the collapsible curtain that divided the two rooms. She made sure the subjects knew that the curtain was unlocked, easily opened, and a means of entry to her office. The representative stayed in her office, shuffling papers, opening drawers, and making enough noise to remind the subjects of her presence. Four minutes after leaving the testing area, she turned on a high-fidelity stereophonic tape recorder.

If the subject listened carefully, he heard the representative climb up on a chair to reach for a stack of papers on the bookcase. Even if he were not listening carefully, he heard a loud crash and a scream as the chair collapsed and she fell to the floor. "Oh, my God, my foot. . . . I . . . I . . . can't move it. Oh . . . my ankle," the representative moaned. "I . . . can't get this . . . thing . . . off me." She cried and moaned for about a minute longer, but the cries gradually got more subdued and controlled. Finally she muttered something about getting outside, knocked over the chair as she pulled herself up, and thumped to the door, closing it behind her as she left. This drama lasted about two minutes.

Some people were alone in the waiting room when the "accident" occurred. Some 70 percent of them offered to help the victim before she left the room. Many came through the curtain to offer their assistance, others simply called out to offer their help. Others faced the emergency in pairs. Only 20 percent of this group—eight out of forty—offered to help the victim. The other thirty-two remained unresponsive to her cries of distress. Again, the presence of other bystanders inhibited action.

And again, the noninterveners seemed to have decided the event was not an emergency. They were unsure what had happened, but whatever it was, it was not too serious. "A mild sprain," some said. "I didn't want to embarrass her." In a "real" emergency, they assured us, they would be among the first to help the victim. Perhaps they would be, but in this situation they did not help, because for them the event was not defined as an emergency.

Again, solitary people exposed to a potential emergency reacted more frequently than those exposed in groups. We found that the action-inhibiting effects of other bystanders works in two different situations, one of which involves risking danger to oneself and the other of which involves helping an injured woman. The result seems sufficiently general so that we may assume it operates to inhibit helping in real-life emergencies.

Diffused Responsibility

Even if a person has noticed an event and defined it as an emergency, the fact that he knows that other bystanders also witnessed it may still make him less likely to intervene. Others may inhibit intervention because they make a person feel that his responsibility is diffused and diluted. Each soldier in a firing squad feels less personally responsible for killing a man than he would if he alone pulled the trigger. Likewise, any person in a crowd of onlookers may feel less responsibility for saving a life than if he alone witnesses the emergency.

If your car breaks down on a busy highway, hundreds of drivers whiz by without anyone's stopping to help; if you are stuck on a nearly deserted country road, whoever passes you first is apt to stop. The personal responsibility that a passerby feels makes the difference. A driver on a lonely road knows that if he doesn't stop to help, the person will not get help; the same individual on the crowded highway feels he personally is no more responsible than any of a hundred other drivers. So even though an event clearly is an emergency, any person in a group who sees an emergency may feel less responsible, simply because any other bystander is equally responsible for helping.

This diffusion of responsibility might have occurred in the famous Kitty Genovese case, in which the observers were walled off from each other in separate apartments. From the silhouettes against windows, all that could be told was that others were also watching.

To test this line of thought, Darley and Latané simulated an emergency in a setting designed to resemble Kitty Genovese's murder. People overheard a victim calling for help. Some knew they were the only one to hear the victim's cries, the rest believed other people were aware of the victim's distress. As with the Genovese witnesses, subjects could not see each other or know what others were doing. The kind of direct group inhibition found in the smoke and fallen-woman studies could not operate.

For the simulation, we recruited male and female students at New York University to participate in a group discussion. Each student was put in an individual room equipped with a set of headphones and a microphone and told to listen for instructions over the headphones. The instructions informed the participant that the discussion was to consider personal problems of the normal college student in a high-pressure urban university. It was explained that, because participants might feel embarrassed about discussing personal problems publicly, several precautions had been taken to ensure their anonymity: they would not meet the other people face to face, and the experimenter would not listen to the initial discussion but would only ask for their reactions later. Each person was to talk in turn. The first to talk reported that he found it difficult to adjust to New York and his studies. Then, very hesitantly and with obvious embarrassment, he mentioned that he was prone to nervous seizures, similar to but not really the same as epilepsy. These occurred particularly when he was under the stresses of studying and being graded.

Other people then discussed their own problems in turn. The number of other people in the discussion varied. But whatever the perceived size of the group—two, three, or six people—only the subject was actually present; the others, as well as the instructions and the speeches of the victim-to-be, were present only on a prerecorded tape.

When it again was the first person's turn to talk, after a few comments he launched into the following performance, getting increasingly louder with increasing speech difficulties:

I can see a lot of er of er how other people's problems are similar to mine because er er I mean er it's er I mean some of the er same er kinds of things that I have and an er I'm sure that every everybody has and er er I mean er they're not er e-easy to handle sometimes and er I er er be upsetting like er er and er I er um I think I I need er if if could er er somebody er er er er er give me give me a little er give me a little help here because er I er I'm er h-h-having a a a a a real problem er right now and I er if somebody could help me out it would it would er er s-s-sure be sure be good be . . . because er there er er a cause I er uh I've got a a one of the er seiz—er er things coming on and and and I c-could really er use er some h-help s-so if somebody would er give me a little h-help uh er-er-er-er-er c-could somebody er er help er uh uh uh [choking sounds] . . . I'm gonna die er er I'm . . . gonna . . . die er help er er seizure er er . . . [chokes, then quiet].

While this was going on, the experimenter waited outside the student's door to see how soon he would emerge to cope with the emergency. Rather to our surprise, some people sat through the entire fit without helping; a disproportionately large percentage of these nonresponders were from the largest-size group. Some 85 percent of the people who believed themselves to be alone with the victim came out of their rooms to help, while 62 percent of the people who believed there was one other bystander did so. Of those who believed there were four other bystanders, only 31 percent reported the fit before the tape ended. The responsibility-diluting effect of other people was so strong that single individuals were more than twice as likely to report the emergency as those who thought other people also knew about it.

The Moral Dilemma Felt by Those Who Do Not Respond

People who failed to report the emergency showed few signs of apathy and indifference thought to characterize "unresponsive bystanders." When the experimenter entered the room to end the situation, the subject often asked if the victim was "all right." Many of these people showed physical signs of nervousness; they often had trembling hands and sweating palms. If anything, they seemed more emotionally aroused than did those who reported the emergency. Their emotional arousal was in sharp contrast to the behavior of the nonresponding subjects in the smoke and fallen-woman studies. Those subjects were calm and unconcerned when their experiments were over. Having interpreted the events as nonemergencies, there was no reason for them to be otherwise. It was only the subjects who did not respond in the face of the clear emergency represented by the fit who felt the moral dilemma.

Why, then, didn't they respond? It is our impression that nonintervening subjects had not decided *not* to respond. Rather, they were still in a state of indecision and conflict concerning whether to respond or not. The emotional behavior of these nonresponding subjects was a sign of their continuing conflict; a conflict that other people resolved by responding. The distinction seems an academic one for the victim, since he gets no help in either case, but it is an extremely important one for understanding why bystanders fail to help.

The evidence is clear, then, that the presence of other bystanders and the various ways these other bystanders affect our decision processes make a difference in how likely we are to give help in an emergency. The presence of strangers may keep us from noticing an emergency at all; group behavior may lead us to define the situation as one that does not require action; and when other people are there to share the burden of responsibility, we may feel less obligated to do something when action is required. Therefore, it will often be the case that the *more* people who witness his distress, the *less* likely it is that the victim of an emergency will get help.

Thus, the stereotype of the unconcerned, depersonalized *homo urbanis*, blandly watching the misfortunes of others, proves inaccurate. Instead, we find a bystander to an emergency is an anguished individual in genuine doubt, concerned to do the right thing but compelled to make complex decisions under pressure of stress and fear. His reactions are shaped by the actions of others—and all too frequently by their inaction.

And we are that bystander. Caught up by the apparent indifference of others, we may pass by an emergency without helping or even realizing that help is needed. Aware of the influence of those around us, however, we can resist it. We can choose to see distress and step forward to relieve it.

agencies, between public purpose and private market-place, Urban Renewal turns out to be a super rivers-and-harbors bill, or a conventional American movement to "beautify downtown" (at whose expense and for what purpose seldom are questions raised by the actors involved).

Our local democracies, our cities, are the arenas of politics most accessible to the individual citizen, and they are the areas most easily studied by the social scientist. What do we know about them? Some cities are weak in their formal governmental power, frag-mented and conflicted in formal terms, but strong in their political structure. Chicago is a case in point; the Democratic machine makes possible government where it is theoretically improbable if not impossible. Other cities are strong in their governmental powers but practically impotent because of the weakness of their political system; many new cities of the West Coast and Southwest are cases in point. And many lie in between.

A Picture of City Political Structures

A recent study by Claire Gilbert of Florida Atlantic University gives us a summary picture not of all Ameri-can city political structures, but of all that have been studied. Using the 167 studies in "Community Power Structure" in the United States, she was able to make certain conclusions despite the variation in background of the observer, quality of research, and nature of the city studied.

Using the data-quality-control technique, she con-cluded that *most* small towns studied were dominated by the formally elected political officials; most of the towns ranging from 20,000 to 50,000 population were dominated by nonpolitical persons or coalitions between such persons and elected officials, while most cities of real size were ruled not by a sinister power elite lurking behind the arras, but by the men who held formal political office and power. Thus the American image of the city government as, in Marx's terms, "the executive committee of the *bourgeoisie*" applies precisely to the outmoded American city, the city of *Main Street.*

But government of the small towns is chiefly house-keeping government, with major decisions postponed indefinitely. As Arthur Vidich and Joseph Bensman show, in their study of *Small Town in Mass Society,* the purpose of local government is to maintain a status quo, while all real forces affecting the community are gen-erated far from its boundaries—in Albany, Washington, or New York City. Local government is of little practi-cal interest to the citizens.

In the small cities there is contact and coalition between elected officials and the "nonpolitical" eco-nomic and organizational leaders. Under such circum-stances it is possible to aggregate enough consent, among those representing enough interests, to use the powers of government positively. They may be used in

ways one does not approve, of course; the point is that power can be used.

In the great cities, our metropolitan complexes, map-ping the power grid is a much more complex matter. There is first, of course, the complex maze of formal jurisdictions; "too many governments and not enough government" is the slogan. The old center city from which the complex takes its name usually includes less than half the population of the metropolitan area; the rest lives in the suburbs and in the unincorporated fringe. There is no government for the metropolis as a whole.

I have said that the great cities are governed by elected officials. It is more correct to say that what government occurs passes through their hands, yet how much they can initiate and execute is problematic. Because of the near unbeatable Democratic organiza-tion in Chicago, Mayor Richard Daley has considerable power, yet as Edward Banfield argues, he may use it only at a cost, and he generally prefers to endorse whatever the major forces from outside impinge upon the city, as with pressure and bribes (grants) from Washington, one may see action. And, when scandal of such proportions as to threaten the party breaks, when police officers are hiring burglars and sharing the loot, one may see action. The government of Chicago is primarily a response mechanism, not an initiator.

When one turns to other, politically less organized cities, the situation is even more ambiguous. In New York, according to Wallace Sayre and Herbert Kauf-man, there is not even a real job for the Mayor as referee among contending interests. Nor can he wield the patronage power available to Daley, for the great bureaucracies have developed near complete autonomy from the general government of the city. His major power lies in his newsworthiness: he can project his own image and his concerns and aspirations for the city through the great magnifier, the mass media. Thus John Lindsay's excursions to Harlem and his expressed con-cern for his Negro citizens have undoubtedly been among his more effective political acts.

The cost of a reactive, rather than an active, govern-ment is obvious and it is high. It means that prevention of ills, planning of long-term improvements—even a coherent image of what the city is and should be—are impossible. It is a view of government as broker among conflicting interests—not of government as expressing the common purpose of the citizenry. In the past we could afford it, at least in the sense that our cities have survived and many citizens have prospered.

Can We Afford Do-Nothing City Government?

Perhaps we can continue with do-nothing local govern-ments. But if there is no radical change in American urban government (and I do not expect it in the near future), if we continue to operate within the frozen

The Shaky Future of Local Government

Scott Greer

The cities themselves are in as much distress as were Kitty Genovese, Andrew Mormille, and Eleanor Bradley. The inner core of most large American towns is rapidly becoming the home of the black and the poor, the tired and huddled masses, while the suburbs spread rich and white across the green landscape. The social and economic problems generated in the city ghettos by the flight of white America to the suburbs are, for the most part, ignored by the suburbanites. Even those concerned citizens who do stop to ask, "What can we do?" do not find a very satisfactory answer. As Scott Greer points out, the aim of small-town government is typically to maintain the status quo; yet the aim of city government must be to change the shape of things before disaster overwhelms. If the urban way of life is to continue in America, there must be drastic changes in our form of local government. Just how extensive these changes must be is suggested in this article.

We have, in terms of technological and economic capabilities, the power to do anything we want with our cities. But we do not have a policy capable of deciding in unambiguous and effective terms what it is that we want. This political incapacity derives from the inescapable dilemmas of power distribution that have been built into the American system of local governments. And the dilemma of power distribution is what a considerable portion of the urban crisis is all about.

History, according to Robert McIver, is largely the story of conflict between the larger and the smaller community. McIver, writing before World War I with an evolutionary background of thought, saw the larger community always winning in the long run: from increasing interdependence among local groups evolves the dominant center, for one must coordinate behavior if people are truly interdependent. The next-door neighbor cannot be allowed to poison the water supply.

But Emile Durkheim, looking at this proposition from a democratic socialist point of view, underlined the great danger. If there are no groups with real power between the individual and the state, the individual is helpless and the result is tyranny. Therefore Durkheim urged the creation and maintenance of separate power centers that may represent the individual against the state. Then, because he saw how easily such groups may also tyrannize, he urged the state act as counterbalance.

Out of the tensions between subgroup (city, labor union, corporation) and the nation-state, he saw the possibilities for maximizing and protecting individual freedom.

American politics, and the politics of the American city, are concrete applications of Durkheim's theory. We have systematically divided power between state and local governments. We have also, and importantly, divided power between the freely choosing individual or group (maximizing their chances as best they can) and the public purpose, whether at municipal, state, or local level. In short, we have encouraged a plethora of subgroups between individual and nation-state. In the process we encourage not only areas of potential innovation and leadership, but coercive veto groups. We have built in conservatism. Thus the very limited kinds of government American cities get are no accidents. The dialectic of city government goes thus: Limit discretion and you limit action; allow discretion and you allow the opportunity for chicanery and the corruption of pur pose. Protect interests by checks and balance, and yo increase the probability of stalemate. Too many cool not only spoil the stew—they may prevent its ever bei assembled in the pot.

Consequently, the fiasco of a national program si as Urban Renewal must be seen as chiefly a *polit* failure. Splitting powers between cities and nati

framework of our political culture and our legal structure, I see this future: Major conflicts within the city
between Negroes and whites, between the vested interests of labor unions and public bureaucracies, between
the prosperous and the poor will continue, and indeed
the fever will rise. Mayors of Lindsay's talent will do
their best to ameliorate, temporize, buy time. But time
for what? Essentially, time to be bailed out by the
national government.

Meanwhile, in many of our great cities there will be a
quiet revolution. City Hall will go black. In the process,
Negroes will have formal political power, patronage,
and, most important, *symbolic representation* in the
power elite. The big screen will be available, the mega-
phone of the press, the charisma of office. Our public
landscape as reflected in the media rarely includes
Negroes as anything other than "problems" to be
solved. As problem solvers they may look better to the
indifferent, scared, or hostile whites, *who are the major
social problem of American society.* Thus I consider the
elections in Gary and Cleveland a sign of hope—not
because they show a breakdown in bigotry among
whites, for they do not. What they show is that our
inability to re-form the boundaries of our cities has
created an opportunity for Negroes to gain major political power where it counts, and that they are able and
willing to do so.

There are, however, two developing trends that must
be considered. Neither points to radical, short-term
change, but each suggests some alternatives to do-
nothing government. The first of these is, simply, the
increasing professionalization and bureaucratization of
local government. It is the concrete expression of that
American yearning to take politics out of government
that so degrades our public life. Yet it also reflects the
sheer increase in organizational scale of the society as a
whole and the cities within it. The command posts of
large city government require highly qualified people;
the decisions to be made with respect to traffic planning
or the abolition of poverty are just too complex and
technical for the "average citizen" to have a responsible
opinion. Even the Mayor is, typically, endorsing or
rejecting programs that he may understand only in
terms of their short-run usefulness for his regime.

Thus we are moving toward the administrative state,
the administered city. Not so much because of the
active thrust for power among the bureaucrats as because of the functional requirements of large-scale government. And indeed, in my more pessimistic moments,
I sometimes believe that the country would be in better
shape to face its problems if we abolished local democracy altogether, putting decision making at the state
and national levels, and running the cities with men
from elsewhere appointed by the higher-level governments. The danger, of course, is the one Durkheim
points out: to remove the groups that protect citizens
from a national government agency is to gamble indi-

vidual rights. And indeed, one major reason for the
Watts riots was the intransigent (and inefficient) behavior of a police department whose chief was, in cold
fact, accountable to *nobody at all.* He was not elected
by the people, nor could he be fired by the mayor and
council; in Los Angeles the situation has given rise to
the term *blue fascism.*

The New Organizations

A second important trend in our cities is the burgeoning
of neighborhood and community organizations. It is an
old tradition, growing out of the concentration of those
with similar life style and life chances in given areas; we
find it in the activities of Jane Addams and the other
pioneers of the "settlement house movement." It had
fallen into disarray during the 1940s and 1950s, largely
because of the surge of prosperity in the United States
and the acculturation of most immigrant groups to the
lower middle-class American culture. Its rebirth was due
in part to such liberals as Saul Alinsky, searching for a
more direct and radical mode of attacking the problems
of the powerless. It has been greatly accelerated by the
increased awareness among those excluded from the
affluent society—Negroes, Puerto Ricans, Mexicans,
rural migrants, and the other poor—that they are indeed outsiders.

Such organization works best, as Alinsky notes, when
it is focused on an enemy. And enemies are available in
plenty for the urban poor. (It should not be forgotten
that neighborhoods of the more prosperous can be
organized in a similar way *against* the poor, to keep
them out.) Thus some of the strength of the "Back of
the Yards" movement was the fear among Polish residents that the Negroes would move in as the area
declined.

Let it not be forgotten that, when one organizes
against, he is generating and structuring intergroup
hostility.

What are the consequences of such organization?
There is, first, the hope for redevelopment (or at least
maintenance at the same level) of the declining neighborhood. While such possibilities are limited, they are
real. And this is particularly important when the goal is
combined with a confrontation of the race problem—
when the effort is made to achieve a stable, integrated
neighborhood. As long as such neighborhoods are rare,
as long as good neighborhoods that admit Negroes are
in such short supply, the long-run promise of such
efforts is not great. Only with a quota system could it
work, and this has been declared unconstitutional by
the Supreme Court.

A more important task for the community organization is what I call the "labor-union function." The local
organization can survey and evaluate the goods and
services provided in the area by local government; it can

represent the citizens before the elected officials; it can arbitrate and negotiate between individuals and the welfare workers, the school administrators and the police. Thus the West Side Organization in Chicago, led by men including those whose background was often in the underworld before they became devoted to the cause of their community, has in the last three years helped over 1,000 welfare recipients in their dealings with the Cook County Department of Public Aid.

The original Economic Opportunity Act included substantial plans and some funds for the encouragement of community organizations. However, it was discovered that such organization was potentially political and, therefore, dangerous to the existing party organizations. These men began working either to: (1) preempt the organization, or (2) prevent it, or (3) destroy it if it existed. We might consider the costs of community organization. I have already noted their potential for creating and structuring intergroup hostility. While this may have healthy side effects, as in the increase of self-respect among the insulted and injured of the society, it may also accelerate the tendency toward intergroup violence in the city. It may create a small order within the immediate community at the cost of greater disorder in the city. And if it is effective, we might very well face the impingement of power groups, made up of ignorant and, in the larger sense, irresponsible people, upon the educational, welfare, and police functions of the society. Nobody can countenance a school board that refuses to allow Darwin's theory to be taught; by the same token, one cannot allow radicals, black or white, to rewrite history for polemical reasons.

We have some data on a nation that has really tried participatory democracy on a large scale. The Yugoslavian system of local government gives separate representation not only to neighborhoods but also to age groups, to ethnic groups, to the workers in factories, and to many others. The individual belongs to many cross-cutting organizations that are democratically controlled; thus plant managers are appointed and serve at the pleasure of an executive committee of workers, as in our city-manager governments. The results are, of course, more participation. But there is still less than one would have expected and there are certain costs: (1) the situation builds uncertainty and therefore anxiety into the role of, say, manager; (2) one can only have so much uncertainty if a system is to function (and if managers are to stay sane); (3) therefore one moves toward preemption of the executive board by the manager—or staff domination. But there is, at any rate, a residue of power for the individual to fall back upon in his confrontation with administrative rule; perhaps this is the most that can be expected of participatory democracy.

A more important cost the Yugoslavian system has in common with our own community organizations is that the subgroups fractionate the society. Thus the cleav-

ages in Yugoslavian society, particularly ethnic schisms, which are very great, are structured for good by the present arrangement. Yet they are cleavages within a larger order, and perhaps the lesson we could learn is the necessity for some formalization of the hundreds of community organizations in a large metropolis. People belong to a "society" only through their group affiliations. American society is highly race conscious, if not racist; if we believe in local democracy we must expect local groups to express what they are. Thus we should build an organizational framework to contain, arbitrate, and organize at a larger level than, say, the West Side Organization.

I return to the question: Will the American system of local government change? I will consider three kinds of change: radical structural reordering; the ameliorative and reformist; and crescive change—that change which results from the unanticipated effects of allowing what is happening to keep on happening, while new things emerge from the accumulation and interaction of the happenings.

I can see a possibility of truly radical change in the extreme pressure being generated in the cities and focusing on local government. Catastrophe may be the mother of invention, as floods and dam breaks lead to new and more effective forms of government. Thus the racial tensions that exist in our great cities, and that result in thousands of acts of violence daily, and that spread in some cases to widespread civil disorder may lead to an extreme form of the administrative state. They may result in formal *apartheid*, though by another name; and this may be enforced not only by the local police but by the Pentagon. The recent formation of a riot-control center in the Department of Defense is an ominous note.

The Resiliency of Government

On the other hand, the American system of government, sloppy and inefficient as it is, has some major virtues. One is a resiliency with respect to maintaining a minimum degree of allegiance among a multitude of people. Thus ameliorative change may prevent the spread of *blue fascism*.

Community organizations may continue to grow in numbers, expand their networks of communication for joint action, and aggregate real political power. This does not demand that black mayors bring the dissatisfied into the system; it does demand formal power.

Then too, we may invent ways of maintaining continuous and static-free communications between the dissatisfied and the formal agencies of government; police review boards could be such a device. And we may create new laws and norms so that, for example, compensatory action for the disadvantaged is accepted as normal and right.

As for crescive change in local government, it grows

out of the larger trends in the larger society. I will mention four of these—social rank, ethnicity, life style, and age grading.

In terms of social rank the entire distribution as a whole is moving upward. Income is increasing steadily; formal education takes a larger proportion through high school and into college; the requirements and prestige of the average job are increasing as brute labor is abandoned. As a result one would predict, among other things, an increasingly literate and sophisticated public. The average man would be knowledgeable not only about baseball but also about politics, which is, after all, the best game.

Ethnicity in the society has never been a stable, unchanging dimension. With the closing of immigration in the 1920s, we initiated a long period of acculturation to American norms. The distinctive *cultural* differences among Americans have been considerably blurred, where they have not disappeared altogether. Thus the barriers that remain, social in nature and formidable, are still less dangerous because we can increasingly talk to one another. One result of this that is not so palatable, however, is that Negroes and other colored minorities are much more alone with their problems than were, say, the Irish and Jews at the turn of the century when a majority of urban America was composed of minorities. (The same alienation is, incidentally, true of the poor.) In short, there is more onus on the unfortunate in a society where almost everybody is fortunate—and almost all of them are convinced that they deserve to be so.

Our life style has been increasingly one that emphasizes family, home, neighborhood, local community. With increasing social rank it has resulted in new families abandoning the dense city neighborhoods and moving to the horizontal acres of suburbia. We are decentralizing our cities at a rapid rate, for commerce and industry are also building on the peripheries rather than in the center. If we do not change—radically—our philosophy of municipal expansion and formation, we can expect an increasing majority of metropolitan citizens to live in the toy government world of suburbia. This could further disable local government: there would be no effective government with jurisdiction covering the area where problems are generated.

Suburbs, as walls against invasion by the colored population, keep pressure on the central city. But suburban governments also involve and educate a larger proportion of their citizenry, and this is true without respect to social rank. Perhaps the small suburbs may be

conceived of as serving the same functions as community organizations within the central city; perhaps a network at this level might cross the boundary lines that now give us our schizophrenic metropolitan areas.

The Old and the Young

With respect to age grading, it is interesting to note the increasing importance of needs and demands based upon one's age status. At one pole we have the poorly regarded and poorly rewarded old. As they increase in numbers, they become more visible and potentially more powerful. Their vote is important, and they do vote.

At the other extreme we have the young. Rewarded well enough usually (some would say overrewarded), they still suffer from a contradiction in the society. With increasing complexity in the economic order, increasing education is demanded for a job. Thus the young person who, in a simpler society, would be married, working, and head of his own household may in contemporary America have five or ten more years of dependency to look forward to. During this period he is in the society but not completely of it; the result is to exaggerate the intergenerational conflict that is, in some degree, inevitable. And, with increasing affluence, the young are listened to not only by disk jockeys but by the merchants and politicians. They are a source of political pressure on the city government and they also are capable of rioting and fighting police. Their numbers and influence will increase. Their present interest in community organization, should it remain and grow, could be an important catalyst.

Of one thing we can be certain: local government in America will change. Whether the change will be catastrophic, moving us toward a police state at a rapid rate, or whether it will be ameliorative and ambitious for American goals depends upon our ability to act. "Politics," as Norton Long remarks, "is an act of will." What are we to will? First, of course, we must be concerned that the basic tasks of government are performed, beginning with safety of person and property. But that is minimal; how do we optimize? What do we want of our cities? I personally am haunted by the high aspirations of the Greek for his Polis, of Calvin for Geneva, of the Puritans for the Bay Colony. But to approach these creations within this massive nation, so interpenetrated by continental organizations and power grids, requires a greater consensus than we have yet achieved.

The Lessons of New Haven—
the Erstwhile Model City

Allan Talbot

Man is the communicating animal. According to the noted cultural anthropologist Leslie White, man is set apart from the rest of the animal kingdom by his ability to manipulate symbols, to impart symbolic information to his fellow human beings. When one man speaks only English, and another only Russian, communication becomes difficult because the two men have different symbolic systems. All of us can see the problem when different languages are involved, but how many of us realize that the words and phrases that ghetto dwellers use—the terms that represent their hopes, desires, fears, and frustrations— can have quite different symbolic meaning than the same words and phrases when employed by upper-middle-class whites, who hold the reins of power in urban government. The real "generation gap" that plagues America today is one that cuts across socioeconomic classes as much as across age groups. As Allan Talbot points out, it took the leaders of New Haven a decade or so to build their model city but only a few weeks to learn that the word-symbol "model" meant one thing to them and quite another to the ghetto groups.

One of the wiser counsels in Washington these days is Harold Fleming, president of the Potomac Institute. While peering over the sordid details of the nation's urban ills one day, Fleming offered the shockingly optimistic view that "it's earlier than we think."

Having grabbed the attention of conference participants, who at that juncture were wallowing in the usual litany of racial and city problems, Fleming suggested there were two reasons for hope. One was the enormous wealth of experience in urban programs that the nation has developed over the past ten years. The very least one can say of it is that now we know how not to fight poverty, slums, and all the other problems of our cities. His second reason was the impact of millions of young Americans who each year bring new perceptions of what the problems are and what ought to be done about them. Unlike most of us, they are unshackled by the lingering failures of their assumptions.

What are the lessons and what new directions ought we be taking in urban affairs? That is a tall order. But to start the discussion, it would be useful to examine briefly one city—New Haven, Connecticut—which until recently was regarded as a national model in planning, urban renewal, and antipoverty programs.

Like a scout sent out to bring reinforcements to a besieged garrison, New Haven was once the source of comfort and hope to many harried urban planners and administrators. But then, one day in August 1967, it, too, got mowed down by riots. Richard Lee, mayor of New Haven for fourteen years, was often awed by the national confidence placed in his city. "If we're supposed to be this good," he would say, "then the others must really be in bad shape."

The reasons for the favorable attention directed to New Haven are not hard to find. It did everything right according to the ground rules of the past ten years. New Haven was very, very good at getting money out of the federal bureaucracy—a frustrating, time-consuming business that draws too much talent away from program delivery.

In urban renewal, it attracted four times more money (measured in per capita distribution) than any other city. But I'm afraid the whole business of grantsmanship leads to false, albeit understandable, visions of job accomplishment.

New Haven also had a very able staff for such a small (population, 142,000) city. The New Haven alumni include high officials in HUD, program directors in New York, New Jersey, and Washington, and individuals now making major contributions in planning, housing, human resource programs, and in the private foundations. At the head of the list is, of course, Mayor

Lee. He's not a young Mickey Mantle any more, but he can still swing.

New Haven as Pacesetter

Perhaps most important (and most depressing) is the city's continued role as a pacesetter. The wisdom being passed out in many consultant and planning reports these days is a *fait accompli* in New Haven. Somewhere in America tonight a mayor or city manager is resting comfortably on one of the accomplishments that New Haven found were useful prerequisites to action, but hardly solutions.

Some examples: Washington, D.C., is trying to make an independent planning commission part of a new, action-oriented development agency. This is an important fight going on now in many cities. New Haven won it in 1954, when Mayor Lee simply told the planning director that's the way it had to be.

New York City has finished a two-year struggle to lump urban renewal, code enforcement, and rehabilitation programs into one department. New Haven accomplished that in 1955.

Pontiac, Michigan, has put together a citizen commission composed of business, labor, and civic leaders to back its social and physical renewal. New Haven did that in 1955.

Columbus, Indiana, is struggling to get a tricounty antipoverty program going. New Haven got a $5 million commitment from the Ford Foundation to start the nation's first antipoverty program in 1962—two years before the federal government got in the business.

Dallas is starting an ambitious rebuilding program in its downtown area as part of a new city hall complex. New Haven tore down its old central business district in 1958 and had rebuilt most of it by 1964.

The list of apparent progress could go on to include the city's pioneer activities in rehabilitation, code enforcement, rent supplements, and nonprofit, moderately priced housing. It all looks very good indeed. But in view of the riots last summer and continued racial tension experienced in New Haven over the winter months, looks seem to be deceiving.

What went wrong?

There appear to be two major pitfalls in New Haven, although some who have been closer to the city in the past few months than I have may disagree. One is the significant conflict between achieving efficiency in programs and making programs responsive; the other is the frustration and absurdity of waging war on poverty, slums, and racism on the very restricted ground of the central city.

Efficiency and Responsiveness

By program efficiency, I am not talking about saving money. It has been pointed out that Robert McNamara sought to make the Defense Department efficient, and in the process its expenditures rose significantly. In New Haven terms, efficiency meant forcing the city bureaucracy to grind out Mayor Lee's programs quickly. This often frantic activity was shaped by the requirements of the mayor's two-year term and the early hostility and doubts generated by the then central plank of his administration, urban renewal.

Under urban renewal, New Haven's government centered on high-powered administrators who, with Lee's urging and support, pushed the program over, around, and through potential obstacles. The democratic check on these proceedings—the two-year term—was, ironically, their reason for being.

In the early 1960s, urban renewal began to expose on a grand scale the problems of poverty. And the city's efforts to combat those were marked by strong similarities to the earlier urban renewal effort—namely, firm executive control, close ties to the mayor, and a very heavy emphasis on delivery. In this case it was jobs, school programs, training, and health care.

With hindsight, one can see that there was a certain inevitability in hostile reactions that followed these physical and social probes into the ghetto. The public process was affecting people never touched before. Some benefited, others were hurt, but all of them suddenly had a specific outlet for grievances that went far deeper than their attitude toward one local Democratic administration.

One can also see in the prelude to New Haven's riots the conflict between delivering programs quickly and the imperative to deliver them democratically. At the head of the list of ghetto grievances is, very simply, the total lack of control or influence over what happens. In this context, the problems of joblessness, dreadful schools, or poor housing are just symbols of impotence. When relief comes from above, as it did in New Haven because it is really *quicker* and more *efficient* that way, the problem of impotence remains.

It has been said that what the ghetto really wants is the same blissful inefficiency that the rest of society enjoys—in the way taxes are collected, buildings constructed, or even presidents chosen. They do not want to be recipients of efficiently or benevolently planned programs. They want a piece of the action.

It could also be argued that if our urban programs were truly efficient, that is, if they were properly funded and administered to eliminate the physical and financial symbols of poverty, then the need for control or influence from the ghetto would diminish. I believe that is correct, but academic.

No City Is an Island

The second major dilemma in New Haven—and it is closely related to the question of efficiency—is that the city is really incapable of solving its problems alone. This is an awareness a city gets only after it really tries to do something about its needs, and discovers they are really more pervasive than the need for a new downtown, or schools, or jobs. The inability of the cities to deal with all the problems that fall within their boundaries is perhaps the crucial lesson to be drawn from the experience of the past ten years.

Take the case of housing alone. A lot of the criticism leveled at Mayor Lee is that he never replaced all the low-cost housing (roughly 5,000 units) that he tore down. That is correct, but misleading if one is trying to uncover some root causes of the city's housing ills. For those answers one really has to look at some of the broader national trends affecting all cities.

New Haven's population has dropped by more than 20,000 since 1950. During the same period its nonwhite population, which is most affected by the housing problem, increased by 28,000, and is still rising. At the same time, the nonwhite population in the areas outside New Haven increased by only 6,000, most of these locating along urban corridors leading to run-down sections of the suburbs. This trend of racial concentration and isolation in the central cities is national. Presently, urban racial ghettos are swelling at the rate of 420,000 persons a year.

Perhaps the most damning thing one can say about urban renewal in New Haven is that it has been irrelevant to Negro housing problems in view of the national and regional trends. The irrelevance is serious. But what can be done about it?

Very little until the range of housing choice for Negroes and other racial minorities is much greater. For at the heart of urban renewal is the planning goal to reduce existing core-city densities of people per acre. That means rehousing families. But where? Available open sites for new housing are scarce in the city. The suburbs are alien. And so the ghetto expands.

New Directions

If New Haven is no longer a model of what cities ought to be doing, it does begin to suggest the new directions that should be taken. It also demonstrates the capacity of the political system for self-readjustment. A city cannot be frozen in a description. During the past several months some significant changes can be discerned in the way decisions in New Haven are being made. Mayor Lee is no longer attempting to exercise the control he assumed in the early days of his administration. City executives are beginning to release some power, chiefly to New Haven's elected Board of Aldermen and newly emerging ghetto organizations. Yale is forging direct links with the ghetto, and the city page of the local newspaper is dotted with brand-new names.

It would be useful if the national government could also swing a little more freely in response to the experience of New Haven and other cities. Some basic needs have been uncovered.

Principal among these is the need to build a permanent economic platform for the poor of the nation—*below which no one should fall*. This rather revolutionary proposal has been made many times, but in checking the record I discover that in the terms I have just used, I am paraphrasing a priority urged first by that conservative's conservative, the late Senator Robert A. Taft, in 1949.

The planning, staffing, funding, program implementation, and indigenous involvement of the federal antipoverty program is no substitute for a direct cash flow to the poor. The gap separating the 24 million poor (excluding the aged) from a bare minimum standard of living has been estimated at $11.5 billion. Much of that amount can be found in the pressing program needs in education, housing, or health.

For example, in urban education there are at least one million jobs that should be created and filled in city schools for teacher aides and community workers. These are not "make" work, but crucial positions that can help achieve some of the basic goals of compensatory education such as reduced class size, closing the cultural gap between teachers and ghetto youth, and providing greater community involvement. Indeed, as one surveys some of the other basic needs in the ghetto, the possibilities for meaningful employment and self-determination are immense.

In 1966, the National Commission on Technology, Automation, and Economic Progress suggested that there could be as many as 5.3 million useful public service jobs to be filled by people with low skills. By useful, the Commission meant that the jobs represented important social needs not being adequately met. There is also increasing evidence that the private sector is willing to assume major responsibilities for training and employing the poor.

Assuming the nation aggressively pursued these employment opportunities and transformed many of them into useful jobs, there would still be people living in poverty because they simply cannot work. In 1966, it was estimated that 7.3 million Americans fell into that category. For them the nation must provide a permanent system of income maintenance to replace the current patchwork of welfare programs.

It has been estimated that to mount the required education, job and income support, housing and physical improvement programs, the nation needs to be spending an additional $25 billion a year. This is not beyond reason when one considers that the President's tax surcharge and economic growth projections could produce an additional $20 billion for domestic spending in 1969, assuming no change in Vietnam.

There is disagreement among those who are paid to make judgments in these areas as to precisely where these resources could be invested—that is, on what specific level of government. There are, for example, at least three basic plans for income maintenance, each of which has several variations. So, too, are there several different versions and some sharp disagreements over

the idea of providing more money to be used more flexibly by states and cities. It is likely that the divisions would melt somewhat if the money were available. There are at least two general financial goals that seem to be widely accepted. One is that the federal government should assume most, if not all, of the financial burden for providing basic economic support to the poor, regardless of the precise means chosen. The second is that states and cities must have more money to improve their capacity to be responsive to local conditions.

Assuming we can lick the economic disparities that exist in America (and we can), we would still be left with some large problems. These stem from the relatively restricted area—the cities—in which we are currently waging our various wars on poverty, racism, and slums; and the precious little attention we pay to the quality of what we do.

The New Haven example is just part of the evidence that it has become impossible to do business in the city. The costs are too high in frustration and hostility. It is possible, with greater emphasis on self-determination and increased cash flows to the poor, for the ghettos to become staging areas for advancement. But very few gains will be made until ghetto residents have a wider range of choice in where they can live, hold jobs, and get their children educated.

The economist and political scientist Anthony Downs has suggested that just to keep big city ghettos at their current levels in the next five years, there will have to be an annual movement of 480,000 to 560,000 nonwhites to the suburbs. This—compared to an annual growth of nonwhite suburban residents of 74,000 during the last decade! Yet achieving that kind of flow is possible if we adopt the proper policies.

The nation is now fairly well blanketed with fair-housing laws. The experience in places like Levittown, New Jersey, indicates that these laws can be highly useful. We also know that, despite all our statistical success in painting a dreary picture of the Negro condition in America, there are many families with the income to move to privately developed housing in the suburbs. In 1962, roughly 20 percent of New Haven's Negro families, all of whom were renters, could be matched to privately developed housing in the suburbs. This finding led to a successful effort to create a local fair-housing commission and ordinance, which, by duplicating a perfectly adequate Connecticut fair-housing law, had the practical effect of getting city staff enforcing a state law in the suburbs.

But fair-housing laws, adequately enforced, are clearly not enough. The suburbs and the new growth areas beyond have to be made relevant to the problems and needs of people in the cities. That can only happen if a substantial portion of the 6 million units of low- and moderate-income housing called for by President Johnson over the next ten years is provided outside of the city, near jobs and schools. Specifically, at least 3 million such units should be built in the next ten years outside central cities, not just to provide greater housing choice, but to assure that the housing gets built, for there are not enough sites in the cities.

Right now there is no chance that we can get anywhere near that number of publicly assisted low- and moderate-income units outside the cities. One obstacle is a perfectly benevolent federal requirement that before a community can qualify for publicly assisted housing, it must develop a workable program to guide its growth. By not developing a workable program, suburban communities have a ready-made barrier against housing for low-income families. Another problem is large-lot and single-family suburban zoning. Both can be eliminated or mitigated with federal policies that would cost nothing. Aside from amending the workable program requirement, the federal government could package its major suburban grant-in-aid programs to require or help suburbs find suitable sites for publicly assisted housing.

But for the really large opportunities to create new housing and living choices for all Americans, one has to go beyond existing suburbs to the underdeveloped fringes of our present metropolitan areas, where we know that most of our growth and development will occur. In less than thirty years, another 100 million Americans will be urban, and most of them will be located out there somewhere. How they are housed, what their communities will look like, where they will work, and even who they will be are open questions. Right now it looks as though this future development will involve a massive duplication of already intolerable conditions—not just of racial isolation, but of transportation frictions, air and water pollution, diminishing open space, and ugliness.

Presently there is no public policy to guide and shape this growth. We really could use one. Within the next few years it can be expected that serious proposals will be advanced for federal encouragement of state- and city-sponsored development corporations. These new agencies will have the legal and financing power to acquire large chunks of open land on metropolitan fringes. The land will then be covered by a comprehensive development plan, not just for one community or town, but for major economic growth centers. Borrowing from the precedents of urban renewal, the development corporation will install basic facilities and parcel off the land, by lease or sale, to private developers who agree to conform to the physical and social objectives of the plan.

Will ideas like these and some of increased financial commitments to urban growth and problems come to pass? There is enormous change under way in the United States, and as Harold Fleming says—prophetically, I believe—"It's earlier than we think."

The City as a Distorted Price System

Wilbur Thompson

The importance of systems of rewards and punishments in shaping human behavior is hard to over-estimate; if we are given a choice, we typically choose an action pattern that yields us the greatest bene-fits or that costs us the least in terms of work or money. Urban planners often seem to forget these facts, believing, apparently, that by legislative fiat they can repeal basic psychological and economic laws. Thus they treat the scarcest thing in our cities—street space at the rush hour—as if it were a free good. They offer "free" such public facilities as museums, marinas, golf courses. They insist on equal pay for teachers everywhere throughout the urban area. These are but a few instances of poor management that result from the failure to understand the city as a price system. But the complex set of prices that shape the city are largely subtle and hidden, a subterranean maze of rewards and penalties. As Wilbur Thompson demonstrates, it is doubtful that the local public managers of any city in the country can even roughly describe, much less defend, the network of "prices" that push and pull at the fabric of the city.

The failure to use price—as an *explicit* system—in the public sector of the metropolis is at the root of many, if not most, of our urban problems. Price, serving its historic functions, might be used to ration the use of existing facilities, to signal the desired directions of new public investment, to guide the distribution of income, to enlarge the range of public choice and to change tastes and behavior. Price performs such functions in the private marketplace, but it has been virtually elimin-ated from the public sector. We say "virtually elimi-nated" because it does exist but in an implicit, subtle, distorted sense that is rarely seen or acknowledged by even close students of the city, much less by public managers. Not surprisingly, this implicit price system results in bad economics.

We think of the property tax as a source of public revenue, but it can be reinterpreted as a price. Most often, the property tax is rationalized on "ability-to-pay" grounds with real property serving as a proxy for income. When the correlation between income and real property is challenged, the apologist for the property tax shifts ground and rationalizes it as a "benefit" tax. The

tax then becomes a "price" that the property owner pays for benefits received—fire protection, for example. But this implicit "price" for fire services is hardly a model of either efficiency or equity. Put in a new furnace and fireproof your building (reduce the likeli-hood of having a fire) and your property tax (fire service premium) goes up; let your property deteriorate and become a firetrap and your fire protection premium goes down! One bright note is New York City's one-year tax abatement on new pollution-control equip-ment; a timid step but in the right direction.

Often "urban sprawl" is little more than a color word that reflects (betrays?) the speaker's bias in favor of high population density and heavy interpersonal inter-action—his "urbanity." Still, typically, the price of using urban fringe space has been set too low—well below the full costs of running pipes, wires, police cars, and fire engines farther than would be necessary if building lots were smaller. Residential developers are, moreover, seldom discouraged (penalized by price) from "leapfrogging" over the contiguous, expensive vacant land to build on the remote, cheaper parcels.

Ordinarily, a flat price is charged for extending water or sewers to a new household, regardless of whether the house is placed near to or far from existing pumping stations.

Again, the motorist is subject to the same license fees and tolls, if any, for the extremely expensive system of streets, bridges, tunnels, and traffic controls he enjoys, regardless of whether he chooses to drive downtown at the rush hour and thereby pushes against peak capacity or at off-peak times, when it costs little or nothing to serve him. To compound this distortion of prices, we usually set the toll at zero. And when we do charge tolls, we quite perversely cut the commuter (rush-hour) rate below the off-peak rate.

It is not enough to point out that the motorist supports road building through the gasoline tax. The social costs of noise, air pollution, traffic control, and general loss of urban amenities are borne by the general taxpayer. In addition, drivers during off-peak hours overpay and subsidize rush-hour drivers. Four lanes of expressway or bridge capacity are needed in the morning and evening rush hours whereas two lanes would have served if movements had been random in time and direction, that is, near constant in average volume. The peak-hour motorists probably should share the cost of the first two lanes and bear the full cost of the other two that they alone require. It is best to begin by carefully distinguishing where market tests are possible and where they are not. Otherwise, the case for applying the principles of price is misunderstood; either the too-ardent advocate overstates his case or the potential convert projects too much. In either case, a "disenchantment" sets in that is hard to reverse.

Much of the economics of the city is "public economics," and the pricing of urban public services poses some very difficult and even insurmountable problems. Economists have, in fact, erected a very elegant rationalization of the public economy almost wholly on the *non*marketability of public goods and services. While economists have perhaps oversold the inapplicability of price in the public sector, let us begin with what we are *not* talking about.

The public economy supplies "collectively consumed" goods, those produced and consumed in one big indivisible lump. Everyone has to be counted in the system, there is no choice of *in* or *out*. We cannot identify individual benefits, therefore we cannot exact a *quid pro quo*. We cannot exclude those who would not pay voluntarily; therefore we must turn to compulsory payments: taxes. Justice and air-pollution control are good examples of collectively consumed public services.

A second function of the public economy is to supply "merit goods." Sometimes the majority of us become a little paternalistic and decide that we know what is best for all of us. We believe some goods are especially meritorious, like education, and we fear that others might not fully appreciate this truth. Therefore, we produce these merit goods, at considerable cost, but offer them at a zero price. Unlike the first case of collectively consumed goods, we could sell these merit goods. A schoolroom's doors can be closed to those who do not pay, *quite unlike justice*. But we choose to open the doors wide to ensure that no one will turn away from the service because of its cost, and then we finance the service with compulsory payments. Merit goods are a case of the majority playing God and "coercing" the minority by the use of bribes to change their behavior.

A third classic function of government is the redistribution of income. Here we wish to perform a service for one group and charge another group the cost of that service. Welfare payments are a clear case. Again, any kind of a private market or pricing mechanism is totally inappropriate: we obviously do not expect welfare recipients to return their payments. Again, we turn to compulsory payments: taxes. In sum, the private market may not be able to process certain goods and services (pure "public goods"), or it may give the "wrong" prices ("merit goods"), or we simply do not want the consumer to pay (income-redistributive services).

But the virtual elimination of price from the public sector is an extreme and highly simplistic response to the special requirements of the public sector. Merit goods may be subsidized without going all the way to zero prices. Few would argue for full-cost admission prices to museums, but a good case can be made for moderate prices that cover, say, their daily operating costs (for example, salaries of guards and janitors, heat and light).

Unfortunately, as we have given local government more to do, we have almost unthinkingly extended the tradition of "free" public services to every new undertaking, despite the clear trend in local government toward the assumption of more and more functions that do not fit the neat schema above. The provision of free public facilities for automobile movement in the crowded cores of our urban areas can hardly be defended on the grounds that: (a) motorists could not be excluded from the expressways if they refused to pay the toll, or (b) the privately operated motor vehicle is an especially meritorious way to move through densely populated areas, or (c) the motorists cannot afford to pay their own way and that the general (property) taxpayers should subsidize them. And all this applies with a vengeance to municipal marinas and golf courses.

Prices to Ration the Use of Existing Facilities

We need to understand better the rationing function of price as it manifests itself in the urban public sector: how the demand for a temporarily (or permanently) fixed stock of a public good or service can be adjusted to the supply. At any given time the supply of street, bridge, and parking space is fixed; "congestion" on the streets and a "shortage" of parking space express demand greater than supply at a zero price, a not too surprising phenomenon. Applying the market solution, the shortage of street space at peak hours ("congestion") could have been temporarily relieved (rationalized) by introducing a short-run rationing price to divert some motorists to other hours of movement, some to other modes of transportation, and some to other activities.

Public goods last a long time and therefore current additions to the stock are too small to relieve shortages quickly and easily. *The rationing function of price is probably more important in the public sector where it is customarily ignored than in the private sector where it is faithfully expressed.*

Rationing need not always be achieved with money, as when a motorist circles the block over and over looking for a place to park. The motorist who is not willing to "spend time" waiting and drives away forfeits the scarce space to one who will spend time (luck averaging out). The parking "problem" may be reinterpreted as an implicit decision to keep the money price artificially low (zero or a nickel an hour in a meter) and supplement it with a waiting cost or time price. The problem is that we did not clearly understand this function (time price; money price) and so cannot explicitly agree to do just that.

The central role of price is to allocate—across the board—scarce resources among competing ends to the point where the value of another unit of any good or service is equal to the incremental cost of producing that unit. Expressed loosely, in the long run we turn from using prices to dampen demand to fit a fixed supply to adjusting the supply to fit the quantity demanded, at a price that reflects the production costs.

Prices that ration also serve to signal desired new directions in which to reallocate resources. If the rationing price exceeds those costs of production that the user is expected to bear directly, more resources should ordinarily be allocated to that activity. And symmetrically a rationing price below the relevant costs indicates an *uneconomic* provision of that service in the current amounts. Rationing prices reveal the intensity of the users' demands. How much is it really worth to drive into the heart of town at rush hour or launch a boat? In the long run, motorists and boaters should be free to choose, in rough measure, the amount of street and dock space they want and for which they are willing to pay. But, as in the private sector of our economy, free choice would carry with it full (financial) responsibility for that choice.

We need also to extend our price strategy to "factor prices"; we need a sophisticated wage policy for local public employees. Perhaps the key decision in urban development pertains to the recruiting and assignment of elementary- and secondary-school teachers. The more

able and experienced teachers have the greater range of choice in post and quite naturally they choose the newer schools in the better neighborhoods, after serving the required apprenticeship in the older schools in the poorer neighborhoods. Such a pattern of migration certainly cannot implement a policy of equality of opportunity.

This author argued six years ago that:

Egalitarianism in the public school system has been overdone; even the army recognizes the role of price when it awards extra "jump pay" to paratroopers, only a slightly more hazardous occupation than teaching behind the lines. Besides, it is male teachers whom we need to attract to slum schools, both to serve as father figures where there are few males at home and to serve quite literally as disciplinarians. It is bad economics to insist on equal pay for teachers everywhere throughout the urban area when males have a higher productivity in some areas and when males have better employment opportunities outside teaching—higher "opportunity costs" that raise their supply price. It is downright silly to argue that "equal pay for equal work" is achieved by paying the same money wage in the slums as in the suburbs.

About a year ago, on being offered premium salaries for service in ghetto schools, the teachers rejected, by name and with obvious distaste, any form of "jump pay." One facile argument offered was that they must protect the slum child from the stigma of being harder to teach, a nicety surely lost on the parents and outside observers. One suspects that the real reason for avoiding salary differentials between the "slums and suburbs" is that the teachers seek to escape the hard choice between the higher pay and the better working conditions. *But that is precisely what the price system is supposed to do: equalize sacrifice.*

Prices to Guide the Distribution of Income

A much wider application of tolls, fees, fines, and other "prices" would also confer greater control over the distribution of income for two distinct reasons. First, the taxes currently used to finance a given public service create *implicit* and *unplanned* redistribution of income. Second, this drain on our limited supply of tax money prevents local government from undertaking other programs with more *explicit* and *planned* redistributional effects.

More specifically, if upper-middle- and upper-income motorists, golfers, and boaters use subsidized public streets, golf links, and marinas more than in proportion to their share of local tax payments from which the subsidy is paid, then these public activities redistribute income toward greater inequality. Even if these "semi-proprietary" public activities were found to be neutral with respect to the distribution of income, public provision of these discretionary services comes at the expense of a roughly equivalent expenditure on the more classic public services: protection, education, public health, and welfare.

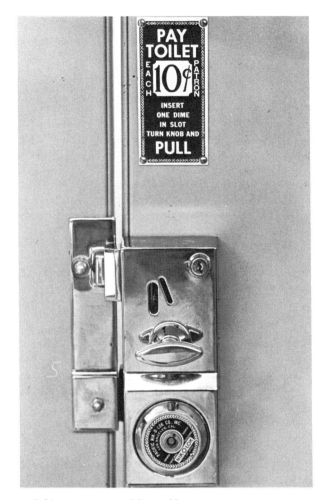

Self-supporting public golf courses are so common and marinas are such an easy extension of the same principle that it is much more instructive to test the faith by considering the much harder case of the public museum: "Culture." Again, we must recall that it is the middle- and upper-income classes who typically visit museums, so that free admission becomes, in effect, redistribution toward greater inequality, to the extent that the lower-income nonusers pay local taxes (for example, property taxes directly or indirectly through rent, local sales taxes). The low prices contemplated are not, moreover, likely to discourage attendance significantly, and the resolution of special cases (for example, student passes) seems well within our competence.

Unfortunately, it is not obvious that "free" public marinas and tennis courts pose foregone alternatives— "opportunity costs." If we had to discharge a teacher or policeman every time we built another boat dock or tennis court, we would see the real cost of these public services. But in a growing economy, we need only not hire another teacher or policeman and that is not so obvious. In general, then, given a binding local budget constraint—scarce tax money, to undertake a local public service that is unequalizing or even neutral in income redistribution is to deny funds to programs that have the desired distributional effect, and is to lose control over equity.

Typically, in oral presentations at question time, it is necessary to reinforce this point by rejoining: "No, I would not put turnstiles in the playgrounds in poor neighborhoods, rather it is only because we do put turnstiles at the entrance to the playgrounds for the middle- and upper-income-groups that we will be able to 'afford' playgrounds for the poor."

Prices to Enlarge the Range of Choice

But there is more at stake in the contemporary chaos of hidden and unplanned prices than "merely" efficiency and equity. *There is no urban goal on which consensus is more easily gained than the pursuit of great variety and choice—"pluralism."* The great rural-to-urban migration was prompted as much by the search for variety as by the decline of agriculture and rise of manufacturing. Wide choice is seen as the saving grace of bigness by even the sharpest critics of the metropolis. Why, then, do we tolerate far less variety in our big cities than we could have? We have lapsed into a state of tyranny by the majority, in matters of both taste and choice.

In urban transportation the issue is not, in the final analysis, whether users of core-area street space at peak hours should or should not be required to pay their own way in full. The problem is, rather, that by not forcing a direct *quid pro quo* in money, we implicitly substitute a new means of payment—time—in the transportation services "market." The peak-hour motorist does pay in full, through congestion and time delay. But *implicit choices* blur issues and confuse decision-making.

Say we were carefully to establish how many more dollars would have to be paid in for the additional capacity needed to save a given number of hours spent commuting. The *majority* of urban motorists perhaps would still choose the present combination of "underinvestment" in highway, bridge, and parking facilities, with a compensatory heavy investment of time in slow movement over these crowded facilities. Even so, a substantial minority of motorists do prefer a different combination of money and time cost. A more affluent long-distance commuter could well see the current level of traffic congestion as a real problem and much prefer to spend more money to save time. If economies of scale are so substantial that only one motorway to town can be supported, or if some naturally scarce factor (for example, bridge or tunnel sites) prevents parallel transportation facilities of different quality and price, then the preferences of the minority must be sacrificed to the majority interest, and we do have a real "problem." But, ordinarily, in large urban areas there are a number of near parallel routes to town and an unsatisfied minority group large enough to justify significant differentiation of one or more of these streets and its diver-

sion to their use. Greater choice through greater scale is, in fact, what bigness is all about.

The simple act of imposing a toll, at peak hours, on one of these routes would reduce its use, assuming that nearby routes are still available without user charges, thereby speeding movement of the motorists who remain and pay. The toll could be raised only to the point where some combination of moderately rapid movement and high physical output were jointly optimized. Otherwise the outcry might be raised that the public transportation authority was so elitist as to gratify the desire of a few very wealthy motorists for very rapid movement, heavily overloading the "free" routes. It is, moreover, quite possible, even probable, that the newly converted, rapid-flow, toll route would handle as many vehicles as it did previously as a congested street and not therefore spin off any extra load on the free routes.

Our cities cater, at best, to the taste patterns of the middle-income class, as well they should, *but not so exclusively.* This group has chosen, indirectly through clumsy and insensitive tax-and-expenditure decisions and ambiguous political processes, to move about town flexibly and cheaply, but slowly, in private vehicles. Often, and almost invariably in the larger urban areas, we would not have to encroach much on this choice to accommodate also those who would prefer to spend more money and less time in urban movement. In general, we should permit urban residents to pay in their most readily available "currency"—time or money.

Majority rule by the middle class in urban transportation has not only disenfranchised the affluent commuter, but more seriously it has debilitated the low-fare, mass transit system on which the poor depend. The effect of widespread automobile ownership and use on the mass transportation system is an oft-told tale: falling bus and rail patronage leads to less frequent service and higher overhead costs per trip and often higher fares, which further reduce demand and service schedules. Perhaps two-thirds or more of the urban residents will tolerate and may even prefer slow, cheap automobile movement. But the poor are left without access to many places of work—the suburbanizing factories in particular—and they face much reduced opportunities for comparative shopping and highly constrained participation in the community life in general. A truly wide range of choice in urban transportation would allow the rich to pay for fast movement with money, the middle-income class to pay for the privacy and convenience of the automobile with time, and the poor to economize by giving up (paying with) privacy.

A more sophisticated price policy would expand choice in other directions. Opinions differ as to the gravity of the water-pollution problem near large urban areas. The minimum level of dissolved oxygen in the water that is needed to meet the standards of different users differs greatly, as does the incremental cost that must be incurred to bring the dissolved oxygen levels up to successively higher standards. The boater accepts a relatively low level of "cleanliness" acquired at relatively little cost. Swimmers have higher standards attained only at much higher cost. Fish and fisherman can thrive only with very high levels of dissolved oxygen acquired only at the highest cost. Finally, one can imagine an elderly convalescent or an impoverished slum dweller or a confirmed landlubber who is not at all interested in the nearby river. What, then, constitutes "clean"?

A majority rule decision, whether borne by the citizen directly in higher taxes or levied on the industrial polluters and then shifted onto the consumer in higher product prices, is sure to create a "problem." If the pollution program is a compromise—a halfway measure—the fisherman will be disappointed because the river is still not clean enough for his purposes, and the landlubbers will be disgruntled because the program is for "special interests" and he can think of better uses for his limited income. Surely, we can assemble the managerial skills in the local public sector needed to devise and administer a structure of user charges that would extend choice in outdoor recreation consistent with financial responsibility, with lower charges for boat licenses and higher charges for fishing licenses.

Perhaps the most fundamental error we have committed in the development of our large cities is that we have too often subjected the more affluent residents to petty irritations that serve no great social purpose, then turned right around and permitted this same group to avoid responsibilities that have the most critical and pervasive social ramifications. It is a travesty and a social tragedy that we have prevented the rich from buying their way out of annoying traffic congestion—or at least not helped those who are long on money and short on time arrange such an accommodation. Rather, we have permitted them, through political fragmentation and flight to tax havens, to evade their financial and leadership responsibilities for the poor of the central cities. That easily struck goal, "pluralism and choice," will require much more managerial sophistication in the local public sector than we have shown to date.

Pricing to Change Tastes and Behavior

Urban managerial economics will probably also come to deal especially with "developmental pricing" analogous to "promotional pricing" in business. Prices below cost may be used for a limited period to create a market for a presumed "merit good." The hope would be that the artificially low price would stimulate consumption and that an altered *expenditure pattern* (practice) would lead in time to an altered *taste pattern* (preference), as experience with the new service led to a fuller appreciation of it. Ultimately, the subsidy would be withdrawn, whether or not tastes changed sufficiently to make the new service self-supporting—provided, of course, that no permanent redistribution of income was intended.

For example, our national parks had to be subsidized in the beginning and this subsidy could be continued indefinitely on the grounds that these are "merit goods" that serve a broad social interest. But long experience with outdoor recreation has so shifted tastes that a large part of the costs of these parks could now be paid for by a much higher set of park fees.

It is difficult, moreover, to argue that poor people show up at the gates of Yellowstone Park, or even the much nearer metropolitan area regional parks, in significant number so that a subsidy is needed to continue provision of this service for the poor. A careful study of the users and the incidence of the taxes raised to finance our parks may even show a slight redistribution of income toward greater inequality.

Clearly, this is not the place for an economist to pontificate on the psychology of prices, but a number of very interesting phenomena that seem to fall under this general heading deserve brief mention. A few simple examples of how charging a price changes behavior are offered, but left for others to classify.

In a recent study of depressed areas, the case was cited of a community industrial development commission that extended its fund-raising efforts from large business contributors to the general public in a supplementary "nickel and dime" campaign. They hoped to enlist the active support of the community at large, more for reasons of public policy than for finance. But even a trivial financial stake was seen as a means to create broad and strong public identification with the local industrial development programs and to gain the public's political support.

Again, social-work agencies have found that even a nominal charge for what was previously a free service enhances both the self-respect of the recipient and his respect for the usefulness of the service. Paradoxically, we might experiment with higher public assistance payments coupled to *nominal* prices for selected public health and family services, personal counseling, and surplus foods.

To bring a lot of this together now in a programmatic way, we can imagine a very sophisticated urban public management beginning with below-cost prices on, say, the new rapid mass transit facility during the promotional period of luring motorists from their automobiles and of "educating" them on the advantages of a carefree journey to work. Later, if and when the new facility becomes crowded during rush hours and after a taste for this new transportation mode has become well established, the "city economist" might devise a three-price structure of fares: the lowest fare for regular off-peak use, the middle fare for regular peak use (tickets for commuters), and the highest fare for the occasional peak-time user. Such a schedule would reflect each class's contribution to the cost of having to carry standby capacity.

If the venture more than covered its costs of operation, the construction of additional facilities would begin. Added social benefits in the form of a cleaner, quieter city or reduced social costs of traffic control and accidents could be included in the cost accounting ("cost-benefit analysis") underlying the fare structure. But below-cost fares, taking care to count social as well as private costs, would not be continued indefinitely except for merit goods or when a clear income-redistribution end is in mind. And, even then, not without careful comparison of the relative efficiency of using the subsidy money in alternative redistributive programs. We need, it would seem, not only a knowledge of the economy of the city, but some very knowledgeable city economists as well.

The Small-World Problem

Stanley Milgram

Fred Jones of Peoria, sitting in a sidewalk cafe in Tunis, and needing a light for his cigarette, asks the man at the next table for a match. They fall into conversation; the stranger is an Englishman who, it turns out, spent several months in Detroit studying the operation of an interchangeable-bottlecap factory. "I know it's a foolish question," says Jones, "but did you ever by any chance run into a fellow named Ben Arkadian? He's an old friend of mine, manages a chain of supermarkets in Detroit . . ."

"Arkadian, Arkadian," the Englishman mutters. "Why, upon my soul, I believe I do! Small chap, very energetic, raised merry hell with the factory over a shipment of defective bottlecaps."

"No kidding!" Jones exclaims in amazement.

"Good lord, it's a small world, isn't it?"

And, as Stanley Milgram suggests in the following article, this is also a world in which billions of people may be bound together by a tight but almost invisible social fabric.

Almost all of us have had the experience of encountering someone far from home, who, to our surprise, turns out to share a mutual acquaintance with us. This kind of experience occurs with sufficient frequency so that our language even provides a cliché to be uttered at the appropriate moment of recognizing mutual acquaintances.

We say, "My, it's a small world."

The simplest way of formulating the small-world problem is: Starting with any two people in the world, what is the probability that they will know each other? A somewhat more sophisticated formulation, however, takes account of the fact that while persons X and Z may not know each other directly, they may share a mutual acquaintance—that is, a person who knows both of them. One can then think of an acquaintance chain with X knowing Y and Y knowing Z. Moreover, one can imagine circumstances in which X is linked to Z not by a single link, but by a series of links, X-a-b-c-d . . . y-Z. That is to say, person X knows person a who in turn knows person b, who knows c . . . who knows y, who knows Z.

Therefore, another question one may ask is: Given any two people in the world, person X and person Z, how many intermediate acquaintance links are needed before X and Z are connected?

Concern with the small-world problem is not new, nor is it limited to social psychologists like myself. Historians, political scientists, and communication specialists share an interest in the problem. Jane Jacobs, who is concerned with city planning, describes an acquaintance chain in terms of a children's game:

When my sister and I first came to New York from a small city, we used to amuse ourselves with a game we called Messages. I suppose we were trying, in a dim way, to get a grip on the great, bewildering world into which we had come from our cocoon. The idea was to pick two wildly dissimilar individuals—say a head hunter in the Solomon Islands and a cobbler in Rock Island, Illinois—and assume that one had to get a message to the other by word of mouth; then we would each silently figure out a plausible, or at least possible, chain of persons through which the message could go. The one who could make the shortest plausible chain of messengers won. The head hunter would speak to the head man of his village, who would speak to the trader who came to buy copra, who would speak to the Australian patrol officer when he came through, who would tell the man who was next slated to go to Melbourne on leave, etc. Down at the other end, the cobbler would hear from his priest, who got it from the mayor, who got it from a state senator, who got it from the governor, etc. We soon had these close-to-home messengers down to a routine for almost everybody we could conjure up . . .

The importance of the problem does not lie in these entertaining aspects but in the fact that it brings under discussion a certain mathematical structure in society, a structure that often plays a part, whether recognized or not, in many discussions of history, sociology, and other disciplines. For example, Henri Pirenne and George Duby, important historians, make the point that in the Dark Ages communication broke down between cities of western Europe. They became isolated and simply did not have contact with each other. The network of acquaintances of individuals became constricted. The disintegration of society was expressed in the growing isolation of communities and the infrequent contact with those living outside a person's immediate place of residence.

There are two general philosophical views of the small-world problem. One view holds that any two people in the world, no matter how remote from each other, can be linked in terms of intermediate acquaintances, and that the number of such intermediate links is relatively small. This view sees acquaintances in terms of an infinitely intersecting arrangement that permits movement from any social group to another through a series of connecting links.

The second view holds that there are unbridgeable gaps between various groups and that therefore, given any two people in the world, they will never link up because people have circles of acquaintances that do not necessarily intersect. A message will circulate in a particular group of acquaintances but may never be able to make the jump to another circle.

The Underlying Structure

Sometimes it is useful to visualize the abstract properties of a scientific problem before studying it in detail; that is, we construct a model of the main features of the phenomenon as we understand them. Let us represent all the people in the United States by a number of points. Each point represents a person, while lines connecting two points show that the two persons are acquainted (see Figure 1). Each person has a certain number of first-hand acquaintances, whom we shall represent by the letters $a, b, c, \ldots n$. Each acquaintance in turn has his own acquaintances, connected to still other points. The exact number of lines radiating from any point depends on the size of a person's circle of acquaintances. The entire structure takes on the form of a complex network of 200 million points, with complicated connections between them (see Figure 2). One way of restating the small-world problem in these terms is this: Given any two of these points chosen at random from this universe of 200 million points, through how many intermediate points would we pass before the chosen points could be connected by the shortest possible path?

Research at MIT

There are many ways to go about the study of the small-world problem, and I shall soon present my own approach to it. But first, let us consider the important contributions of a group of workers at the Massachusetts Institute of Technology, under the leadership of Ithiel de Sola Pool. Working closely with Manfred Kochen of IBM, Pool decided to build a theoretical model of the small world, a model that closely parallels the idea of points and lines shown. However, unlike my own model, which is purely pictorial, Pool and Kochen translate their thinking into strict mathematical terms.

To build such a model they needed certain information. First, they had to know how many acquaintances the average man has. Surprisingly, though this is a very basic question, no reliable answers could be found in the social science literature. So the information had to be obtained, a task that Michael Gurevitch, then a graduate student at MIT, undertook. Gurevitch asked a variety of men and women to keep a record of all the persons they came in contact with in the course of 100 days. It turned out that on the average, these people

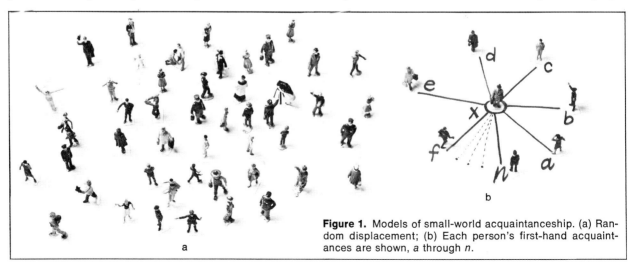

Figure 1. Models of small-world acquaintanceship. (a) Random displacement; (b) Each person's first-hand acquaintances are shown, *a* through *n*.

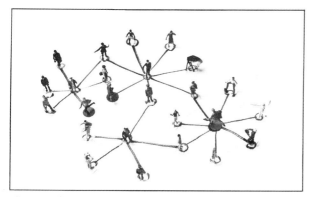

Figure 2. Interconnected network of acquaintances.

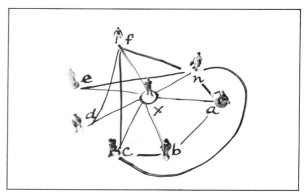

Figure 3. Inbred network of acquaintances.

recorded names of roughly 500 persons, so this figure could be used as the basis of the theoretical model. Now, if every person knows 500 other people, what are the chances that any two people will know each other? Making a set of rather simple assumptions, it turns out that there is only about one chance in 200,000 that any two Americans chosen at random will know each other. However, when you ask the chances of their having a mutual acquaintance, the odds drop sharply. And quite amazingly, there is better than a 50–50 chance that any two people can be linked up through two intermediate acquaintances. Or at least, that is what the Pool-Kochen theory indicates.

Of course, the investigators were aware that even if a man has 500 acquaintances, there may be a lot of inbreeding. That is, many of the 500 friends of my friend may actually be among the people I know anyway, so that they do not really contribute to a widening net of acquaintances; the acquaintances of X simply feed back into his own circle and fail to bring any new contacts into it (see Figure 3). It is a fairly straightforward job to check up on the amount of inbreeding if one uses only one or two circles of acquaintances, but it becomes almost impossible when the acquaintance chain stretches far and wide. So many people are involved that a count just is not practical.

So the big obstacle one runs up against is the problem of social structure. Though poor people always have acquaintances, it would probably turn out that they tend to be among other poor people, and that the rich speak mostly to the rich. It is exceedingly difficult to assess the impact of social structure on a model of this sort. If you could think of the American population as simply 200 million points, each with 500 random connections, the model would work. But the contours of social structure make this a perilous assumption, for society is not built on random connections among persons but tends to be fragmented into social classes and cliques.

A Harvard Approach

The Pool and Kochen mathematical model was interest-

ing from a theoretical standpoint, but I wondered whether the problem might not be solved by a more direct experimental approach. The Laboratory of Social Relations at Harvard gave me $680 to prove that it could. I set out to find an experimental method whereby it would be possible to trace a line of acquaintances linking any two persons chosen at random.

Let us assume for the moment that the actual process of establishing the linkages between two persons runs only one way: from person A to person Z. Let us call person A the *starting* person, since he will initiate the process, and person Z the *target* person, since he is the person to be reached. All that would be necessary, therefore, would be to choose a starting person at random from the 200 million people who live in the United States, and then randomly choose a target person.

This is how the study was carried out. The general idea was to obtain a sample of men and women from all walks of life. Each of these persons would be given the name and address of the same target person, a person chosen at random, who lives somewhere in the United States. Each of the participants would be asked to move a message toward the target person, using only a chain of friends and acquaintances. Each person would be asked to transmit the message to the friend or acquaintance who he thought would be most likely to know the target person. Messages could move only to persons who knew each other on a first-name basis.

As a crude beginning, we thought it best to draw our starting persons from a distant city, so we chose Wichita, Kansas, for our first study and Omaha, Nebraska, for our second. (From Cambridge, these cities seem vaguely "out there," on the Great Plains or somewhere.) To obtain our sample, letters of solicitation were sent to residents in these cities asking them to participate in a study of social contact in American society. The target person in our first study lived in Cambridge and was the wife of a divinity school student. In the second study, carried out in collaboration with Jeffrey Travers, the target person was a stockbroker who worked in Boston and lived in Sharon, Massachusetts. To keep matters straight, I will refer to the first study as the Kansas Study, and the second as the Nebraska Study. These terms indicate merely where the starting persons were drawn from.

Each person who volunteered to serve as a starting person was sent a folder containing a document that served as the main tool of the investigation. Briefly, the document contained:

1. The name of the target person as well as certain information about him. This oriented the participants toward a specific individual.

2. A set of rules for reaching the target person. Perhaps the most important rule was: *"If you do not know the target person on a personal basis, do not try to contact him directly. Instead, mail this folder . . . to a personal acquaintance who is more likely than you to know the target person . . . it must be someone you know on a first-name basis."* This rule set the document into motion, moving it from one participant to the next, until it was sent to someone who knew the target person.

3. A roster on which each person in the chain wrote his name. This told the person who received the folder exactly who sent it to him. The roster also had another practical effect; it prevented endless looping of the folder through participants who had already served as links in the chain, because each participant could see exactly what sequence of persons had led up to his own participation.

In addition to the document, the folder contained a stack of fifteen business reply, or "tracer" cards. Each person receiving the folder took out a card, filled it in, returned it to us, and sent the remaining cards along with the document to the next link.

Several other features of the procedure need to be emphasized. First, each participant was supposed to send the folder on to one other person only. Thus, the efficiency with which the chain is completed depends in part on the wisdom of his choice in this matter. Second, by means of the tracer card, we had continuous feedback on the progress of each chain. The cards were coded so we knew which chain it came from and which link in the chain had been completed. The card also provided us with relevant sociological characteristics of the senders. Thus, we know the characteristics of completed, as well as incompleted, chains. Third, the procedure permitted experimental variation at many points.

In short, the device possesses some of the features of a chain letter, though it does not pyramid in any way; moreover, it is oriented toward a specific target, zeroes in on the target through the cooperation of a sequence of participants, and contains a tracer that allows us to keep track of its progress at all times.

Would It Work?

The question that plagued us most in undertaking this study was simply: Would the procedure work? Would any of the chains started in Kansas actually reach our target person in Massachusetts? Part of the excitement of experimental social psychology is that it is all so new

we often have no way of knowing whether our techniques will work or simply turn out to be wispy pipe dreams.

The answer came fairly quickly. It will be recalled that our first target person was the wife of a student living in Cambridge. Four days after the folders were sent to a group of starting persons in Kansas, an instructor at the Episcopal Theological Seminary approached our target person on the street. "Alice," he said, thrusting a brown folder toward her, "this is for you." At first she thought he was simply returning a folder that had gone astray and had never gotten out of Cambridge, but when we looked at the roster, we found to our pleased surprise that the document had started with a wheat farmer in Kansas. He had passed it on to an Episcopalian minister in his home town, who sent it to the minister who taught in Cambridge, who gave it to the target person. Altogether the number of intermediate links between starting person and target person amounted to *two!*

How Many Intermediaries?

As it turned out, this was one of the shortest chains we were ever to receive, for as more tracers and folders came in, we learned that chains varied from two to ten intermediate acquaintances, with the median at five (see Figure 4). A median of five intermediate persons is, in certain ways, impressive, considering the distances traversed. Recently, when I asked an intelligent friend of mine how many steps he thought it would take, he estimated that it would require 100 intermediate persons or more to move from Nebraska to Sharon. Many people make somewhat similar estimates, and are surprised to learn that only five intermediaries will—on the average—suffice. Somehow it does not accord with intuition. Later, I shall try to explain the basis of the discrepancy between intuition and fact.

On a purely theoretical basis, it is reasonable to assume that even fewer links are essential to complete

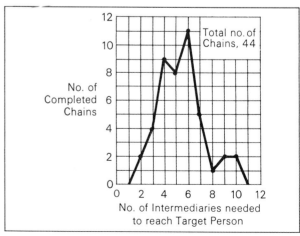

Figure 4. In the Nebraska study two to ten intermediate acquaintances were needed to complete the chain; the median was five.

the chains. First, since our participants can send the folder to only one of their 500 possible contacts, it is unlikely that even through careful selections, they will necessarily and at all times select the contact best able to advance the chain to the target. On the whole they probably make pretty good guesses but surely, from time to time, they overlook some possibilities for short cuts. Thus, the chains obtained in our empirical study are less efficient than those generated theoretically.

Second, by working on a highly rational basis, each intermediary moves the folder toward the target person. That is, a certain amount of information about the target person—his place of employment, place of residence, schooling, and so forth—is given to the starting subject, and it is on the basis of this information alone that he selects the next recipient of the folder. Yet, in real life, we sometimes know a person because we chance to meet him on an ocean liner, or we spend a summer in camp together as teenagers, yet these haphazard bases of acquaintanceship cannot be fully exploited by the participants.

There is one factor, however, that could conceivably have worked in the opposite direction in our experiments, giving us the illusion that the chains are shorter than they really are. There is a certain decay in the number of active chains over each remove, even when they do not drop out because they reach the target person. Of 160 chains that started in Nebraska, 44 were completed and 126 dropped out. These chains die before completion because on each remove a certain proportion of participants simply do not cooperate and fail to send on the folder. Thus, the results we obtained on the distribution of chain lengths occurred within the general drift of a decay curve. It is possible that some of the incomplete chains would have been longer than those that were completed. To account for this possibility, Harrison White of Harvard has constructed a mathematical model to show what the distribution of chain lengths would look like if all chains went through to completion. In terms of this model, there is a transformation of the data, yielding slightly longer chains.

Examining the Chains

Several features of the chains are worth examining, for they tell us something about the pattern of contact in American society. Consider, for example, the very pronounced tendency in our Kansas Study for females to send the folder on to females, and males to send it on to males. Of the 145 participants involved in the study, we find:

Female to female:	56
Male to male:	58
Female to male:	18
Male to female:	13

Thus, participants were three times as likely to send the folder on to someone of the same sex as to someone of the opposite sex. Exactly why this is so is not easy to determine, but it suggests that certain kinds of communication are strongly conditioned by sex roles.

Participants indicated on the reply cards whether they were sending the folder on to a friend, a relative, or an acquaintance. In the Kansas Study, 123 sent the folder to friends and acquaintances, while only 22 sent it to relatives. Cross-cultural comparison would seem useful here. It is quite likely that in societies that possess extended kinship systems, relatives will be more heavily represented in the communication network than is true in the United States. In American society, where extended kinship links are not maintained, acquaintance and friendship links provide the preponderant basis for reaching the target person. I would guess, further, that within certain ethnic groups in the United States, a higher proportion of familial lines would be found in the data. Probably, for example, if the study were limited to persons of Italian extraction, one would get a higher proportion of relatives in the chain. This illustrates, I hope, how the small-world technique may usefully illuminate varied aspects of social structure.

Specialized Channels

Each of us is embedded in a small-world structure. It is not true, however, that each of our acquaintances constitutes an equally important basis of contact with the larger social world. It is obvious that some of our acquaintances are more important than others in establishing contacts with broader social realms; some friends are relatively isolated, while others possess a wide circle of acquaintances, and contact with them brings us into a far-ranging network of additional persons.

Referring to our Nebraska Study, let us consider in detail the pattern of convergence crystallizing around the target person—the stockbroker living in Sharon, Massachusetts, and working in Boston (see Figure 5). A total of sixty-four chains reached him. (Forty-four chains originated in Nebraska and twenty chains, from an auxiliary study, originated in the Boston area.)

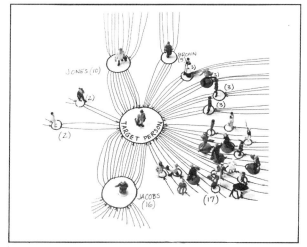

Figure 5. The roles of Jacobs, Jones, Brown, and others illustrate specialized contact channels.

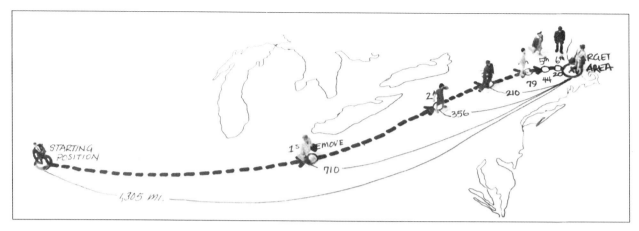

Figure 6. Movement of one folder from Omaha to Boston. Note the progressively smaller distances as the target area is approached.

Twenty-four of the chains reached him at his place of residence in the small town outside of Boston. Within Sharon, sixteen were given to him by Mr. Jacobs, a clothing merchant in town. Thus, the clothing merchant served as the principal point of mediation between the broker and a larger world, a fact that came as a considerable surprise, and even something of a shock for the broker. At his place of work, in a Boston brokerage house, ten of the chains passed through Mr. Jones, and five through Mr. Brown. Indeed, 48 percent of the chains to reach the broker were moved on to him by three persons: Jacobs, Jones, and Brown. Between Jacobs and Jones there is an interesting division of labor. Jacobs mediates the chains advancing to the broker by virtue of his residence. Jones performs a similar function in the occupational domain, moving ten chains enmeshed in the investment-brokerage network to the target person.

More detail thus fills in the picture of the small world. First, we learn that the target person is not surrounded by acquaintance points, each of which is equally likely to feed into an outside contact; rather, there appear to be highly popular channels for the transmission of the chain. Second, there is differentiation among these commonly used channels, so that certain of them provide the chief points of transmission in regard to residential contact, while others have specialized contact possibilities in the occupational domain. For each possible realm of activity in which the target person is involved, there is likely to emerge a sociometric star with specialized contact possibilities.

Geographic and Social Movement

The geographic movement of the folder from Nebraska to Massachusetts is striking. There is a progressive closing in on the target area as each new person is added to the chain (see Figure 6). In some cases, however, a chain moves all the way from Nebraska to the very neighborhood in which the target person resides, but then goes round and round, never quite making the necessary contact to complete the chain. Some chains died only a few hundred feet from the target person's house, after a successful journey of 1,000 miles. Thus we see that social communication is sometimes restricted less by physical distance than by social distance.

The next step is to see what happens when we change the relationship between the starting person and the target person. That is, if the two are drawn from different class backgrounds, does this then decrease the probability of completing the chain? Does it increase the number of links?

In collaboration with Charles Korte, I am now applying the small-world method to the study of communications between subgroups in American society—Negro and white. We will have both Negro and white starting persons, but only Negro target persons, and try to trace the lines of communication between them. First, we want to ask: In what degree are the racial lines surmounted? Can any sizable fraction of the communications get through the racial barrier? If the answer is yes, we then want to identify the typical locus of transmission. Does it occur at the neighborhood level, or at the place of work? We are particularly interested in the persons who serve as links between Negro and white groups. In what way do they differ from others in the chain? Do they tend to occupy particular professional categories, such as minister, teacher, and so forth? Is the communication flow between Negroes and whites easier in Northern or in Southern locales? Perhaps some new light can be cast on the structural relationships between Negro and white communities by probing with the small-world method.

Intuition and Fact

As we saw above, many people were surprised to learn that only five intermediaries will, on the average, suffice to link any two randomly chosen individuals, no matter where they happen to live in the United States. We ought to try to explain the discrepancy between intuition and fact.

The first point to remember is that although we deal directly with only five intermediaries, behind each of them stands a much larger group of from 500 to 2,500 persons. That is, each participant has an acquaintance pool of 500 to 2,500 persons from which he selects the person who, he thinks, is best able to advance the chain. Thus we are dealing only with the end product of a radical screening procedure.

The second thing to remember is that geometric progression is implicit in the search procedure, but nothing is more alien to mathematically untutored intuition than this form of thinking. As youngsters, many of us were asked the question: If you earned a penny a day and the sum were doubled each day, how much would you have earned by the end of a thirty-day working period? Most frequently people give answers on the order of $1.87 or $6.45, when in fact the sum is more than $10 million for one thirty-day working period, the last day alone yielding $5,368,709.12. Elements of geometric progression with an increase rate far more powerful than mere doubling underlie the small-world search procedure, and thus, with only a few removes, the search extends to an enormous number of persons.

Finally, when we state there are only five intermediate acquaintances, this connotes a closeness between the position of the starting person and the target person. But this is in large measure misleading, a confusion of two entirely different frames of reference. If two persons are five removes apart, they are far apart indeed. Almost anyone in the United States is but a few removes from the President, or from Nelson Rockefeller, but this is true only in terms of a particular mathematical viewpoint and does not, in any practical sense, integrate our lives with that of Nelson Rockefeller. Thus, when we speak of five intermediaries, we are talking about an enormous psychological distance between the starting and target points, a distance that seems small only because we customarily regard "five" as a small man-

ageable quantity. We should think of the two points as being not five persons apart, but "five circles of acquaintances" apart—five "structures" apart. This helps to set it in its proper perspective.

There is a very interesting theorem based on the model of the small world. It states that if two persons from two different populations cannot make contact, then no one within the entire population in which each is embedded can make contact with any person in the other population. In other words, if a particular person, a, embedded in population A (which consists of his circle of acquaintances), cannot make contact with a particular person, b, embedded in population B, then:

1. No other person in A can make contact with b.

2. No other person in A can make contact with any other person in B.

3. In other words, the two subpopulations are completely isolated from each other.

Conceivably, this could happen if one of the populations were on an island never visited by the outside world. In principle, any person in the United States can be contacted by any other in relatively few steps, unless one of them is a complete and total hermit, and then he could not be contacted at all.

In sum, perhaps the most important accomplishment of the research described here is this: Although people have talked about the small-world problem, and have even theorized about it, this study achieved, as far as I know, the first empirically created chains between persons chosen at random from a national population.

Although the study started with a specific set of questions arising from the small-world problem, the procedure illuminates a far wider set of topics. It reveals a potential communication structure whose sociological characteristics have yet to be exposed. When we understand the structure of this potential communication net, we shall understand a good deal more about the integration of society in general. While many studies in social science show how the individual is alienated and cut off from the rest of society, this study demonstrates that, in some sense, we are all bound together in a tightly knit social fabric.

Political Attitudes in Children

Robert D. Hess

Does the government rule the people, or do the people rule the government? Most adults interested in politics would probably insist that the people rule themselves, that they participate in political decision making in many ways. But what about children? How do they see themselves in relation to the government? Where do their political attitudes come from? Robert Hess, describing his own research in this area, believes that teachers in our schools impart to their charges an idealized concept of government, that the children come to confuse how things ought to be with how things are. Later, when the children reach early adulthood and the discrepancy between fact and fiction becomes apparent to them, they either retreat to disillusioned cynicism or react with open rebellion against the governmental system itself. But the real culprits, according to Hess, are the teachers who failed to present the political and social facts of life to the children and who failed to teach them the many effective ways that our governmental institutions can be influenced and changed.

"Sandra, in what way could our country be harmed?"

"By war, we can be harmed, and if the President of the United States don't do the right job that he should be doing he can lead us into trouble too."

"Which is worse?"

"I think war is worse. No, wait—I don't think war is worse. I think the other one is worse, because in war you can fight back but when the President doesn't do his job right, there can be nothing done about it. You just can't get a new President—you just have to wait."

Sandra is a sixth-grade girl from the working class, the daughter of a police detective in a large Midwestern city. She is somewhat more sophisticated about political matters than many children her age. It is unusual for an elementary school child to suggest the possibility that the President might not "do his job right." More typical is Sandra's implicit assumption that the United States would be on the defensive side in the event of war. Most young children believe that the government and its representatives are wise, benevolent, and infallible, that whatever the government does is for the best, and that the United States is a highly effective force for peace in the world.

The average child would agree with Sandra that, if something *is* wrong, "you just have to wait." They know that a citizen can write letters to the President

and to Congress, but they see virtually no other way to influence political affairs in the period between elections. They know almost nothing about pressure groups, for instance. In fact, group political activity of any sort, including that of political parties, seems unimportant to them. They believe that the way the citizen affects the government is through the vote, the individual vote; that is almost the only thing that counts, and it counts very heavily indeed.

Political socialization, the process by which attitudes like these are learned, is a special, socially oriented form of political learning. It is accomplished *by* the society and *for* the society, mostly through the institution of the schools. Its purpose is to transmit to each new generation the political attitudes and behavior patterns that the society deems useful in its adult citizens. That is, political socialization is based on and is intended to preserve stability and consensus in the adult population.

In the United States today, stability and consensus are conspicuously lacking. There is strong, open conflict between ethnic groups and the dominant society, between the affluent and the poor, and between generations. The conflict concerns wealth and other material resources, but the basic issue is the division of political power.

In my opinion, children in this country are being

socialized in ways that contribute to the very fragmentation that political socialization is meant to prevent.

In 1961 and 1962, David Easton and I, together with Judith Torney and Jack Dennis, collected data on the political knowledge, attitudes, and behavior of 12,000 children in grades two to eight. The children were from eight cities, two in each major region of the United States. In each region we used a large city and a small one; and in each city, two schools from working-class areas and two from middle-class areas.

We found, among other things, that elementary-school children have a highly idealized view of the government and a very high estimate of the power of the individual vote, combined with an ignorance of other legitimate channels of influence. These views are unrealistic (a fact that is becoming increasingly obvious today to children themselves), and they do not offer a good foundation for active, effective participation in a democratic process. They seem to point more toward compliance and complacency on one hand, and toward disillusionment, helplessness, anger, and perhaps even rejection of the system on the other.

The child's early conception of the nation and its government is vague but very favorable. In the early grades, almost all children agree that "the American flag is the best flag in the world," and that "America is the best country in the world." As one girl put it, "if it wasn't for the United States, there probably would be a lot of wars and regular Dark Ages."

"President" and "government" are almost synonymous for the young child. Both are regarded as powerful and benevolent, though there is some confusion about the functions they perform:

"Judy, do you know of anyone in the United States government?"

"Well, the President."

"What do you know about the President?"

"Well, that a . . . oh, dear . . . he . . . ah, makes laws and a . . . and . . . ah . . . well, he tries to do good."

"Tommy, what is the government?"

"The government is like the President, but he isn't actually a President. . . . Maybe he makes the laws of the country. Maybe he tells the numbers on the license plates. . . . I heard on the radio that he's in charge of the income tax. He can higher it or lower it."

"What does he spend the money on?"

"How should I know? Like, the government doesn't know what we spend our money on. He spends it for food, clothing, things for his wife, and that sort of thing."

In the second grade, the average child believes that the President would be nearly as helpful to him as a policeman or his father if he were in trouble. Children express strong emotional attachment to the President and expect him to protect them. They think he is personally responsive to children's wishes; if necessary they could even go to the White House and talk to him.

Responses to one question show especially clearly how concerned children think the President is about them. The question was: "If you write to the President, does he care what you think?" The possible answers were that he cares "a lot," "some" or "a little." Three-fourths of the children in second grade and 43 percent of those in eighth answered "a lot." (Interestingly, this answer was also chosen by 47 percent of the teachers.)

Laws, like government, are viewed as powerful and benevolent. They are helpful and protective, just and unchanging. Most young children think laws were made a long time ago, probably by the President, and his stamp of approval carries weight: "The President okays them before they're obeyed, so I guess if it is good enough for him, it is good enough for anybody."

The young child's idealization of the figures and institutions of government is supported by what he learns in school, but it does not seem to originate there. Its source is probably the child's psychological need to compensate for his own inferior and vulnerable place in the system. Attachment to the President, for example, begins with an awareness that there is a very powerful "boss" of the United States. If he is benevolent and concerned with the child's welfare, the child need not be afraid of him. The child apparently sees his own position in the nation as similar to his position in the family, a conclusion borne out by what we learned from children with working-class backgrounds. Working-class children tended to have less positive attitudes toward their fathers than children from the middle and upper classes, and to invest the President with correspondingly more paternalistic qualities. They expressed very strong emotional ties to him.

In the later grades, children begin to transfer their allegiance from officials to offices and institutions. The average seventh-grader thinks that the Supreme Court and the government know more and are less likely to make mistakes than the President. Since support for offices rather than for particular officials is an important ingredient in peaceful political change, the transfer of allegiance from personal figures to roles and institutions is a step toward political stability.

However, older children have not so much abandoned their belief in the benign qualities of governmental authority as redirected their expectations of protection toward institutions. In all grades, 80 to 90 percent of the students agreed that "the United States government knows what is best for the people." Agreement on a related item, "What goes on in government is all for the best," declined with age, from 90 percent in grade three to 76 percent in grade eight, but this is still a very high percentage. (Among teachers, agreement had dropped to 46 percent.)

An idealized acceptance of the authority, omniscience, and benevolence of the political system does not fit well with the need, in a democratic society, for a critical examination of public policy. Without abandoning his positive attachment to government, law, and structures designed to regulate dissent, the citizen must see a need to watch—and to influence—the government's actions.

Older children do show more awareness than younger ones that all is not necessarily perfect. Though agreement with positive statements about how the system *should* be stays high in all grades, perceptions of how things actually are become more realistic with age. Most children in all grades agree that the policeman's job is to make people obey laws, but the belief that punishment inevitably follows crime declines from 57 percent in second grade to 16 percent in eighth (and to 2 percent in teachers). Similarly, children of all ages agree that "laws are to keep us safe," but there is more and more reluctance to agree that "all laws are fair." In general, responses to idealized statements of how things ought to be were more stable than perceptions of the way the system really functions.

How Does the System Work?

The discrepancy between the ideal and the actual could be the basis for disillusionment and cynicism, but it might also be an incentive to act. Let us assume the latter—that at least some older children are motivated to do more than admire the status quo and comply with the law. Let us also assume (for the moment) that these children have two other prerequisites to political action, a view of themselves as effective and a view of the system as responsive. What then?

Children believe that democracy is "rule by the people," but they have a limited understanding of how this rule operates. As one sixth-grade boy tried to explain it, "Oh, in the United States the people are supposed to rule the government . . . but that is kind of complicated because the government rules over the people. . . . It is kind of mixed-up, but it's a good set-up, but yet there's no real rule. Everybody has power; that is, everybody's power is limited."

The idea of a reciprocal relationship between an individual citizen and the government is difficult to grasp, even for adults. Young children do not try: they see government at the top and themselves at the bottom, with influence moving down but not up. In general, children in the early grades say that the duties of the citizen are compliance and "good" behavior. Asked what a citizen can do to help the country, one fourth-grader replied, "Well, follow the laws, don't get in accidents, and do practically everything as hard as he can." Children this age, presented with a list of seven characteristics of the good citizen and asked to choose two, opted for "helps others" (48 percent) and "always obeys laws" (44 percent).

Older children said that the good citizen "is interested in the way the country is run" (65 percent) and "votes and gets others to vote" (45 percent). Almost all eighth-graders think it is important to vote, and most of them are convinced that the ideal citizen "makes up his own mind" about a candidate, rather than turning to parents, teachers, television, newspapers, and so forth. Just where the ideal citizen *does* turn for political information is unclear, though estimates of usefulness of the mass media began to rise in the later grades.

A similar spirit of independence shows itself when eighth-graders are asked what they think of voting along party lines. The ideal citizen, they say, votes for "the man, not the party," and he splits his ticket.

Parties and Pressure Groups

Attitudes toward political parties are fairly late in developing. Most children first learn the words "Democrat" and "Republican" when they label a Presidential candidate as one thing or the other. Young children identify the party with the candidate rather than vice versa; since they see the candidates as different, they also believe the parties are different.

To older children, the Democratic and Republican parties look almost identical. "Well, basically they both want the same things," said an eighth-grade girl. "Just peace and happiness and want our country to be free."

Children are eager to minimize political conflict of all sorts. They usually take sides in a campaign and hope their man wins, but this does not mean they condone strong disagreement between the candidates. Unity and cohesion should surely reign *after* an election, and perhaps before as well. Here, for instance, is what one seventh-grader remembered about the 1960 election: "[I remember] the morning of the election when Kennedy was elected, and Nixon said that Kennedy would be a nice President. Kennedy said how sorry he was that Mr. Nixon wasn't elected. He would have been just as good a President as he was himself, and that he wished they could both be President together. I would have liked them to go together instead of going through this big thing that they go out in the streets and talk to all the people and giving the impression that they got a better impression than the other one. It would have been easy if they both went together. Then there wouldn't have been much quarreling and fighting."

Conflict between parties is just as undesirable as conflict between candidates. One question we asked the children was, "If the Democrats and Republicans disagreed on important things, would it be good or bad for the country?" On a scale from 1 (very bad) to 5 (very good), the responses ranged from a little under 2 in the fifth grade to a little over 2 in eighth. Teachers were better able to tolerate disagreement, and the difference between them and eighth-graders on this item was one of the largest in our data.

Although most older children believe that adults should belong to parties, they think a decision between the two should be deferred until after high-school graduation. Asked to specify the party they would join if they were adults, 32 percent specified "sometimes Democrat, sometimes Republican." This percentage is somewhat higher than estimates of the number of independent voters in the adult population, though much lower than the 55 percent of teachers who reported themselves "sometimes Democrat, sometimes Republican."

Very little material on partisanship and political conflict finds its way into the elementary-school curriculum. Teachers apparently stress the virtue of independent political action oriented toward an assessment of candidates' worth rather than an alignment with a party. They may do this from a desire to avoid controversial issues or to present political material without bias. But the result for the students is an awareness of the need for consensus and majority rule without a complementary appreciation of the role of debate, disagreement, and conflict.

As for pressure groups, children's understanding of the role they play in government is shown in Figure 1. Until the seventh grade, children rated the policeman's influence in law-making as higher than that of any other individual or group except the President and labor unions. In a clear demonstration of faith in the importance of the individual, older children saw the average citizen's influence on law-making as equal or superior to the influence of big companies, rich people, newspapers, and churches. Teachers differed greatly from eighthgraders on this matter, rating the influence of unions, big companies, rich people, and newspapers nearly equal, and much greater than that of the average citizen.

The sharp divergence between students and teachers suggests that this topic, like partisanship, is not discussed at school. Schools concentrate on the formal aspects of government, teaching that Congress makes the laws but not recognizing the influence of interest groups. It is not easy to teach children that groups who promote their own (as opposed to the public) interest can be influential, even decisive, in legislative matters, but it would make for a more realistic view of how a complex democracy operates.

Effectiveness

Exerting an effect on the course of government requires more than an awareness of the need to do so and a knowledge of how to go about it. As I mentioned earlier, it also requires a belief in one's own effectiveness and in the government's responsiveness. A child who thinks the government is benevolent and protective may fail to see why he *should* interfere, but he also believes that if he *does* speak, the government will listen. And a child who thinks the government pays more attention to the average person than to, say, U.S. Steel or *The New York Times* may confine his political activities to the voting booth, but he unquestionably has a high opinion of his own effectiveness.

There is a house-of-cards air to this structure of beliefs; misguidedly or not, however, most children do believe that the government is responsive and that they, as individuals, can be effective in the political arena. Most, but not all. For example: "Richard, if the President did something that people didn't like, what could they do?" "The people can't do anything. They can't go to the White House and tell him what to do because he makes all the decisions. If the people don't like it, too bad for them."

Richard is from a working-class home. A difference in feelings of effectiveness was one of the most striking

Figure 1. Teachers' attitudes and changes in those of children about the relative influence of groups and individuals on law-making.

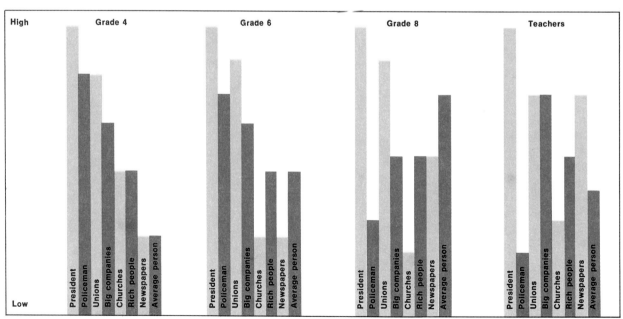

social-class discrepancies in our data, one of the few variables on which there was considerable difference between the middle- and the low-status groups. Even in third and fourth grade, low-status children see themselves and their families as having substantially less ability to influence government than high-status children award themselves; the difference increases with age.

Differences between IQ groups on effectiveness were even more marked than those between social classes, and they also increase with age. Children of low intelligence were three or four years behind children of high intelligence in developing a sense of effectiveness; the eighth-grade child of low intelligence was scarcely above the highly intelligent third- or fourth-grader.

On effectiveness, as on most matters where there were variations by both social class and level of intelligence, the difference between low- and high-status children was less than, but in the same direction as, the difference between children of low and high intelligence (see Figure 2). In addition to feeling less effective, children from the lower class and children with low IQs tend to be more loyal, accepting, and compliant and less interested and involved in politics than children from the middle and upper classes and children with high IQs—in short, to be more trusting and apathetic.

Another way of putting it is to say that children from low-status homes and children of low intelligence are retarded in their socialization to effective participation in the political system. But perhaps they are only a little more retarded than children from other groups.

Children of all classes and all levels of intelligence seem to be learning an incomplete, simplistic, and cognitively fragmented view of the political process, and the situation is likely to persist as long as the schools stress values and ideals, the individual and his vote, and

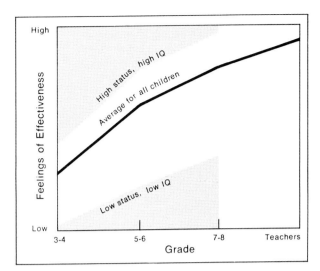

Figure 2. Effect of IQ and social status on feelings of ability to influence government.

the need for compliance and consensus at the expense of social realities, the role of groups, and the uses of controversy and argument.

The strength of current protests against social and political conditions, and the fact that they are focused on institutions, is a sign of vigor: it indicates at least a hope that remedies can be found short of full revolution. However, under the circumstances it makes very little sense to instill in children a superficial faith in the institutions under attack, to gloss over social realities, and to obscure many of the routes effective action can take. More useful would be a candid acknowledgment of political and social facts and, especially, a clear explanation of the ways that institutions can be influenced and changed.

II
Race and Race Relations

The Other Bodies in the River

Lloyd T. Delany

What is it like to be a black American? Will white Americans every really know, and, if they don't, will they really care about the problems that black citizens face? Probably no social problem in the United States today is as important as the color confrontation now taking place. But does everyone, particularly every-white-one, understand that a problem exists? In the following article, Lloyd T. Delany insists that white America suffers from a massive case of color shock, that it sweeps its guilts and anxieties under the carpet of continuing indifference, justifying its pathological behavior toward Negroes in a variety of predictable ways. And in this case, the pathology far too often leads to a brick smashing into a five-year-old's mouth or unaccounted-for bodies floating strangely, silently down a brackish Southern river.

On April 4, 1968, a bullet speeding across an open courtyard smashed Martin Luther King in the face. He died soon after. National response ran from open joy or indifference to deep shock, horror, and grief. Yet the breath was hardly out of King before the racism of the white American began to manifest itself in its characteristic ways.

King's death was not the first time in recent years that white America was to be "shocked" by the display of white violence. He had been preceded by Emmet Till, a fourteen-year-old child who had been lynched in Mississippi for "looking at a white girl." In 1963, the civil rights leader Medgar Evers was left sprawled on his front lawn, shot to death before the eyes of his wife and children. The nation was to be "shocked" again in 1963

with the bombing of a church and the death of four black children who were in it attending Sunday school classes. In 1964, James Chaney, Andrew Goodman, and Michael Schwerner were shot down by a lynch mob near Philadelphia, Mississippi, a mob that included members of the sheriff's office. Reverend James L. Raab was beaten to death on the streets of Selma, and Mrs. Viola Gregg Liuzzo was shot to death on the road between Selma and Montgomery. The murderers, in each instance, were white. Most were never brought to trial, and the few who did get tried either were acquitted or received light jail terms.

These murders, though soon forgotten, did receive some degree of attention. But what of the thousands of other bodies? In that summer of 1964, while searching for the bodies of Chaney, Goodman, and Schwerner, the nearby rivers were dragged. The bodies of the three civil rights workers were not found in the dragging operation of the Pearl and Okatibee rivers, but others were found—one in the Mississippi was cut in half. The press of the nation gave only the most cursory coverage to these other bodies. Not one official in or out of Mississippi called for an investigation as to how or why these bodies came to be there. The pathology of American racism is nowhere more evident than in this vignette. We cannot ignore the death of Martin Luther King or of John Kennedy, but we can and do overlook the bodies of the nameless, poor and black.

Two black men, commenting seventy-four years apart, both illuminated the sickness of American racism and demonstrate that its roots pervade not only the assassins but the total society.

Frederick Douglass, in 1892, wrote:

Where rests the responsibility for the lynch mob? . . . It is evident it is not entirely within the ignorant mob. . . . They are simply the hangmen, not the court, judge, or jury. They simply obey the public sentiment . . . the sentiment created by wealth and respectability, by press and pulpit . . .

Dr. Benjamin Mays, retired president of Morehouse College, was to restate the words of Douglass in his eulogy of Martin Luther King.

We all pray that the assassin will be apprehended and brought to justice, but make no mistake, the American people are in part responsible for the death of Martin Luther King. The assassin heard enough condemnation of King and Negroes to feel that he had public support. He knew that there were millions of people in the United States that wished that King were dead. He had support. The Memphis officials must bear some of the guilt for Martin Luther King's assassination.

The sickness of racism runs deep in the history of this nation. No institution is immune. Our "honored" leaders past and present exhibit it as do our churches, synagogues, our schools, courts, and our laws. It is found in newspapers, on radio, and television; our books overflow with racist ideology and myths. No vestige of the American community is free of it, no American citizen evades its expression or its impact on his life.

Few Americans know that black men were with Columbus when he discovered the West Indies; one was a pilot of one of the three ships. Estevanico explored and discovered the southwest in this nation. A black man, Du Sable, founded Chicago. The first man to fall for the independence of all the white racists was Crispus Attucks, a black man. Americans do not know that black men and a black woman fought with the Minutemen at Lexington and Concord, and that five thousand black men fought in the American Revolution. Blacks fought with Jackson in New Orleans in 1812. And 186,000 black men fought in the Civil War

to preserve the unity of this nation. Blacks rode with Teddy Roosevelt's Rough Riders in the Spanish American War. Black units received special commendations for their valor and bravery in World War I, and hundreds of thousands of black men fought German racism in World War II in a segregated army. Black men fought in Korea, and black men are dying today in Vietnam in higher proportions than their white American compatriots.

A superb irony lies in the fact that the lives of thousands of Americans in World War II were saved by a black man, Dr. Charles Drew, who established the method for preserving blood plasma. Even though Dr. Drew was the discoverer of this method, he himself would have been subjected to the irrational practice at that time that separated black and white blood; there is no difference between the blood of humans. This is a clear demonstration of the irrationality of American racism.

Racism in this nation has generally taken two forms. They are not mutually exclusive, but for the purposes of clarity they may be separated in discussion. The most obvious is the overt expression of racist ideology and actions.

The most explicit, unequivocal expression of racism can be found in the utterance of a former Chief Justice of the United States Supreme Court. In 1859, Roger B. Taney, in rendering the Dred Scott Decision, wrote that the statements in the Declaration of Independence and the phrase in the Constitution, "We the people of the United States," was not intended to include Negroes. He expanded in his decision, writing:

This unfortunate class have, with the civilized and enlightened portion of the world, for more than a century, been regarded as being of an inferior order, and unfit associates for the white race, either socially or politically, having no rights which white men are bound to respect . . .

Taney's views are shared today by millions in American society, and their acts express those beliefs.

The other form of American racism is less obvious, often cloaked in respectable-sounding phraseology. Thomas Jefferson, who wrote, "All men are created equal and endowed by their Creator with . . . life, liberty and the pursuit of happiness," held in bondage 106 men, women, and children. In a letter to a friend, Edward Coles, dated August 25, 1814, Jefferson wrote:

Nothing is more certainly written in the book of fate, than that these people ought to be free; nor is it less certain than that the two races, equally free, cannot live in the same government. Nature, habit, opinion, have drawn indelible lines of distinction between them.

Taney and Jefferson, both learned, both holding the highest positions of power and authority in the society —both espousing racism, one unequivocally, the other cloaked in pseudo-compassion and respectability.

Black Violence and White Violence

It is of some pertinence here to discuss the difference between black violence and white violence, since the recent ghetto riots are used to such an extent by whites to justify their racism.

The report of the National Advisory Commission on Civil Disorders documents historically that until World War II the riots and racial conflicts that occurred in this nation were almost invariably instigated by whites. They involved personal attacks and injury to blacks; they involved the destruction of property within the ghetto areas. There have been no riots over the past twenty-five years involving blacks during which blacks have invaded white areas. Very few whites have been personally attacked in any of the hundreds of major and minor racial disorders that have occurred in the twenty-

five years. The number of blacks who were injured in the riots prior to World War II far exceeded the number of whites who were injured, because they were personally attacked by white citizenry and officials. The few attacks on whites were incidental, and nothing demonstrates this more clearly than the fact that a white reporter can stand in the midst of a so-called riot, interview the rioters, and leave that community entirely unscathed. Yet, can anyone conceive of a black reporter standing in the midst of a Klan meeting, interviewing Klansmen? Or see a black reporter standing in Milwaukee, interviewing the demonstrators who opposed open housing there?

The Pathology of Racism

The presence of racism, some would argue, is not perforce evidence of pathology. As a psychoanalyst and psychologist, the pathology of racism is obvious to me; it can be documented and supported by evidence in clinical analogy. One of the major clinical examples of pathology in individuals is the utilization of certain defense mechanisms. These mechanisms can also be recognized as operating in racism for the society. I intend, therefore, to trace some societal defense operations that, if seen in an individual by a clinician, would be considered ipso facto pathological.

| ACTING OUT | Acting out is invariably an indication of pathology. In acting out, feelings like resentment or frustration that cannot be traced to a cause or are too dangerous to release on their real targets are vented on inappropriate but safe victims. Racism has often been expressed in the acting out of feelings of hate and rage. One section of the Report of the National Advisory Commission on Civil Disorders traces the history of violence in the society. The Commission describes the Cincinnati riot of 1829:

In 1829 white residents invaded Cincinnati's "little Africa," killed the Negroes, burned their property and ultimately drove half the colored population from the city.

The riot of 1865 in New York City:

The crowd refused to permit firemen into the area and the whole block was gutted. Then the mob spilled into the Negro area, where many were slain and thousands forced to flee town. The police were helpless . . .

The East St. Louis riot of 1917:

The authority for the event records that the area became "a bloody half mile" for three or four hours; streetcars were stopped, and Negroes, without regard to age or sex, were pulled off and stoned, clubbed and kicked, and mob leaders calmly shot and killed Negroes who were lying in the blood in the street. As the victims were placed in an ambulance, the crowds cheered and applauded. Other rioters set fire to Negroes' homes, and by midnight the Negro section was in flames and Negroes were fleeing the city. There were 48 dead, hundreds injured and more than 300 buildings destroyed.

Other examples of the pathological acting out of hate can be found in the statistics on lynching: A study (*Thirty Years of Lynching*, 1919) conducted by the National Association for the Advancement of Colored People proved that between 1892 and 1918 a black man, woman, or child was lynched every three and one-half days in some part of the United States. The report cites specific instances in addition to the overall statistics:

For the crime of killing a white man's cow, William Carr, a Negro, was killed at Planquemies, Louisiana. The lynching was conducted in a most orderly manner, Carr being taken from the sheriff without resistance by a mob of thirty masked men, hurried to the nearest railroad bridge and hanged without ceremony.

The acting out of hate is not limited to ordinary

citizens. The Commission Report quotes General Sheridan's description of the 1870 New Orleans riot:

At least nine-tenths of the casualties were perpetrated by the citizens and police by stabbing and smashing in the heads of many who had already been wounded and killed by policemen . . . It's not just a riot but an absolute massacre by the police . . . A murder which the mayor and police . . . perpetuated without a shadow of necessity.

A more recent example of the acting out of hate by law enforcement officials is described by an eyewitness in the Commission's Report of the Newark riots: He stated that National Guardsmen who were brought in to subdue the riot shot up stores that had signs indicating they were black owned. These stores had been passed over by the rioters for that reason, but the National Guardsmen shot them up.

| DENIAL | Another mechanism that demonstrates the pathology of the individual is denial. Denial is a response to the environment in which the person merely says that something that actually occurred did not occur. It is a direct denial of reality. Denial is also pathologically present in American society, particularly in reference to racial conflicts. A few cogent examples follow.

An examination of the Mississippi press reaction during the period when the bodies of Chaney, Goodman, and Schwerner were still missing shows classical examples of denial. From the *Meridian Star*, July 26, 1964:

Now about these so-called missing civil rights workers. They are no more missing than I am. They are in a safe place. Most likely in a northern state in a swanky hotel. They dropped out of sight for one reason and that was to get the FBI into our state. Mississippi people are not fools and they don't believe that these men met any form of foul play.

From the Jackson *Clarion-Ledger*, August 3, 1964:

If they were murdered, it is by no means the first case of such disposition by communists of their dupes to insure their silence. However, the careful absence of clues makes it seem likely that they are quartered in Cuba or another communist area awaiting their next task. There is no reason to believe them seriously harmed by citizens of the most law-abiding state in the Union.

Sometimes the mechanism of denial is accompanied by a thought disorder. This is exemplified by the response of the Governor of Georgia, Lester G. Maddox, following the assassination of Martin Luther King, as quoted in the *New York Times*, April 11, 1968:

Could it be that the communists had decided that he [Dr. King] had lost his effectiveness and this was a way to revitalize their efforts or was this only a blind to pass the Civil Rights Bill? I believe they [the communists] done him in and I will continue to believe that until they apprehend the killer and they prove otherwise. I hope I am wrong and the guilty person is apprehended.

The final statement of the Governor contradicts everything he said previously, indicating a thought disorder. | PROJECTION | Projection enables an individual to attribute his own undesired characteristics to others; consequently, it is commonly used to avoid personal conflict. James Baldwin, in his book *The Fire Next Time*, comments on how whites use this device in handling their conflicts over racial interactions:

If one examines the myths which proliferate in this country concerning the Negro, one discovers beneath these myths a kind of sleeping terror of some condition which we refuse to imagine. In a way, if the Negro were not here, we might be forced to deal within ourselves and our own personalities with all those vices, all those conundrums, and all those mysteries with which we invest the Negro race. . . . The Negro is thus penalized for the guilty imagination of the white people, who invest him with their hates and longings, and the Negro is the principal target of their sexual paranoia. . . . We would never allow Negroes to starve, to grow bitter, to die in ghettoes all over the country if we were not driven by some nameless fear that has nothing to do with Negroes.

Projection is one of the most widespread psychological mechanisms underlying the stereotypes and myths that have evolved around what being black means in the minds of white Americans.

| DISASSOCIATION | Closely related to denial but considerably more sweeping is the process of disassociation, in which large segments of one's actions and/or experiences are treated as if they do not exist. The response of the American society to people of Japanese ancestry during World War II exemplifies not only the virulent racism in the nation but the pathological manner by which the society avoids a confrontation with its racist character.

The history of racist attitudes and acts toward the Japanese, especially along the West Coast, is long. As early as 1908, racist legislation against them was instituted. The culmination of this occurred during the days following our entry into World War II, when all Japanese—citizens and aliens alike—were evacuated from their homes to "relocation camps" in other parts of the country. The camps' euphemistic title was belied by the barbed wire and armed guards. Franklin Delano Roosevelt, the Jefferson of his day, executed the order. The American society sat in movie houses watching the newsreels or listened impassively to their radios while an act was being committed in this nation the racist nature of which was exceeded only by the genocide of the red man and the enslavement of blacks. They disassociated it. After all, we were busy fighting a war against racism. | TRANSFER OF BLAME | One of the major mechanisms employed by emotionally ill people is transfer of blame: The individual disowns the responsibility for his own acts by finding another person who can be blamed. Per-

haps no characteristic of American racism is more common than this. It enables the American white racist to turn over to the black man blame for the black's difficulties—difficulties that were, in fact, created by racism. For instance, whites blame blacks for being lazy, when, of course, blacks don't work because they are not hired or are paid starvation wages when they do work. The Report on Civil Disorders states:

Pervasive unemployment and underemployment are the most persistent and serious grievances in minority areas. They are inextricably linked to the problem of civil disorder. Despite growing federal expenditures for manpower training development programs, sustained general economic prosperity, and increasing demands for the skilled workers, about two million —white and nonwhite—are permanently unemployed. About 10 million are underemployed, of whom 6½ million work full time for wages below the poverty line.

Whites blame blacks for living in squalor. In reference to housing, the Commission Report states:

Nearly 6 million substandard housing units remain occupied in the United States. The housing problem is particularly acute in the minority ghettoes. . . . Many ghetto residents simply cannot pay the rent necessary to support decent housing. In Detroit, for example, over 40% of the nonwhite occupied units required rent of over 35% of the tenants' income. Discrimination prevents access to many nonslum areas, particularly the suburbs where good housing exists . . . To date, federal programs have been able to do comparatively little to provide housing for the disadvantaged. In the 31-year history of subsidized federal housing only about 800,000 units have been constructed, with recent production averaging about 50,000 units per year. By comparison, over a period only three years longer, FHA insurance guarantees have made possible the construction of over 10,000,000 middle and upper income units.

The mechanism of transfer of blame operates to prevent any confrontation by whites of the nature and character of racism in American society.

| JUSTIFICATION | Another device commonly used by people with emotional disorders is justification; the individual attempts to provide a "reasonable" explanation for his behavior, and to the extent that he can accomplish this, he can avoid confrontation of his unacceptable feelings.

Racism in American society is pervaded with attempted justification. A cogent example is a letter to the editor of *Newsday*:

I am a white middle class American who along with tens of millions of other middle class Americans, both white and black, have been roundly criticized and condemned as "racists" by the President's Commission on Civil Disorders. I am a white, middle class American who served his country in World War II, who managed via 22 years of hard work and initiative to pull himself and his family out of the slums . . . to live in a middle class community in a house which will require 19 more years of labor to pay for. . . . I am tired of hearing "whitey" blamed for all the plights and ills of the Negro in Harlem and elsewhere, and I am sick and tired of the "get whitey" slogans of the black extremists who would like to take what "whitey" possesses rather than break their collective backs working for it like this "whitey" has.

Yes, I am a white, middle class American, tired but proud of my accomplishments and my heritage, proud of the community in which I reside, proud of my country . . . I shall continue to pay my taxes to support my community and my beloved America and be darn glad of the opportunity to do so. If this effort be labeled "racist" by the learned gentlemen of the President's panel, then I shall wear this label with pride. . .

The pathology of the man who pulled the trigger in Memphis is obvious, that of the men who dumped the bodies in the rivers is clear. The pathology of this letter-writer and the "tens of millions" like him often escapes us. American society is our letter-writer. He is sick, and far more dangerous because he denies his illness while in the very act of displaying it. He cannot see any connection between his beliefs, attitudes, and actions and the actions of the trigger man in Memphis.

He is dangerous because he cannot be reached as long as he wraps himself in the self-righteousness of his bigotry. He is sick because in reading the Commission's Report, he refused to face what he read, and like millions of other whites, he disassociates his blatant, obvious distortions of attitudes towards blacks and other minorities.

He is sick because his grasp of reality is tenuous. He lives in a world peopled by his unrealistic fantasies of himself and others. He interprets what he sees in ways to perpetuate this unreal self-concept. He is sick because he has never asked himself why. He has never asked himself why because he would have to confront his responsibility. He would have to confront, for example, the fact that his middle-class community is all white not because there are no blacks who could live there but because he and all his neighbors will not sell to a black man. He would have to confront himself and know that if a black man who had "pulled himself out of the slums" moved next door, he would quickly sell his house in panic, creating another fantasy about deterioration of property values or about his two-year-old daughter marrying the black man's three-year-old son.

The author of that letter puts the issue where it belongs. He is an American, heart and soul. He is a racist from the tip of his shoes to the crown of his hat. He is a racist because he has a systematic value system, a bias toward people who are different from him. He is a racist because his bias is based on preconceived attitudes and values and unfounded in fact. He is a racist because he lacks an awareness of his common humanity with all men.

Facts will not change his views, for facts do not change values and attitudes that are grounded in emotions. These attitudes and emotions serve a need that facts by themselves cannot assuage. No form of racism is more difficult to confront than that which is unconscious and uses the mechanisms of acting out, transfer of blame, projection, denial, or the other mechanisms discussed.

Uses of Guilt

The sanctimony, the mourning that went on following the death of Martin Luther King is one of the chief characteristics of American racism. In America we often attempt to dull our racism by excessive displays of guilt. Guilt, psychologically, is a mechanism that can easily become a tool for permitting us to continue acting the way we wish to act; once we have admitted our guilt, once we have displayed our remorse, we are relieved and can continue to do what we did in the first place, having established to ourselves and others that we are indeed good, decent people.

The response of many Americans following the death of Martin Luther King reveals how guilt is used to cover and mute confrontation with racism. Following his death, the communications media, government officials —national and local—citizens on corners, preachers in pulpits, rocked and rolled with self-pitying, platitudinous epitaphs. The nation was smothered in rhetoric, copious in self-praise as to how great a nation we were to mourn and honor this black man. But almost ignored in this display was the fact that Martin Luther King was slain by white violence and is a victim of white racism, as are the thousands of other bodies.

We must ask ourselves: What kind of society are we to have created and given birth to such virulent and pervasive hate? The question has been answered by the whole history of racism in America. It was answered by the Commission on Civil Disorders in its Report:

What white America has never fully understood—but what the Negro can never forget—is that white society is deeply implicated in the ghetto. White institutions created it, white institutions maintain it, and white society condones it.

Nothing more clearly demonstrates the tragic components of our sick society than an account by Dick Gregory, published in *Newsday*, of the first days of school integration in the South:

You ought to try to integrate those schools like we did in Greenwood, Mississippi. Spent the whole summer talking to colored folk trying to get them to commit their kids. Had to lie to them, tell them the government was going to protect them, but we knew damn good and well we were all going to get killed. And you finally get 12 black kids committed. But the morning school is opened you only got 8. Maybe you got to feel what it feels like to be walking down that street with that little black kid's hand in the palm of your hand and your hand is soaking wet—from *your* sweat because you know what's going to happen but the kid don't. And as you approach those steps to that school, not only are you attacked by the white mob but also by the sheriff and the police.

Next thing you know you're knocked down in the gutter with that cracker's foot in your chest and a double barrel shot-gun in your throat saying "move, nigger, and I'll blow your brains out"—which is interesting 'cause the only time that a cracker ever admits we got brains is when he says what he's going to do to them.

Maybe you have to lay in that gutter, knowing it's *your* time now, baby, and then you look across the street, laying down in the gutter, from the gutter position, and see the FBI standing across the street taking pictures. . . . And then as you lay there in that gutter, man, it finally dawns on you that that little five-year-old kid's hand is not in the palm of your hand anymore. And that really scares you . . . and you look around trying to find the kid and you find him just in time to see a brick hit him right in the mouth. Man, you wouldn't believe it until you see a brick hit a five-year-old kid in the mouth.

Racism
and Strategies for Change

Lloyd T. Delany

If the Negro is to assume his rightful place in American society, if further bodies floating down the river are to be avoided, and internecine war between racial groups is to be prevented, there will have to be changes in the ways that blacks and whites treat each other. Many such changes will come about only when the white citizen learns to perceive the black citizen more humanely and more realistically; but it is also true that the Negro must come to see himself in a different light. Lloyd T. Delany now suggests several ways in which we might all help bring these perceptual changes about.

Not all whites are racist, but most racists are white. For the racist, the accident of birth becomes the most important determinant of his interaction with others. His actions and attitudes are generated and sustained by a persevering preoccupation with minor biogenetic differences. And he generalizes from these differences.

A new society in which racism is a major theme quickly establishes a network of institutions to perpetuate its racist actions and attitudes. And eventually racism affects all the members of the society. Such is the nature of American bigotry.

How do we overcome the problem?

Self-delusion is self-destructive, therefore any strategy for change requires self-awareness. To eradicate racism it is necessary first to understand its historic roots and the myriad manifestations this particular and unique form of bigotry has taken.

Racism in nations other than the United States in the Western Hemisphere is a minor form of bigotry—if not totally absent. One of the most thorough and cogent statements of the history of racism is in Frank Tannenbaum's book *Slave and Citizen: The Negro in the Americas.*

Tannenbaum traces the history of slavery in the Western Hemisphere, documenting how early attitudes toward slavery influenced present-day attitudes toward blacks in the various parts of the Western Hemisphere.

There were three major influences on slavery in this part of the world: Dutch-English, French, and Spanish-Portuguese. Tannenbaum describes the Spanish and Portuguese attitudes toward slavery:

The element of human personality was not lost in the transition to slavery from Africa to the Spanish or Portuguese dominions. A slave remained a *person* though a slave. He retained his right to buy his freedom and thus the essential elements of moral worth that make freedom a possibility. He was not considered chattel, never defined or treated as unanimated property. Though excesses and cruelties existed, the master was not supposed to hold life and death power over the slave.

In contrast with this was the Dutch-English system. "The slave had no rights in law and acquired none by contract," Tannenbaum explains. "In the absence of either religious or legal provisions for the slave, it was not illogical for the planter in the West Indies and in the American Colonies to settle the legal issue involved by legally defining the slave as chattel." And these attitudes toward the black remained in each of the systems after the emancipation of the slave.

In Latin America the Negro was encouraged toward obtaining his freedom, and once free, there were no obstacles to his incorporation in the community. In Brazil, for instance, it was from the ranks of the Negroes and mulattoes that some of the great artists, musicians, and sculptors came.

In the United States, Tannenbaum points out:

The Negro was considered a slave by nature, and he could not escape his natural shortcomings even if he managed to evade their legal consequences. Freedom was made difficult for achievement and made to be undesirable both for the Negro and the white man's community in which the Negro resided.

This distinction had been drawn in absolute terms, not merely between the slave and the free man, but between the

Negro and the white man. The contrast was between color—the Negro was the slave.

As long as the slave owner could regard the slave as nonhuman or chattel then any form of behavior was acceptable. After all, one can do with property what one chooses: one can break up families, if they are not families of human beings. The selling of children and the other barbarities and atrocities that have been well documented about slavery stemmed from this depersonalization of the black. Although slavery has been abolished, the depersonalized attitude toward the black exists. Too many Americans still think of Little Black Sambo stereotypes.

A critical paradox confronting America exists because even the institutions designed to combat prejudice and bigotry too often are agents for perpetuating racism. It is this paradox that shadows any simple confrontation and resolution of American racism.

The key to effective strategies in handling prejudice is this: depersonalization of blacks and other minorities in our society can be reversed by invoking the *same* strategies and techniques originally employed to depersonalize blacks in the past.

Using this general guiding principle, it is possible not only to examine specific ways in which depersonalization of the black man has occurred in this society, but also to look at ways out of the tangled mess. Let us examine the two important problem and strategy areas —utilization of police power and the communications media. Each provides a model that can be superimposed on any of the other strategies that have been employed or can be employed to bring about changes in America.

Depersonalization in Law Enforcement

Law enforcement agencies are replete with instances of the most obvious forms of racism. In recent years there have been increasing attempts on the part of some police departments to change the direct expression of the racism within the departments and to alter the attitudes of police toward minorities generally, and black people specifically.

But it is well to point out that many authoritative studies, including the Report of the President's Advisory Commission on Civil Disorders and a fine book by George Edwards, Justice of the United States Court of Appeals, Sixth Circuit, show that racism in northern police departments is just as prevalent as in the South.

Judge Edwards, a former Detroit police commissioner, makes this comment in his book *The Police on Urban Frontiers:* "Policemen in the North and South became deeply imbued with the idea that the major part of their responsibility was to keep the Negro in his place . . . often did not heed to distinguish between law-abiding and lawless Negroes. . . ." This is strikingly similar to the National Advisory Commission

Report's statement: "In practically every city that experienced racial disruptions since the summer of 1964, abrasive relationships between police and Negroes and other minority groups have been the major source of grievance, tension and ultimate disorder. . . ."

Professor Albert Reiss, Director of the Center of Research on Social Organization, University of Michigan, found in his study of police methods and action:

In predominantly Negro precincts over three-fourths of the white policemen express prejudice or highly prejudiced attitudes toward Negroes. Only one per cent of the officers expressed attitudes which could be described as sympathetic toward Negroes. Indeed, close to one-half of all the officers in the predominantly Negro high-crime-rate areas show extreme prejudice against Negroes.

This is only one aspect of the problem of racism in police work. The National Advisory Commission found: "The proportion of Negroes on the police force still falls far below the proportion of Negroes in the total population. . . ." And there are too many documented cases of police brutality toward minorities for a healthy nation to endure.

A frequently overlooked factor is the prevalence of disturbed personnel in police departments. Very few police departments have any standards for screening police personnel either in terms of psychiatric problems or of intellectual competence. Only one-fourth of police departments in the country have any kind of screening for emotional fitness. In those few that require psychiatric tests to spot racial bias, sadism, and panic response, an amazing number of applicants have been dropped. In Portland, 25 percent of police applicants fail to pass a psychiatric screening.

| SUCCESSFUL NEW STRATEGIES | Notwithstanding the history of racism in police departments, there are strategies that have been employed by some police departments, often with success. Herbert T. Jenkins, the police chief of Atlanta, Georgia, has made a serious attempt to bring about changes in his department. It is one of the most successful programs because it has not made the error common to many other such attempts. In Atlanta, the Crime Prevention Bureau established a good relationship with the community, and the National Advisory Commission reports:

It is concentrated [the Atlanta Crime Prevention Bureau] on social services persuading almost 600 drop-outs to return to school, assisting 250 hardship cases with food and work, arranging for dances and hydrant showers during the summer, working quickly and closely with families of missing persons. The result is close community rapport.

Bureau staffers perform such other tasks—historically alien to police work—as directing people to appropriate social agencies, helping job hunters, and delaying evictions. Quite simply the emphasis is on help rather than traditional hard-nosed law enforcement.

Operation Friend, the program in New York's 24th Police Precinct, has been successful. Judge Edwards describes it:

Operation Friend has produced everything from kite-flying contests for children to seminars for elders and classes in Puerto Rican *mores* for policemen. Operation Friend cuts two ways: persuading the citizenry that the police are human and humane servants of the public; persuading the policeman that they can win the backing of the community in functioning better. . . . The police decided to meet the Puerto Ricans half way. Teachers from the Board of Education went to the 24th Precinct and held classes in Spanish. Like a merchant who learns a language to sell his wares, the men of the 24th are learning to communicate. . . . Policemen have taken bus loads of youngsters to museums, the Hayden Planetarium, local beaches and to Washington, D.C. . . .

Last February, 39 children and a contingent of policemen went to a camp at Rifton, New York, for a winter vacation. . . . A small foundation grant made it possible for 11 policemen from the area to spend two weeks in Puerto Rico with local families to gain an insight into the problems of the Puerto Rican and the frustrations of the Puerto Rican when he came to New York.

The Harlem riot of 1964 was in response to a police incident in which an off-duty police lieutenant shot and killed a fourteen-year-old youngster. As a direct result of that riot, a black police officer was appointed to head the 32nd Police Precinct in the heart of Harlem. In the midst of seething tension, Captain Lloyd Sealy did more in the relatively short time he held the Harlem post than anyone had been able to do in the preceding 30 to 40 years of police relationships in the Harlem community. And not just because he was black. Quite obviously, his blackness to him was only incidental to his approach. The approach was straightforward. He regarded the residents of Harlem as people and put into effect programs and specific strategies based on this premise.

He immediately made it quite clear to those police officers under his command that he would not tolerate any unwarranted use of force, any deprecation of black citizens in that community. And he meant what he said. Sealy sought to educate his officers about underlying socioeconomic factors in the black community. He began a program of education aimed at developing police awareness of who the Harlem residents were, where they came from, what motivated them. Most important, he stressed their individuality.

He attended community meetings night and day, his presence was felt in that community not as the usual black perception of the policeman—the enforcer of the status quo, the enforcer of racism and bigotry of the white community—but as a man who was there to support the community, to give protection, and to extend needed service.

Unfortunately, because of his stunning success, Lloyd Sealy's stay in Harlem was short. He was promoted, and he has left that community. And, sadly, too little has been done since to continue strongly the programs he instituted.

If daily communication continues over a long enough period of time, there follows necessarily a mutual change in perceptions on the part of the community and on the part of the police officer. This day-to-day communication means that both the cop on the beat and black man on the street can and will begin to see one another as people. There is a recognition on the part of the police that there are various kinds of citizens in the community.

The effective police officer must have knowledge of the community, including understanding of all of community leadership—the indigenous leaders as well as the political leaders; not only those who have national prominence or local prominence, but the people who, to use the cliché, are the real grass-roots leaders—the opinion leaders on the street corners.

The most influential people may not be particularly well educated or even particularly articulate. But their opinions are highly regarded by their neighbors. They exercise direct and immediate influence. If one moves into these communities and gets to know the social structure, one can quickly begin to spot the true indigenous leaders in that community.

There is need in all of these strategies to evaluate the complaints of citizens, to take them seriously, and to be willing to act on those complaints. And definitely *not* to act as though in every instance where there is a confrontation between a black citizen and a policeman, the citizen is wrong, the policeman right. This is just not necessarily so.

Law enforcement agencies must make it clear that any officer who abuses his position will be reprimanded as required. We should not move from the extreme of denying that abuses exist to the extreme of dismissing an officer for the slightest abridgment of regulations. The punishment should fit the proved crime, nothing more, nothing less. There are few institutions in our society which claim that every member's conduct is above question. Most police departments do. And no group personifies this more clearly than the Police Benevolent Association of New York, which automatically supports every single policeman in every single interaction with a citizen, be he black or white.

During the struggle for the perpetuation of a Civilian Review Board in New York City, the black policemen and their organization came out strongly in support of a Civilian Review Board.

That the Civilian Review Board was a racial issue is made clear by the fact that the black policemen supported it totally, while white policemen by and large opposed creation of such a board. The New York press made almost no attempt to distinguish between the positions of the black and white policemen.

The black citizenry's ability to voice grievances and

to have legitimate recourse for unwarranted police acts is, of course, basic to successful police functioning, and basic to the success of any strategy in changing racism.

Depersonalization in Media

The communications media have encouraged racism—press, radio, television, movies, and books. In the day-to-day process, the media with the most direct impact on the lives of people are newspapers, radio, and TV. In long-range attitudes, motion pictures, the theater, and books not only have shaped the racist nature of our society, but have perpetuated it. In its report on the role of the communications media, the National Advisory Commission on Civil Disorders said:

Far too often the press talks and acts about Negroes as if they did not read the newspapers or watch television, give birth, marry, die, or go to PTA meetings. . . . Most newspaper articles and television programming ignore the fact that an appreciable part of their audience is black. The world that television and newspapers offer to their black audience is almost totally white, both in appearance and attitude.

This is another expression of racial depersonalization in our society. The absence of any significant number of blacks in the communications field is another important factor. In 1964, for instance (the latest figures available), the American Newspaper Guild could name only forty-five Negroes working as reporters, copy readers, or desk men on the metropolitan daily newspapers in the United States. The most generous employment estimates put the number of Negroes in news jobs at 100 out of a total of 50,000 men and women.

Ignoring blacks and failing to employ them is not, however, the only racial affliction suffered by the communications media. Ted Poston, a black reporter of long experience on the oldest newspaper in the country, *The New York Post,* has written: "During my 35 years in this business, I have observed northern editors and publishers creating a subtle myth: that northern Negroes are really a monolithic mass, not plain individual Americans, and that they must be reviewed and reported in that context." Though directed toward newspapers, Poston's remarks are equally applicable to all communications media. There are only rare attempts in press, radio, television, plays, movies, or books to depict the black person as human, as varying, as having individuality and an identity—something quite separate from the monolithic mass to which Poston refers.

No one in white America would point to a single individual whom they could designate as *the* leader of whites. Even President Johnson, elected with the largest majority of any president in our history, could not stake such a claim. Yet there is no hesitancy on the part of the media to designate any number of people at different times as "*the* black leader."

Television, the newest of the media, is not free from racism either. A hullaballoo started when Harry Bela-fonte was to appear on a TV special as the guest star of Petula Clark. Quite spontaneously, during the filming of this special, Miss Clark placed her hand on Harry Belafonte's arm. And the show's directors wanted to cut out this film segment. Only because of considerable resistance from Miss Clark and Mr. Belafonte did the fragmentary moment of warmth remain in the show.

A number of years ago, a major TV network wanted to film a community agency program on New York's Lower East Side. This agency is integrated, with young people of all races and ethnic groups; they come to the center and play together, play Ping-Pong together, shoot pool together, sit and talk together, join clubs together, dance together.

When camera crews arrived and saw the teenagers dancing, some white and black youngsters were dancing together. The TV directors insisted that there could be no such interracial dancing during the filming of this show, a "spontaneous" portrayal of the agency program. The agency personnel refused to comply with this request. Eventually the show was presented naturally, as the community agency insisted, and, so far as we know, there were none of the dire consequences the TV directors seemed to fear.

Our literature is replete with racism. William Styron's best-selling *The Confessions of Nat Turner* (Random House, 1967) says something about American racism. Fine book that it is, *Nat Turner* is a comfortable novel for whites, fulfilling all the myths they have about black people. Most black publications, black reviewers, and some whites have attacked this novel as falling into a racist trap.

| POSSIBLE NEW STRATEGIES | What strategies in this context would seem necessary to reverse the racist nature of the communications media? There are, of course, the obvious strategies suggested by the National Advisory Commission. The Commission urges that a number of steps be taken by the communications industry, such as the establishment of an Institute for Urban Communication, training and education of black journalists in the field of urban affairs, and recruitment and placement of black journalists.

Recently the Columbia Broadcasting System announced a plan to recruit more Negroes for its staff. Mike Dann, Senior Vice President for Programming, explained: "A reflection of the general racist situation as outlined in the Kerner Report and a realization that television can play an important part in communication between Negroes and Whites requires that these steps be taken."

The steps he refers to involve intensive, immediate portrayal and use of increased numbers of blacks on the entertainment programs, as well as attempts to portray the black man in everyday life.

A most intelligent comment on the role of the news media in relation to race is from Lawrence S. Fanning, former Executive Editor of *The Chicago Daily News.*

"If I have learned nothing else in the last 10 years, certainly we have seen that the man who says 'I treat everybody alike regardless of race, creed or color on a first come first serve basis' is either a fool or a knave," Fanning wrote in *Race and the News Media*. "The differences between people—and what we do about them—is what this racial crisis is all about." The editor, according to Fanning, will not speak out loudly for the necessity of impartial news judgment when he knows, if he cares to face himself with that fact, that his own fashion page or his own society page almost never shows a black face.

The fundamental question rests in decisions about what news to disseminate and what news not to disseminate, and this in itself is a partisan act.

Fanning speculates that: "In the midst of social cataclysm, telling both sides of the story may not always be telling the truth." The perceptiveness of this comment is understood by any who have participated in the civil rights movement. Civil rights workers are often frustrated by the press and the communications media—by the façade of impartiality, when to present both sides as if they were equally sound often is to distort the truth.

It is imperative that our communications media rethink their stand of so-called impartiality. Is there such a thing in reality?

Additional strategies are obvious: to present the black person in this nation as a human being, to put him on TV in all kinds of roles. Some blacks are servants, some are judges, some are housewives, some own businesses. They play tennis, ski, read books, eat hot dogs—all the good and bad things that any American citizen does. Any scene that involves general activities could present both blacks and whites in these ordinary everyday-living experiences without comment, without making an issue of it. There is no reason to present the black as either devil or angel.

Consider the kind of role Sidney Poitier plays. He must be above reproach. He is not permitted to have human reactions and responses. He must be kind, always understanding, and he must never make mistakes. He seldom is portrayed as having a wife, or a woman. He is the modern-day version of the "good nigger."

This is not to disparage Mr. Poitier's acting ability, character, or the important contribution he has made to the position of the black artist in the cinema. It is much more a comment on the underlying problem of the movie producers and the directors who fear that the only way they can permit a black actor to play a major role in the movies or television is to have him above reproach.

As long as this continues, they merely perpetuate the myth of depersonalization. The black man is neither better nor worse than the white man. He has no special qualities. He is not a symbol and should not be presented as such.

In Praise of Diversity

Most direct or indirect strategies to change racism fail because these approaches fit into the format of regarding all blacks as the same, as if the problem is not complicated by a host of other factors—psychological, moral, historical, national, geographic. Such strategies often fail to recognize that one kind of approach works in *one* situation, not in every situation; that the way one approaches young people is not the way one approaches old people, that the black urban dweller in Washington is not identical to the black urban dweller of Chicago, nor to the field hand of Alabama, that even within the ghettos there are differences among blacks—in life style, sentiments, and attitudes. For example, there is the simple truth that middle-aged blacks are confronted with the same generation gap as their white counterparts in the parent-teenage lack of contact and communication.

The whole concept of bringing about changes is far more complex than the approach assumed in most of our programs. These programs tend to continue and perpetuate the depersonalization of the black man by regarding him as a symbol, a monolithic mass, for which there is one aspirin that will resolve everything.

In view of the rash of civil disorders that have cropped up in various cities in the past five or six years, it has become a redundant litany among social scientists to talk about the despair of the existing society and the inevitable destruction of the society.

It is far more crucial that we stop our self-indulgent wailing and confront real issues. Racism in American society is one of the most pathological aspects of the society. It is a very complex form of pathology, and the strategies aimed at bringing about a change in our society are vital to all members of that society.

There are no simple solutions. We must accept the complexity of combating racism on the real issue—black and white recognition that the depersonalization that exists in *both* groups perpetuates the problem of racism.

Any strategies must constantly be policed to see whether they are in fact not committing the very mistake that created the problem in the first place. The lines in this black spiritual may be oversimplification, but they state the emphasis of this article clearly.

> *I wish I could share all the love that's in my heart,*
> *Remove all the bars that keep us apart.*
> *I wish you could know what it means to be me,*
> *Then you'd see and agree every man should be free.*

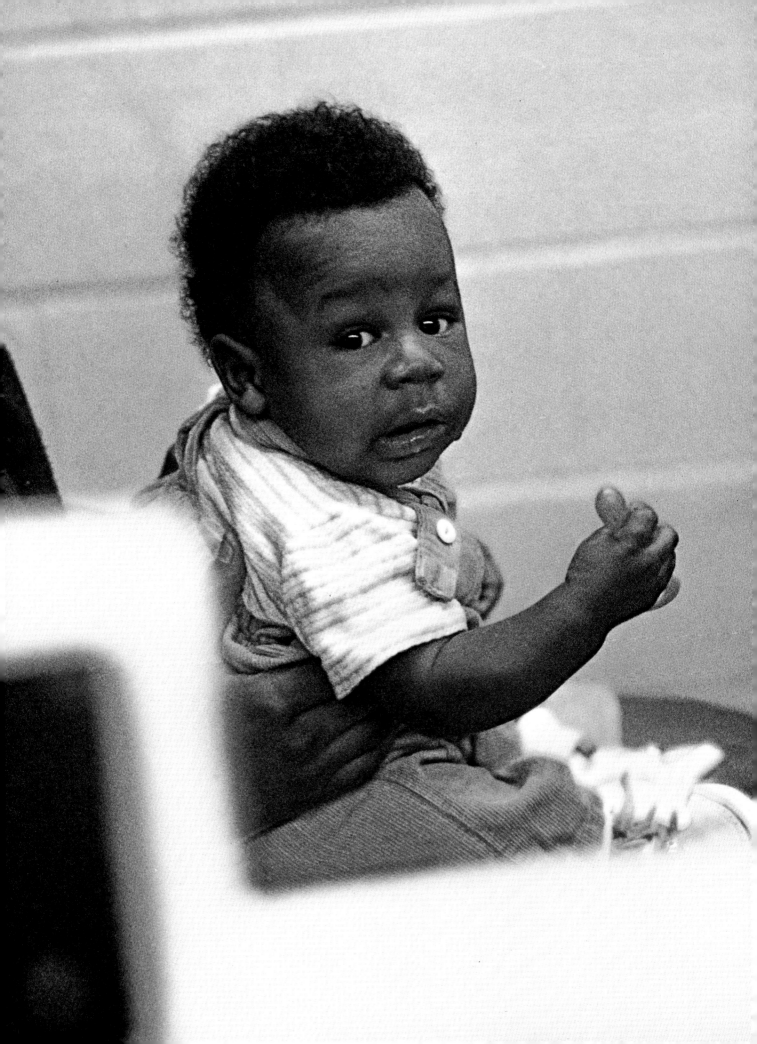

Civil Rights
and the Vote for President

Angus Campbell

That "civil rights" should be a campaign issue at all is a signal that all is not well in the United States; we are all—black and white—citizens, so it should follow that we are all equally entitled to our civil rights. Americans were sensitive to this issue in the 1964 election, and the striking differences in the campaign approaches to it by Johnson and Goldwater drew the battle lines clearly. But after the smoke clears and the ballots are counted, how is one to know whether it really was Johnson's civil rights stand that helped him accumulate all those votes? Angus Campbell, director, and his colleagues at the Survey Research Center, University of Michigan, have been conducting interviews with the electorate for twenty years; what they found about the impact of the civil rights issue on the 1964 vote could give the spirit a lift. Of course, there are his predictions about the shape of issues to come in 1968 . . .

The issue of civil rights divides white Americans more categorically and unites Negro Americans more completely than any political issue or any controversy in our country today. The confrontation that has been building between white and Negro populations over desegregation and civil rights emerged in 1966 in city elections throughout the United States. For the first time, Negroes were elected mayor in major American cities—Carl B. Stokes in Cleveland and Richard G. Hatcher in Gary, Indiana.

For the last two decades my colleagues and I at the Survey Research Center, University of Michigan, have been investigating the growing impact of racial issues on national politics. And one of our specific interests has been the impact of racial issues on the vote for President in the national elections.

In 1964, shortly after President Johnson's victory over Barry Goldwater, we made a particular effort to assess the contribution of the civil rights issue to the votes for each presidential candidate.

Our newspaper and television savants analyze voter intentions with ease after each election, and so it sometimes seems that the motives behind the voter's choice are simple. But in our twenty years of election surveys, we have learned to be suspicious of such simple explanations. The motives for important decisions seldom are clear-cut, and often the people making decisions really understand their own motivations very poorly.

The act of voting imposes a categorical yes-or-no choice upon the voter, and we have found that the voter's final choice frequently is the result of a conflict of motives. The explanations he will give for his choice are often superficial or palpably invalid.

Following each presidential election since 1948, and in four off-year congressional elections, we have conducted interviews with a representative sample of the national electorate. Our objective is to map the political life-space of the American electorate at the time voting decisions are made and to try to understand the interaction of those forces that shape the collective decision.

Our electorate sampling has varied in size from 1,600 to 2,000 persons, with the selection of voters to be interviewed made from records in our office through a probability sampling technique that gives each voter in the country an equal chance of being selected.

We expect our sampling error to be less than 3 percent, and comparison of the distribution of votes obtained in our interviews with the actual national vote shows that the sampling error has ranged from less than 1 percent up to 3 percent.

Our interviews are carried out in each chosen voter's home by a trained member of the Survey Research Center's field staff. It is from these interviews that we have recorded in detail the perceptions, attitudes, group attachments, and past experiences of a representative sample of the American electorate.

To assess the impact of even a single issue on the collective vote of more than 60 million people is a scientific problem of considerable magnitude. We began our search for the influence of the current racial situation on the vote for president by defining the basic attitude involved. The essential political quality of the present crisis in Negro-white relations lies in the growing pressure for the extension of full and equal civil rights to the Negro.

To measure public attitudes toward the civil rights issue we developed a list of five questions on desegregation of schools, open housing, desegregation of hotels and restaurants, and federal legislation concerning fair employment practices (see the questionnaire below).

1. Congress passed a bill that says that colored people should have the right to go to any hotel or restaurant they can afford, just like white people. Do you think the government should support the right of colored people to go to any hotel or restaurant they can afford or should it stay out of this matter?
2. Which of these statements would you agree with:
   White people have a right to keep Negroes out of their neighborhoods if they want to, or
   Negroes have a right to live wherever they can afford to, just like white people?
3. Some people say that the government in Washington should see to it that white and Negro children are allowed to go to the same schools. Others claim that this is not the government's business. Which side do you favor?
4. Some people feel that if Negroes are not getting fair treatment in jobs, the government in Washington ought to see to it that they do. Others feel that this is not the Federal government's business. How do you feel about it?
5. What about you? Are you in favor of desegregation, strict segregation, or something in between?

These five questions are systematically related to each other in such a way that a respondent who scores a favorable reaction to a proposal that generally has acceptance by the public will be disposed favorably to all proposals having greater public acceptability. The scaling technique used in scoring civil rights attitudes is called cumulative, or Guttman, scaling. It assures us that we are measuring a single attitude domain and measuring it with high reliability.

In our sampling, the responses to these questions in the autumn of 1964 revealed some basic and important facts about the civil rights attitudes of Americans.

Not surprisingly, three out of four Negroes expressed strongly favorable attitudes toward civil rights on all five questions. Most of the remaining Negroes expressed favorable attitudes, and none placed themselves at the negative extreme of the scale. This heavy support of Negroes for the listed civil rights questions is readily understandable; after all, it is *their* freedom of choice and *their* equality that are at stake.

Our survey results refute the argument sometimes put forward that Negroes are satisfied with the traditional patterns of segregation and are willing to let them continue. Except for that small percentage of Negro militants currently pressing for a program of "black separatism," American Negroes are generally resentful of segregation and wish to see it brought to an end.

Public opinion on social and political issues when plotted as a graph usually forms curves that are bell-shaped, flat, or J-shaped; the curve is seldom bimodal or U-shaped. Bell-shaped curves indicate that the majority of the voters sampled hold mixed or moderate opinions on the issue. Flat curves indicate that public opinion is evenly distributed. J-shaped curves indicate that the majority of the public place themselves at one extreme of the opinion scale. U-shaped curves indicate that public opinion is sharply divided or polarized. The curve of Negro attitudes to civil rights is J-shaped (see Figure 1a). Foreign-policy attitude curves are bell-shaped, and social-welfare attitude curves are frequently flat or moderately J-shaped.

The distribution of the attitudes of white voters toward the civil rights of Negroes proved to be quite extraordinary in 1964; they were strongly polarized at the two extremes of our attitude scale (see Figure 1b). We found that the issue of civil rights divides white Americans more categorically than any other issue we have examined in our nine national surveys since 1948.

The polarization of white attitudes is to a large extent a reflection of regional differences. White voters in the South, of course, are far less ready than the rest of the country to end segregation practices. The civil rights issue seems to be a modern restatement of the basic issue that brought about the Civil War more than a hundred years ago.

The Effect of the Cause

How has the issue of civil rights of Negroes affected national elections? To answer this question we must briefly step back into history. After the Civil War, the newly enfranchised Negroes rallied to the party of

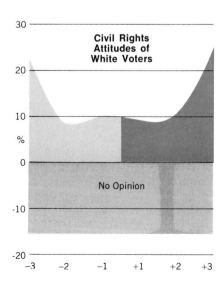

Lincoln. Racial issues were of very great political importance in the Southern states during the Reconstruction period and remained so until the "Black Codes" effectively disfranchised most Negroes and returned political power in the South to the white population. In the North, Negroes comprised such a small proportion of the population that they were easily ignored, and racial issues had little political significance.

In 1936, President Roosevelt's New Deal, with its welfare proposals, caused a dramatic and substantial realignment of the Negro vote from the Republican to the Democratic party. For example, in one Michigan metropolitan area, 19.5 percent of the Negro vote in 1930 went to the Democratic party; in 1936, the Negro vote for the Democratic party was 63.5 percent.

During the era of President Truman, there was some talk about Negro civil rights legislation, but the idea went into cold storage when Dwight D. Eisenhower became president. Pressure for civil rights did not become politically significant until after the 1954 Supreme Court ruling on racial segregation in public schools. From that time, public pressure for civil rights legislation rose until it culminated in the march on Washington in 1963 and the Civil Rights Act in the spring of 1964.

In the presidential elections of 1952, 1956, and 1960, there was no evidence in our surveys that the civil rights issue affected the vote for President in any significant way. This is also supported by evidence that during this period the Negro and the white votes moved in the same directions.

In the 1964 election, however, a new situation emerged. For the first time in four presidential elections, the voters had two presidential candidates with clearly different views on civil rights. President Johnson had sponsored the 1964 Civil Rights Act and had signed it into law. Senator Goldwater was one of the few members of the Senate who had voted against the act. The differences in the positions of the two candidates were more widely known by the voters than are most differences: more than 80 percent of the people we interviewed just after the 1964 election correctly identified the civil rights positions of Johnson and Goldwater. The clearly opposing civil rights platforms offered by Johnson and Goldwater presented a classical situation for the vote to polarize around a specific issue. How, then, did the civil rights issue affect the vote for president in 1964?

In each election, voters bring with them a set of long-standing political commitments; they do not enter a new political campaign as a totally new experience. Most Americans develop an identification with one of the major parties before they are old enough to vote, and their attachment generally grows stronger as they grow older.

Figure 1. Civil rights attitudes of (a) Negro voters, (b) white voters, as plotted from the questionnaire data. The U-shaped curve in (b), indicating polarization, is very unusual.

Three-fourths of the voters we interview invariably tell us that they "usually think of themselves" as either Republicans or Democrats. We know also from repeated measurements over many years that these attachments are highly stable. The remaining quarter of the voters call themselves independent or nonpartisan.

Thus, the impact of a particular issue—such as civil rights in 1964—is superimposed on the "standing commitments" of the voters to their regular parties.

The effect of the issue may reinforce the voter's natural tendency to support the candidate of his own party, or it may create enough conflict to make him desert his party temporarily and vote for the other candidate, whose position on the issue is nearer his own. Some exchanges of this type occur in every election, and in many cases the crossings of party lines balance each other so that neither candidate gains an advantage.

The Party Voter

Analysis of all our survey data from the past fifteen years shows that in the absence of an overriding issue, approximately 90 percent of the voters who call themselves Republican will support the Republican candi-

date. The corresponding figure for Democrats is slightly smaller, about 88 percent. The explanation for the small difference between Republicans and Democrats is not clear but may be due in part to the fact that Republicans tend to come from higher-educated and better-informed classes, and may be more firmly identified with their political party. When a strong issue does not emerge, independent voters, with no attachment to a political party, generally tend to divide their vote about equally between the two presidential candidates.

The responses to our civil rights questions showed that the distribution of attitudes of self-identified Democrats, Republicans, and independents differed only slightly. The attitudes of Democrats tended more toward the two extremes of our scale—strongly opposed or strongly favorable—reflecting the fact that both Southern whites and most Negroes consider themselves Democrats. The distributions of Republican and independent attitudes toward civil rights are similar to each other (see Figure 2a). When we compared our scale of civil rights attitudes for each of the above groups with their vote in the 1964 election, we found that there was a definite relationship.

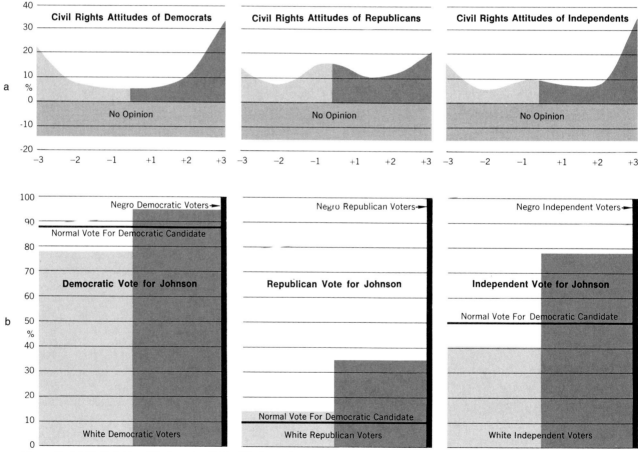

Figure 2. (a) Civil rights attitudes of self-identified members of political parties show similar distributions. (b) Distribution of white votes, by party, for Johnson in 1964. (All Negro voters in the electorate sample said they had voted for him.) It can be seen that the net effect of the vote in sympathy with civil rights worked strongly in Johnson's favor.

Without exception, all Negro voters interviewed in our sample reported that they had voted for Johnson. Since nearly 90 percent of Negroes registered favorable attitudes toward civil rights, the correspondence between their attitudes and their vote is overwhelming. We know, of course, that our survey must contain some sampling error, since the election records from Negro wards in large cities show a small vote for Goldwater. But the vote for Johnson in these wards ran as high as 97 percent, and there is little doubt that in the 1964 election the Negro vote for a presidential candidate was as close to being unanimous as any racial or other group vote is likely to be.

Of particular interest is how the civil rights attitudes of white voters affected their choice of candidate. At the time of the election, there were predictions that a "white backlash" would occur among voters who were disposed unfavorably toward Negro civil rights.

We separated the white respondents in our sample into self-identified Democrats, Republicans, and independents, and within each group compared their civil rights attitudes to how they voted (see Figure 2b).

It can be seen that in 1964, civil rights did affect the presidential vote. White voters favorable to civil rights for Negroes tended to support Johnson much more than white voters who held unfavorable attitudes toward civil rights.

In his own party, interestingly, the civil rights issue seems both to have helped and hindered President Johnson. It helped by reinforcing the voting intention of Democrats, particularly Negroes, who might not have come out to vote. But President Johnson clearly lost votes among that segment of the Democratic party which might have voted for him except for his civil rights stand. These losses were mainly in the South, where Goldwater won several normally Democratic states.

The net effect of the civil rights issue on the white Democratic vote was slightly detrimental to President Johnson. He gained about seven percentage points in the vote from Democrats with positive civil rights attitudes, but lost about ten percentage points among Democrats who disagreed with his civil rights program. The white backlash did not have the effect that had been predicted.

Among Republicans and independents, however, the net effect of the civil rights issue was strongly in Johnson's favor. He won virtually all of the Negro vote regardless of party affiliation. He also won a substantially larger proportion of the white independent vote because of the civil rights issue. The relationship between civil rights attitudes and voting is strongest in the case of the independents. Those with favorable attitudes to civil rights voted heavily for Johnson; those with unfavorable attitudes to civil rights were more likely to vote for Goldwater. In the case of the independents, the net effect of the civil rights issue worked strongly in President Johnson's favor.

Among Republicans, there was a substantial defection from Goldwater to Johnson by those who did not share Goldwater's civil rights views. The desertion rate of Republicans with favorable civil rights attitudes was about three and one-half times higher than normal.

When we subtract the loss of Southern Democrats from gains among Negroes, independents, and Republicans, we see that there was indeed a net displacement of the vote to Johnson that can be attributed to the civil rights issue, and that undoubtedly played a part in making up the extraordinary majority Johnson received at the polls in 1964.

The exact size of this displacement cannot be estimated with precision, but our data suggest that it was in the range of three or four percentage points. The 1964 presidential election was won by a landslide majority, so this may seem relatively unimportant. But in an electoral system as closely balanced as the American one is at present, this is a movement of considerable importance. In past years, presidential elections typically have been won with approximately 5 percent majorities.

The Image Factor

It should be noted, however, that even among Republicans who shared Goldwater's civil rights views the rate of defection was higher than normal—14 percent instead of the expected 10 percent. This suggests that there must have been influences other than the civil rights issue that worked against Goldwater among Republicans, but our data strongly suggest that these other issues did not affect the vote as much as did the civil rights issue.

There is no doubt that the public "images" of Johnson and Goldwater differed substantially. Personality factors that have no specific relation to policy positions can influence the vote, and this could explain why Republicans who shared Goldwater's civil rights views failed to give him the support that a Republican presidential candidate might ordinarily expect.

We have found in our surveys that television has become the most important source of information for voters, and it is quite likely that voters are affected in ways they may or may not be aware of by each candidate's personal attributes—by his apparent sincerity, dependability, physical appearance, and integrity as he appears on television in news reports and campaign speeches. It is interesting to see that while the reported importance of television as an information source increased substantially from 1952 to 1964, the importance of newspapers remained constant, and the importance of radio dropped considerably (see Figure 3).

In assessing the net displacement of votes that might be attributed to the civil rights issue, we carried out a cross-check to assure ourselves that we were not measuring in fact the general influence of political "conservative" and "liberal" attitudes.

We measured attitudes toward two other political issues in our 1964 survey. One was concerned with how

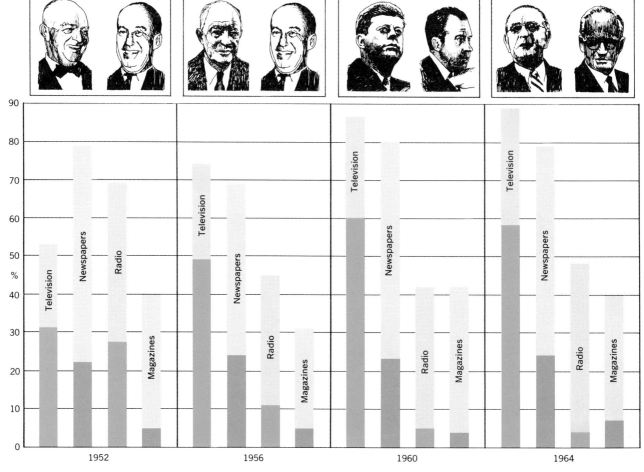

Figure 3. The lighter color in the bars indicates the change over time in number of voters *following* political campaigns via the various media; the darker color indicates those who said they get the *most information* from the specified medium.

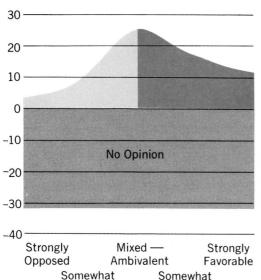

Figure 4. Views of 1964 voters on foreign policy (many voters had no opinion). This issue had little effect on the vote.

Figure 5. Views of 1964 voters on social welfare policy. The displacement of this curve reflects, in a much-reduced way, the displacement effect of the civil rights issue.

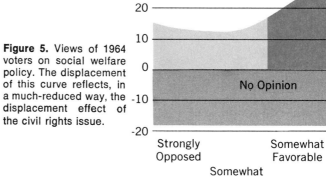

much the federal government should be concerned with welfare legislation, and the second dealt with foreign policy.

Voter attitudes on foreign policy tend to be distributed along a bell-shaped curve with most opinions falling at the center or "moderate" category (see Figure 4). Typically, the number of voters with no opinion on foreign policy was high. Attitudes on social welfare tend to be distributed along a moderately J-shaped curve (see Figure 5). We found that voter attitudes on welfare or on foreign policy were not strongly related to attitudes on civil rights. In other words, the American voter typically does not have his attitudes toward civil rights, welfare legislation, and foreign policy organized in a systematic way, so that knowing his position on one, we could predict his attitudes on the other two.

We found that the displacement of votes associated with attitudes on welfare legislation was sizable although less pronounced than the displacement caused by the civil rights issue, and that foreign policy attitudes affected the vote much less. But in all cases the net effect was prejudicial to Goldwater, and it appears that his conservative views on civil rights and social welfare and his aggressive foreign policy all cost him votes.

Civil Rights Versus Vietnam

The conclusions drawn here regarding the 1964 election inevitably raised the question whether civil rights will continue to have a strong influence on presidential elections. If we could be certain that the circumstances in the 1968 election would be similar to those in 1964, we could predict a similar effect on the vote. But the 1964 election was quite remarkable in the polarity of choice that the presidential candidates offered to the electorate, not only in civil rights but in other issues as well. This is not really in the American political tradition. Typically, both candidates try to stay near the center of all major policy issues in a bid for the support of the entire electorate. Polarizations of this magnitude have occurred very infrequently in the last fifty years—the welfare legislation issue of the New Deal in 1936 gives the most striking earlier example.

If the two presidential candidates in 1968 hold substantially the same attitudes toward civil rights, it will be difficult for voters who are concerned with this issue

to express their desires on their ballots. Under such circumstances, the displacement of the vote for president by the civil rights issue could be very slight, no matter how great the concern of the majority may be.

It is also possible that the distribution of attitudes toward civil rights may change significantly. The years since the 1964 election have brought riots in urban Negro ghettos, Black Power advocates, and increasing use of government authority to enforce compliance to desegregation regulations. We cannot predict what the reaction of the electorate is now and will be to these events. If they have hardened the attitudes of white voters against further extension of civil rights of Negroes, then the white backlash may have a far more potent influence than it did in 1964. One of the most striking facts about the recent election of Negro mayors in Cleveland and Gary was the high polarity of the vote along racial lines.

Finally, it is possible that another issue may become the overriding factor in the 1968 election. We know that foreign policy did not exert a strong influence in the 1964 election. Developments in the Vietnam war may have intensified opinions in the area of foreign policy to the point where it will become a major factor in voter motivation in 1968.

We are planning to conduct another survey following the 1968 election to determine what issues affected the vote for president. It is possible that we may find the foreign affairs issue to be a vote-displacing factor, but in previous surveys we have found that a great many of the voters are confused about foreign policy and do not have organized opinions on this issue.

Psychology of the Voter

The psychology of the voter is a study of attitudes and decision making. To understand decisions made at the polls, we must have data on voter commitment to the major political parties, on voter attitudes toward major policy issues, and on their comprehension of the choices the candidates actually offer. Issues and candidates change, but we are reasonably certain that the pattern of party commitment—the long-standing loyalties to political parties that provide the major stabilizing force in American politics—will *not* change appreciably from the 1964 to 1968 presidential elections.

Encounter in Color

Thomas J. Cottle

Children are born "color blind." In the words of Oscar Hammerstein II, they must be carefully taught to hate people whose skin is a different color than theirs. Psychologists have made a profession out of studying learning in the laboratory. But what can all these laboratory experiments tell us about how children come to hate other children or, more importantly, how children can be taught not to hate others in spite of skin-color differences? Thomas J. Cottle tells how one group of social scientists has approached the problem by bringing together lower- and middle-class white and black children in self-analytic groups that could be studied in a quasi-laboratory setting.

School-busing integration programs normally proceed along fairly predictable lines. Students of both races are told simply that a merger soon will occur; automatically, whites are designated as the home team, the Negroes are the visitors. The outnumbered transients—and Negroes feel like transients—then are plopped into the middle of a familiar and well-rehearsed drama, one in which they are totally uncomfortable. And throughout the entire process, teachers must assume responsibility for making the merger work.

The sadness of the drama is that it takes place with almost no psychological preparation and with no time devoted to the resolution of human and institutional complications. Yet as though by some magic, students are supposed to live together peaceably and to learn something. The drama's irony is that where schools in the past have exulted in their socializing function, when integration becomes a reality they hurriedly retreat to their fundamental didactic activities. School boards try to combine the races in varying ratios—advantageous to the whites but justified by national or regional proportions—with the hope that somehow the kids will work it out. Afterward social scientists are employed to diagnose the existing exigencies and to present the statistics on prior injustices and inequalities.

Social science methodology and sophistication hardly are required, however, to assess contemporary token integration programs, for anyone can observe the difficulties involved for students, teachers, and administrators. Anyone can vibrate to the currents of open and muffled prejudice and of hatreds. And of the inevitable despair. Yet in the design of human environments social science can make one important contribution that provides a workable way in which integration and learning may evolve naturally.

For the past year, a group of us at Harvard have been engaged in a small project aimed at developing an experimental context that permits the observation of integration dynamics. At the same time we have offered an arena for the confrontation of adolescents, who bring to this most complex encounter their conspicuous and well-rehearsed sentiments and less well-understood, newly discovered fears and fantasies.

Our intention was to transport integration to a laboratory setting modeled after the real and often frightening world of contemporary high-school students. Our participants were lower- and middle-class Negro and white boys and girls, and their difficult task was to meet together and to speak directly upon the issues of race and social relations.

Self-analytic Groups

But these were not simple seminars. They were self-analytic groups. In self-analytic groups, an experienced leader "trains" group members to pursue the personal expressions and interpersonal processes that arise "spontaneously." Group members are encouraged to analyze their feelings and verbalize their attitudes, actions, and even fantasies. The emphasis in self-analytic groups rests on the meaning of group interactions, as well as on private revelations.

In such groups, the self-analytic procedures normally are not outlined fully to group members; rather they are insinuated by the leader into the ongoing group processes. The leader guides the group toward more expansive observation and analysis, and the mood generated is one of constrained freedom. Anything can be said by anyone at any time, but the inferred rule is that expression and analysis must run contiguously.

This notion is borrowed from the psychoanalytic tradition, which argues that the ego must be "split" if one is to perform two requisite therapeutic tasks. A second notion, taken from the same source, is that leaders (not unlike classical analysts), by participating minimally, create in the minds of group members a need to construct a viable social system with inherent institutional arrangements and necessary role allocations. (In fact, taciturn leaders, by creating social contracts that are seemingly devoid of normally evident sanctions, accentuate their own positions as the ultimate authority and render ever so complicated the nature of relationships between members.) The starkness of the self-analytic context, by compelling participants to develop for themselves a social order that they then must assess, brings to the laboratory a setting that some authors claim is suitable for studying the most primitive and complex forms of human behavior.

The greatness of such groups comes as they succeed in getting persons to confront both private and public issues normally avoided or not noticed.

The danger in the technique, as we employed it, was that innocent students inadvertently were transformed into cadres of miniature psychotherapists. And, untrained, they may have believed mistakenly that manifest content had little value. The balance fell into the very human hands of the leader, who in the safety of his role and with his dappled moments of real understanding, had the power to drive the group to either end. In the process he came to be perceived, at least by people of his own race, as father, mother, teacher, older brother, therapist, and—if he played it wrong—as God himself.

Three points should be made here about our perspectives on the self-analytic technique. First, we did not consider the groups as psychotherapy. The assumption was *not* illness and the intention was *not* treatment. (This is not to say that people enlisting in self-analytic groups may not have been seeking the therapy context.)

Second, it was expected that when problems were so complex that they could not be verbalized, groups would deal with them in fantasy terms and thus provide both an outlet for their expression and a justification for direct interpretation. The open and direct line to their own fantasies held by adolescents actually increased the significance of this point.

Third, as in psychotherapy, every action of every moment was considered potentially significant. Thus, jokes, member absences, meeting time and place, physical appearance, and apparently casual topics assumed importance.

| DUAL STRUCTURE OF THE GROUPS | The application of self-analytic groups to racial integration barely has been explored. But we selected such groups for our program because we believe this format is ideal and offers stimulating experiences, which also can be observed carefully. Furthermore, because of their flexibility, such groups could be structured in at least two ways to simulate the paradigms for school-busing operations.

The first school-busing program, which may be called the "September plan," is the method by which reluctant administrators throw Negro and white students together in white schools, with instructions to get along. While the previous summer has brought deep and searching thoughts and hopes for the impending merger, as well as pessimism and red-hot antipathies, few professionals, with the exception of men like Robert Coles, author of *Children of Crisis,* have concerned themselves with these months before school integration, either in terms of research or as a time for support and guidance of the equally bewildered white and Negro students. Presumably a bit more humane, the "June plan" grants Negroes and whites a brief moment to discuss their fears and animosities in the privacy of their own academic and racial environments.

Accordingly, our groups were arranged to replicate these two alternative ways of handling school integration. Some of our groups consisted of Negroes and whites together from the start, with the size of groups limited to ten or twelve students. Other groups of four to six youths each began in a segregated fashion and met thus for six sessions. After six meetings, we merged the groups for six more weeks. For these groups, announcement of approaching integration came at the beginning of the first segregated session. Students were asked to participate in twelve group meetings, one per week, with each lasting a little more than an hour. Because of the students' busy school and work programs, the sessions all were scheduled in the early evenings or on Saturday mornings. To avoid administrative complications, meeting rooms were reserved in a Harvard University building; and this meant, of course, that while the "turf" was unfamiliar to both races, it clearly was on the white side of neutral. To accentuate this, we arranged for groups to meet after merger at the same time and in the same room as did white students during the segregated sessions. A community's university, of course, is hardly a neutral stimulus for lower-class adolescents. And the structure symbolized by the university, forbidding to Negroes, may be even more upsetting to white students for whom the university and the very idea of research represent familiar but unattainable objects.

Some forty-five students were selected from local high schools, church groups, and neighborhood youth clubs for our self-analytic group experiment. They volunteered for a project advertised as an experiment in human relations. Ironically, Negro participants had to be reimbursed for taxi fare necessary to transport them from their homes—both distant from and inconvenient to the university. There was no other reimbursement for members because we felt that only would complicate things. Termination of "salaried" students could be interpreted as the firing of inferior employees. (As an incentive and a gesture of nurture, however, students were given beverages and snacks during each meeting.)

Strict obeying of busing statistics would urge white-dominated groups, but the natural anxieties attending self-analytic experiments of this type dictated instead a goal of population equality. Students of about the same age—sophomores and juniors—were assigned to groups in random fashion but with the stipulation that sexes and races should be distributed evenly. Definitely to be avoided in the project (and in schools as well!) was a group with one Negro or only one boy, and other such dramatic imbalances.

As it turned out, several of the students knew each other from school, and though prior acquaintanceship often interferes with group progress, actually it proved beneficial in some instances. In one group, for example, a Negro boy listened intently to a white girl's discussion and then told of his prior distaste for her and of his newly formed admiration. Her performance in the group demonstrated a courage and intelligence he had never seen in the classroom, he said. It was with obvious joy that he announced his change of heart.

| SELECTION OF LEADERS | Just as important as group composition was the selection of group leaders. If leaders were overly specialized, the possible general applicability of the project's results would be greatly decreased. Certainly our resources were limited by the availability of people possessing similar kinds of group experience so that relatively uniform group structures could be set up.

Available to us in almost superabundance, however, was a population of university students, both graduate and undergraduate, who not only had taken part in self-analytic groups but had spent additional months observing groups other than their own. This then became the delicate minimum for leader credentials: one year as a group member, plus at least one semester of observation.

Schoolroom realities suggested using female leaders—for us a sadly rare commodity. Hence, acknowledging both reality guideposts and the characteristics of the university manpower pool, five white males—two graduate and three undergraduate students—were selected as group leaders. None of these young men had previous experience as leaders, but each had been in groups and had worked in areas of race relations. It was through their mature insights and sensitivities, as well as through their natural apprehensions and reticence, that the project was conceived and launched.

It is always difficult to differentiate between rational calculations about what groups should be and the experimental designs drawn according to the less rational and invisible needs of those who direct them. The fact that the subtle expectancies of the experimenter influence the outcomes of research has been more than amply demonstrated by Robert Rosenthal in his book, *Experimental Effect in Behavioral Research.* Similarly, self-analytic groups all have expectations that drive members toward certain demarcated ends. Leaders—or therapists—do not create a vacuum with their ungainly silences and vocally bland penetrations; they build toward a discrete and peculiar atmosphere that often makes normal brain function difficult but putatively yields the desired and desirable ends.

We simply do not know the degree to which our own needs were met by project procedures. For example, our decision to substitute in-group observers and tape recorders for the frequently used one-way mirrors may be explained in several ways: while public-private, formal-informal dimensions exist naturally in groups, there also are nebulous realms of insecurity, intimacy, competence, and potency. On the other hand, private, closed rooms protect leaders and members from outside evaluation.

The influence of leaders on groups, furthermore, varies from man to man, session to session, and probably from moment to moment. Leader strategies and reactions could not possibly be uniform, or even consistent, except perhaps in cases where single leaders ran both the Negro and white segregated groups prior to merging.

At best, leaders could but listen intensely and predicate their utterances upon a concern for their group members and upon what in a word is history, namely that only months before, as group members themselves, they too had struggled with similar problems in similar fashion.

Examples of Interaction

Assessments of our results certainly must be made not only in light of integration factors and more characteristic adolescent social phenomena but also with consideration for the reaction of human beings to the novel, seductive, and perhaps terrifying system offered by group structure and purpose. The early phase of all our groups, for instance, was characterized by a grappling at so-called reality levels with the proposed (white) authority and intimacy, and on fantasy levels with the actual or promised racial merger. The groups sidled into the authority problem by verbal attacks on the University, inquiries into whether Harvard's president, the governor of Massachusetts, and even Senator Robert Kennedy would learn of the project. The groups wanted to know: Would it be written up? Were they guinea pigs? Was all this really confidential? What might result from the excessive freedom and exposure of one's inner self?

Contained within these natural queries, of course, was the students' hope that if they would open up to one another, the leader in turn would approve of their efforts, reveal his involvement with them, and ironically even reward them by declaring negative sanctions.

The major problem in our early meetings was to establish a social order involving trust but also taking account of authority hierarchies and qualities of interpersonal attachment. Sample conversations were: "We're just like the United Nations and he (the leader) is like a silent Secretary General." "What would happen if he weren't here?" "There would be anarchy." "What would that mean?" "Probably free love for everyone." Every single group met and solved that problem: the transference of free minds and open discussions to free love and, to use a neologism often heard in groups, "orgification."

In his silence and manifest sureness, the self-analytic group leader perpetrates what at the beginning can be felt, if not perceived, as a legitimized seduction and human coalescence. If the coalescence is overly sexual, group members must align their sex-role definitions and defenses in reaction to the aroused threats. If in his coalescing the leader appears overly paternalistic, an action not necessarily excluding Negroes, members must align their mutual associations in accordance with social codes appropriate in family and peer realms. Such alignments bring up unconscious interpretations of sexual prohibitions relating to patterns of incest, premarital intercourse, and ensuing illegitimate childbirth. "How many of us here are accidents?" one boy shouted as he attempted to discover a potentially uniting reality—and in so doing planted the seeds of an incestuous sibling rivalry.

No matter how he came across in our group, the leader was the unequivocal agent of integration and, in our segregated groups, he was also the sole person to share communications and histories of Negroes and whites alike. It became apparent that, whatever the source and strength of the leader-member tie might be, this bond necessarily transcended a pure racial identity. In fact, a form of "backlash" emerged as the neutrality of each group leader caused whites to see him often either as a turncoat or as a father abandoning his own children. Negroes began to perceive the leader as an inexplicably trustworthy person and perhaps even as a suitable stepfather. In the first session of one merged group, a Negro girl left her fellow Negroes and pulled her chair halfway around the room so that she might sit down next to (and a bit behind) the white leader.

Actual merger of the segregated groups naturally affected the quality of the transference to the leader. During segregated sessions, the approach of both whites and Negroes changed radically as the whites evidenced fear of abandonment and their disbelief that a member of their own race would lead them knowingly into such a predicament. Negroes tended to drift back to a more primitive self-perception and a stereotype ghetto behavior. Possibly because of this element in their shared group experience, the participants collectively returned to the leader during final sessions before merging in an almost childlike posture of dependence. We interpreted this as symbolizing their hopes that the leader would regulate their activities and thus bring the merger to its desired ending.

The transference, however, changed for a third time as group members gradually realized that they *alone* were the architects and inhabitants of this new community and that their prior real and fantasy histories—both with and without the leader—had to be reconciled or even altered to accommodate a still newer environment. Although less clear, similar transformations occurred in integrated groups as well.

Given these many complexities, how does one interpret one white girl's explosive response to the proposition of racial merger and the presence of white male authority: "Let's talk about premarital sexuality!" And how do we explain the exquisite associations of a slight Negro girl as she nervously wandered through fantasy descriptions: gypsy marriages, desire for racial equality, student demonstrations in Florida, life in her own ghetto, the crimes committed by police, her pleasure at the Boston Strangler's escape from prison (an escape from another kind of ghetto), her terror that the Strangler would come to her home, and her subsequent and *real* preparations: boarding windows and doors and piling knives and scissors under her chair. Poignantly, she ended the verbal fantasy by revealing one more fear—that midst his seemingly uncontrollable psychosis, the Strangler still would discriminate against a Negro and reject her as a murder victim.

Our groups' remarks about premarital sexuality well may refer to what many participants saw as a "marriage" of the races, performed in the group by the integrating "ceremony" of the group leader who had "powers invested in him" and was equally associated with both white and Negro group members.

In one integrated group, an almost Quaker-like ceremony actually was performed as two boys, one Negro and the other white, gradually developed a closeness sufficiently strong and public to unite the entire group as a congregation. The presence of girls presumably kept the boys' intimacy from gaining the pejorative status.

In another experimental group composed of Negro and white gang boys, a similar intended marriage, if it can be called that, became aggressive and atavistic as each side designated one of its members as inferior and agreed to a contract of mutual denigration. Swelling with homosexual overtones, their project fizzled; a basketball game was proposed, with the leader acting as referee. The merger failed as the "bunch" of whites and "pile" of Negroes (their own description) never melded.

Much of the foregoing imagery seems to us related to the group's need for control, particularly in spheres of authority and morality. In our groups, authority assumed heightened significance in light of the racial merger, either scheduled or already enacted. It was not surprising, therefore, that participants made strong pleas for refereeing and social policing; someone must define not only psychospatial limits of the group but the "legal" extent of the merger's penetration.

In one of our integrated groups, an eloquent Negro boy was able to contrive a medium for expressing the vertical intimacies inherent in good authority arrangements. Speaking of the microcosm that was his group, he spelled out the disparities of local and highway police: the former—slow, dark, dirty, irresponsible, inconsistent in their punishment, unavailable when needed; the latter—sleek, neat, tall, strong, quick to

attend. And his poetry continued: "All of us are dark specks on a policeman's badge." Soon afterward, he turned these descriptions into a comparison of Negro and white fathers, and then he concluded by expressing his distaste for his own father in what seemed to the group to be his wish to be ministered to or even adopted by the leader, a man no more than three years his senior.

Comparable feelings were equally prevalent among white group members, but the undeniable existence of the white authority figure must not be overlooked, for it may have inspired what Erik Erikson calls negative identity elements in Negroes in the group and, at the same time, may have made statements of needs for parental-like gratifications more difficult for the whites.

In their attempt to sculpt a social identity it was expected our group members would turn to those aspects of family and peer-group subsystems that seemed sociologically appropriate and psychologically congenial. The group thus provided an unanticipated opportunity to engineer if not a miniature social-psychological Utopia, then at least a stage for rehearsing ideal psychosocial identity. Flexibility and credulity in adolescent role playing made this rehearsal seem like the real thing, but the evolution of a Utopia was not without occasional racial and sexual clashes, replete with fantasies of violence, as the various interest groups bid to build their own special social structures.

One identity component that showed itself in our groups was the urge to become substantially more potent and to increase the felt sense of a free autonomy and naked power. Normal levels of potency and aggression just did not suffice when races and sexes saw themselves in public competition. But how often their concerns were swathed in terror. From white male students

in one segregated group came: "What are they? Colored? Older? Girls? They'll kill us. Make 'em younger . . . real small, pygmies with eyes like poison darts. Why are they coming? They'll want to fight! We'll talk and let them sit in the back of the room."

Then, with no apparent connecting thought: "Do you think there are people on the moon? No atmosphere . . . too low . . . too high . . . too many craters. No human could live there . . . We're not human as far as they're concerned."

From the Negro camp, though the groups were meeting separately, came the reciprocal posture of the aggressor. Negroes, too, spewed platitudes that revealed how deeply lodged the bigotry of ignorance was, and how clear the way in which their self-degradation was transformed into precarious esteem by the stereotyping of whites: "Whites aren't as good; you can't slick the slicker; you can't bullshit the bullshitter . . . The white people slide, we glide . . . We have natural-born rhythm. They can't dance. Can't sing soul . . . We're naturally strong. If you see a strong Whitey, you know he's been lifting weights . . . And we got better girls."

Clearly each side feared the devastation, and even total annihilation, of its own social fabric. In almost revolutionary terms, each group seemed to believe that one social order must be torn down before a new one could be installed. Evident throughout was the recurring disbelief of white students that a white leader could draft his own kind into such a battle; the Negroes showed explicit acceptance of and preparation for battle; and in all the group participants there was the primitive interweaving of both sexual and destructive fantasies.

The basic aggression and the uncertainty about the ultimately victorious and hence superior race came out in discussion about the war in Vietnam, or school experiences involving teachers, which served as conversational starting points for almost every group. Typical talk went this way:

"It's the good white against the bad colored . . . It's the pure and powerful stabilizers versus the vile and unclean troublemakers . . . It's racial violence . . . If the Negroes refused to fight, America would lose . . . Negroes are America's potency and the untapped potential for its continuing strength . . . Let's not confuse Negroes like us with the inferior types that come up from the South and in from Puerto Rico . . . You got to get immigration laws and keep the Puerto Ricans out . . . Who's better, Adam Clayton Powell or Edward Brooke? They're both no good. Powell doesn't help his own people and Brooke takes advantage of the white liberals and gets the rest of the vote by being a Republican. What's more they either marry white people or hire them as secretaries . . . You gotta crawl in and dig those Viet Cong out of their black tunnels . . . and either build a democracy for them or kill 'em!"

This concentration on defeat of the Viet Cong may have symbolized not only the eradication of Negroes, or racial integration. It also may have represented the Negroes' own destruction of existing stereotypes and their desire to be divorced from what they themselves labeled as "black trash."

Certainly Vietnam represented aspects of white aggression, foreign invasion, and draft laws as both races encounter them. Like the war, conquest of the moon also provided a perfect medium for the embroidering of fantasies that ultimately were concerned with racial integration. "Aliens probably look like us," said one Negro boy, "maybe they're a bit bigger with an extra finger . . . maybe just a glob of hair." Thus, intruders were Negroes from different communities, aliens from a different planet, or soldiers from a different country.

As important as the actual theme of fantasies was the fact that without suggestion, groups selected topics on which they could build elaborate fantasies serving the multifarious purposes and needs of *all* contributors. Perhaps the greatest impact of the self-analytic procedure was felt, not when the leader unraveled by interpretation the various intertwined fantasy threads and returned them to their originators, but when group members themselves recognized the various layers of implications as they were built up in the course of such embroidery sessions. Just such an experience was felt by one who tried to act out her unstated sense of a racial perspective by turning off the lights in the group room and leaving them on in the hall, and then reversing the procedure. Irrespective of the illumination or her own physical location, her point about skin-color permanence and the eye of the beholder was forcibly communicated. The more she went on with her fantasy, the more she realized what she was doing.

Typically, fantasy expression increased as experienced reality became more difficult to face head on, but fantasies were not just alternatives to so-called reality considerations. Rather they were less threatening detours to them, or rehearsals for them. Often resembling free-form behavior trials, collective fantasies mirrored the fears, wishes, and defenses of participants as the group attempted to mold new sentiments and action strategies. Nowhere is this more true than during adolescence, a period condoning fantasy experimentation as a way of tasting those public morsels that someday may become reality.

The Two Group Types Compared

One notion stemming from our project was that effecting change in adolescent fantasies may alter more real perceptions and hence change the eventual behavior. And so a question to be answered in our experiments was: how does the evolution of fantasy vary within basic group structures?

In the integrated groups, change came gradually from so-called internal dynamics, because from the start both races contended with a fixed structure.

In those Negro and white groups that were merged after six sessions, the physical merger seemed to render invalid the members' previously constructed fantasies. Even with preparation, the change may have been so disrupting that adaptability could not easily take place. One virtue of such a disruption is that prior belief systems were seen to be inaccurate. Hence a second phase of adaptation was required. A liability of the merger, of course, is that it may have communicated the necessity of relinquishing totally the familiar belief systems and a sense of competence within them.

In the long run as research continues, groups that merge after first meeting separately may prove the more effective paradigm, if only because actual social change becomes part of the process and history that lead to ongoing social engagements. Where the originally integrated groups should develop a sense of earlier-later, the merged groups might experience more of a sense of beforeness-afterness or even oldness—temporal feelings ideal for reinforcing the conception that something has, indeed, been accomplished.

Experiment Findings

Self-analytic groups do not provide *the* solution for all the tensions indigenous to school-integration programs, and the kinds of students volunteering for group membership and for leader roles in our project were not sufficiently representative to permit extensive generalization of any sort. Moreover, the self-analytic process, itself so idiosyncratic, cannot be alleged to work successfully in *all* school settings or in *all* community clubs. But the findings that came even from our small experiment are, to say the least, encouraging.

First, we have learned that the self-analytic technique can be fathomed and used by lower- and middle-class young adolescents. Second, we observed incredibly moving, deeply personal expressions and interpretations in groups that were led by nonprofessionals. The fact that leaders also were young and at times awkward may have helped to establish the trust so necessary for viable working groups.

The racial factor might have made the white leaders appear real and warm to white students while Negroes saw the leaders as the unfamiliar representatives of a hostile group. But our evidence did *not* show this.

Third, the procedure of keeping groups segregated at the start seemed to permit a direct and open confrontation of the realities and fantasies connected with integration, even—or especially—when the authority figure was white. While it is obvious that Negroes cannot grow to their full height in a society incessantly demanding that right be equated with white, the Negroes in our project may have been spared some of the tensions inherent in the existing social comparison.

For different reasons, our university buildings and leaders may have been just as foreign to the whites as to the Negroes. A study of racial integration cannot neglect, therefore, the discrete concerns of white students and the eminent force of social-class differentiations.

Fourth, the power of our self-analytic group to a limited extent came from an ability to cut through the barriers that are built into the "September plan," in which Negro and white students are herded together, neither group knowing what to expect or how to act.

Perhaps the study's outstanding finding is that, even temporarily encountered, the social structure demanded solutions to problems that in their form and intensity tended to blur racial issues. As always in nondirective groups, the dilemmas of intimacy (with threats of homosexuality and heterosexuality) and the definitions of existing and potential power hierarchies had to be resolved, and unequivocal action taken.

Yet these facts also might indicate that the net effect of the self-analytic device was symptom *substitution* rather than *resolution*. Perhaps our efforts did little more than arouse new and different threats, which were met with new and different defenses. Perhaps we did a disservice in fact by creating a structure that linked racial integration with authority, and with sexuality. But what else is the reality?

It cannot be denied that while our intention was to explore integration, our procedures at times deflected the emphasis away from race. By putting boys and girls together in a relatively free culture, we evoked that essence of human beings from which come social facts like interaction norms, incest taboos, prejudicial projections.

But, even if the integration-sexuality-authority linkage does represent a phenomenon underlying racial mergers, a potentially liberating experience still was provided by the group environment, and significant bits of information still were exposed. School integration is not simply a coming together of people. It is a merger of boys and girls, and it is the convergence of their preestablished realities and fantasies. And, while leader strategies certainly pushed our groups in easily definable directions, authorship of group fantasies, contents, and associations still belonged for the most part to the members.

To some people, integration well may symbolize intermarriage or even illegitimate intercourse, and white authority may signify the slave master, Uncle Tom, or even white man (or strangler) looking for a Negro prostitute or victim. Though these images may seem absurd, no one can overlook the fantasies that are stimulated in high-school classrooms, where teachers openly seduce some students, turn others into children or patients, and never bother at all with the rest. Talk in our groups pointed this up: "What about the little child just breaking out of her shell [whom the teacher rejects in favor of some newcomer]? . . . I'll do all in my power to hate that [new] girl. She's gonna take all the love and care out of that room . . . No, she [the teacher] don't have to be my friend if she's gonna be that way . . . I don't like teachers who stick to one person."

We would invite the use of self-analytic techniques in schools, for not only could teachers and counselors learn to lead groups, but their participation as leaders could extricate them from restrictions normally placed on their expressive and integrating abilities.

Where groups seem to offer even greater natural implementations to the environment, however, is in the new concept of the educational park, in which social scientists will have to prescribe ways to bring city and suburban populations together. In such environments the distinction between home team and visiting team will be lost, and the question about who is the aggressor or the intruder will be blurred. In the park plan, there will be no one to confront nor even to approach about the problems in bringing races together in schools. Thus, group encounters might well be built in.

It may be that student group encounters will offer direct roads to social and cultural problem areas. Such groups also can offer a radically new medium in which academic learning may take place. Social integration, after all, must be a part of all school activities, not just an hour a week of isolated research.

For the moment our own efforts are aimed at systematically assessing the value of both segregated and merged groups, as well as in evaluating the reactions to integration by sex, social class, and race. For us, the immediate future holds more groups with both female and Negro leaders and, hopefully, other groups in which parents will join their children in the self-analytic dialogue. Many participants in our first groups have expressed their desire to carry "the thing home." As one girl projected: "So maybe we can talk our problems out and they can go home and tell their parents, and we can go home and tell our parents . . ."

III
Aggression and Rebellion

Civilization and Its Malcontents

O. Hobart Mowrer

Ideally, any culture should be made up of people all of whom have undergone the same amount of socialization. Such an idealized state has never occurred in reality, of course; the mores of any given society always seem to be better instilled in some individuals than in others. The individual who violates the laws or mores of his society is, by definition, a criminal, but some criminal acts are perceived by members of the culture as being worse than others. Among many groups in America today, the most heinous crimes of all are those that involve aggression and violence—wars, murders, rapes, assaults, and riots. These behaviors seem so unnatural, so illogical, so self-defeating that we might wonder how the criminal comes by his behavior patterns, and more than this, how and why these illegal activities are maintained in the face of rather overwhelming punishment. In the following article, O. Hobart Mowrer contrasts the psychoanalytic explanation of this phenomenon with his own insights into the problem of criminality.

Man, they say, is a social animal, but some men are more social than others. Sigmund Freud and his followers have held that the typical neurotic is highly, in fact excessively, socialized—that he is more sensitive to society's rules and prescriptions than is the normal person. But clinical evidence suggests that such is not the case. On the contrary, it appears that the neurotic is *deficient* in socialization.

Deciding between these two points of view is a matter of the highest importance. Their implications are strikingly different. They lead to incompatible conclusions about the treatment of neurotics and criminals, and even about such broad human problems as the rearing of children and the evolution of culture.

The socialized person demonstrates both a well-developed sense of right and wrong and the ability to govern his behavior accordingly. In other words, he has both a strong superego and a strong ego. The normal person is well socialized, he has a strong conscience and good self-control. He seldom behaves in a deviant way, and when he does, he is able to make peace between his superego and his ego without serious difficulty.

The criminal (or sociopath), on the other hand, is very poorly socialized. He has little sense of right and wrong, and little self-discipline. The successful criminal may have a strong ego, but because he has no conscience his deviant behavior does not bother him and he remains fairly happy unless he is caught. However, sociopaths who are ineffectual criminals (disdained by the successful ones) have both weak egos and weak superegos.

The neurotic bears some resemblance both to the normal person and to the sociopath. Like the normal person he has a highly developed conscience, but like the ineffectual criminal he has a weak ego and therefore little self-control (see Figure 1).

If we rate these three groups on a socialization scale, sociopaths clearly belong at the bottom. But who comes next? Freud's contention is that the order, from low socialization to high, is sociopaths, normal persons, neurotics (see Figure 2). Much psychotherapy therefore has been based on the assumption that the neurotic's chief need is for a relaxation of the control of his superego, so that he can move in the direction of normality.

Opposing this view are my research findings, which indicate that the neurotic is undersocialized, though less seriously so than is the sociopath. If this is true, then the order on the socialization scale should be sociopaths, neurotics, normal persons (see Figure 3). This means that the treatment of neurotics should proceed in an opposite direction: Socialization of the neurotic should be increased by the strengthening of his ego and not decreased by the reduction in control of the superego.

Examining the Evidence

At the University of Illinois in 1966, we administered a socialization test to 391 women attending a small Midwestern liberal arts college. The test used was the Socialization Scale of the California Psychological Inventory, which is known to have both high validity and high reliability. Then we asked their instructors to evaluate the students by means of a questionnaire we had designed. The ratings of the instructors made it possible to place more than two-thirds of the students into one of three categories: 190 of them were normal, 51 were neurotic, and 26 sociopathic (delinquent).

When we examined the average scores that the three groups had made on the socialization test, we found, as might be expected, that the sociopaths' average score was the lowest. If Freudian theory were correct, the neurotic group would have turned out to be more highly socialized than the normal group. Such was not the case. The highest scores belonged not to the neurotics but to the normal group (see Figure 4).

At the same time we conducted a related investigation, using as subjects 50 sociopaths, 50 neurotics, and 50 normal persons, so designated, independent of test results, by psychiatric consensus. The three groups were roughly matched for education and age, and all were men between the ages of 20 and 40 who had completed at least the eighth grade of school.

To assess the socialization of these men, we used the part of the Minnesota Multiphasic Personality Inventory (MMPI) known as the Psychopathic Deviate Scale (see Table 1), which is an inverse measure of socialization. Again we discovered that the most highly socialized of the three groups was the normal one—not, as Freudian theory would predict, the neurotics (see Figure 5).

We also analyzed the scores the 150 men had made on the Psychasthenia Scale of the MMPI (see Table 2). This scale probably is the best single measure we have of neuroticism or anxiety. The results confirmed the clinical supposition that both sociopaths and normal persons are relatively low in anxiety, while neurotics are very high (see Figure 6).

When the MMPI data on socialization and on anxiety are combined, an interesting picture emerges. According to Freudian theory, we would expect that anxiety and socialization would increase together (see Figure 7). Instead, though neurotics do suffer far more from anxiety than do sociopaths or normal persons, they fall between the two groups in degree of socialization (see Figure 8).

New Directions

Taken in conjunction with the results reported by numerous other investigators, our findings seem decisive. The implication for psychotherapy is clear. Any form of therapy, and this includes the majority of both past and present efforts, that tries to move the neurotic in the direction of reduced socialization is seriously suspect. A different approach is called for, such as the one offered by *integrity therapy*.

The underlying assumption of integrity therapy is that neurosis is not a disorder or disease produced by oversocialization but that it is a state of personal immaturity, irresponsibility, and concealed deviance. The neurotic has done something that he feels, probably with good reason, should be hidden. So he forgets it, denies it, rationalizes it, or whatever, trying to escape the danger that his strong superego (or an outside agent) will discover the forbidden act or impulse and punish him for it, again probably with good reason.

In a sense, integrity therapy works *with* the superego instead of against it. The neurotic's chief problem is a lack of communication between superego and ego, rather than between id and ego (see Figure 9). So the

TABLE 1

Some Items from the Psychopathic Deviate Scale of the MMPI

1. These days I find it hard not to give up hope of amounting to something.
2. My way of doing things is apt to be misunderstood by others.
3. I am sure I get a raw deal from life.
4. At times I have very much wanted to leave home.
5. Someone has it in for me.

TABLE 2

Some Items from the Psychasthenia Scale of the MMPI

1. There seems to be a lump in my throat much of the time.
2. Sometimes I become so excited that I find it hard to get to sleep.
3. I usually have to stop and think before I act even in trifling matters.
4. Often I cross the street in order not to meet someone I see.
5. Bad words, often terrible words, come into my mind and I cannot get rid of them.

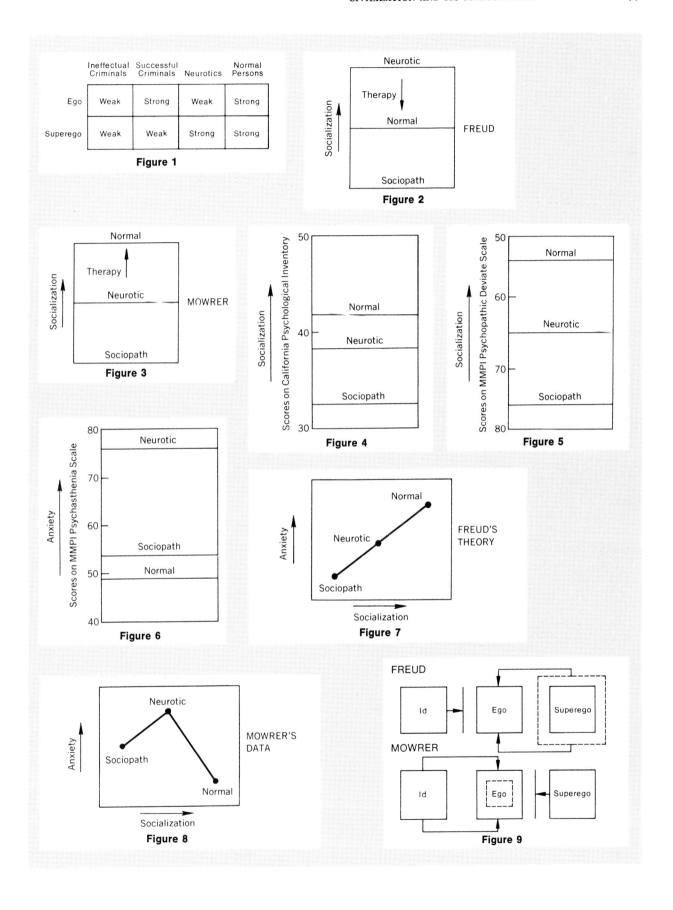

Figure 1

Figure 2

Figure 3

Figure 4

Figure 5

Figure 6

Figure 7

Figure 8

Figure 9

task of therapy, in my opinion, is not to undermine conscience, as the Freudians do, but rather to support it and to help the ego recognize the legitimacy and potential of the superego.

The therapist attempts to divest the patient of the cloak of secrecy and dishonesty in which he shrouds himself—to get him to admit who he is and what he has done, and then to take whatever steps he can toward restitution. What the conscience says is, of course, subject to change. What does not change is the requirement that, having made an interpersonal commitment, either tacit or explicit, the patient does not secretly violate it.

Freud also saw the neurotic's problem as essentially a moral one, involving a discrepancy between moral standards and personal conduct. But Freud thought the discrepancy was caused by individual standards that were too high. In fact, it appears that the neurotic is a person whose standards are normal enough but whose conduct leaves something, often quite a lot, to be desired. Once the neurotic sees that this is the case, and that the responsibility for his behavior lies squarely on his own doorstep, then he can if he wishes—and he usually does—begin to change. His ego strengthens its control over his behavior, his self-discipline improves, and he is able to level with himself and with others.

Consider the Criminal

Does it make any difference to the sociopath whether he is a great deal less socialized than the neurotic and somewhat less socialized than the normal person, or vice versa? At first glance, it might appear that the rehabilitation of criminals would take the same course regardless. In either instance, normality would lie in the direction of increased socialization: the criminal must somehow acquire a conscience as well as a willingness to listen to it.

According to Freud, the criminal can move directly to normality. However, I am convinced that he must pass through the neurotic stage first.

New evidence that this is indeed what happens came my way in November, 1966, when I helped conduct an integrity training workshop at Daytop Village in Swan Lake, New York. Several residents of the Village, which was established for the self-rehabilitation of drug addicts, attended one of my lectures, and some of them reacted with obvious discomfort and incredulity to the implication that they would have to "get sick" before they could become normal. This reaction was not hard to understand, but later some of the older residents told me privately, with dramatic illustrations from their own lives, that this was precisely what their own experience had been.

An article by Seymour Halleck, based on his observations as staff psychiatrist in a hospital for federal offenders, substantiates what I was told at Daytop Village. Inmates who became mentally ill while in prison and were transferred to the hospital, where life was generally easier and some psychiatric treatment was provided, made strenuous efforts to return to the prison. They did so even when, in the opinion of the doctors, they were far from ready to resume prison life. Halleck wrote:

There are definite social advantages to the person who chooses the criminally deviant role. The attractions of the criminal culture can be enormous. It is a seductive culture in which guilt feelings are easily rationalized away and in which the rewards for effective performance are great . . . While some offenders are probably unable to form close interpersonal relationships, others can do so, and associations between offenders may be close and sometimes meaningful.

In order to be effectively rehabilitated, Halleck said, the criminal offender often must pass through a period of conflict that has clearly neurotic, sometimes psychotic, overtones. In a report in which he described his work at three different institutions that were in the process of improving their rehabilitation programs, Halleck wrote:

In each case, as the program improved, the neurotic and psychotic symptoms among the institution population increased. Apparently the average delinquent remains fairly comfortable as long as he is allowed to associate with other delinquents and is not forced to delve too intensively into his own motivations. [But] an increasing emphasis on rehabilitation makes it difficult for him to continue his identification with the "bad" role. Older staff members at these institutions have made such comments as "We just don't get the same type of tough offenders any more; they're just a bunch of sick, helpless people." Such statements are usually indicators that the program is moving forward.

Halleck's observations are the more remarkable because he is psychoanalytic in orientation, and there is nothing in the Freudian scheme that would require or even permit the criminal to become neurotic before he becomes normal. According to Freud, normality is "next door" to sociopathy; in this frame of reference, it would not be at all necessary for the criminal to pass through a neurotic stage. On the other hand, if the alternate scheme I am suggesting is correct, then Halleck's observations are precisely what we would expect. The sociopath must show, or at least develop the capacity for, neurotic responses before he can reach normality.

One of the reasons sociopaths ordinarily experience relatively little anxiety is that their personality structure is not well enough developed to produce this reaction. But there is the further consideration that, although some criminals are "loners" and truly unsocialized, many are quite highly socialized—in criminal societies. These societies may, as Halleck pointed out, prove quite satisfying psychologically. So the sociopath faces a double disadvantage: He has to leave a society that has been rewarding in many ways, and he must encounter conflict and anxiety before he can enter the more conventional social order. In the light of these facts, it is not surprising that the rehabilitation of criminal offenders is so difficult.

Consider the Child

What about children? It is generally conceded that in the beginning they, too, are quite unsocialized and have to be made "fit to live with" by a long process of training and education. Must they pass through what Edgar Allan Poe has called "the misty midregion of Weir"? If, as Freud supposed, the neurotic is oversocialized, then children would have to become normal before they could become neurotic.

The observations of the analysts themselves speak otherwise. Freud and his students have written extensively about the "infantile neurosis," or Oedipus complex, which children supposedly show between the ages of two and five, and they note a second edition of this complex at puberty. Here, again, the movement toward socialization is sociopath, neurotic, normal—not sociopath, normal, neurotic.

Consider Culture

A few months ago, several students and I were discussing the broader implications of socialization. It suddenly occurred to us that groups of people tend to become increasingly socialized as they progress from a stage of lawlessness and disorder to civilization—with many periods of moral struggle and conflict in between. In *Civilization and Its Discontents*, Freud argues that man puts up with civilization, and indeed has evolved it, not because it makes him happy but merely because it increases his security. However, according to the psychoanalytic scheme, the more highly socialized or civilized a person is, the more anxious, and therefore the more insecure, he will be. If Freud's conception of the relationship between socialization and anxiety were valid, there would be no real incentive for mankind to abandon savagery (sociopathy) and move toward civilization (morality), since such a course would entail a steady increase in anxiety.

In my opinion, it is clear why societies tend to move toward civilization, or at least toward a moral order of some kind, and why individuals also have a kind of stability, once they have approximated the norms of their particular group. A high degree of socialization provides mankind with more security than does neurosis, as well as with more security than the original sociopathic state. Similarly, a person who has reached normality is likely to remain there, held by the threat of a greater anxiety.

Student Activists: Result, Not Revolt

Richard Flacks

Societies typically change their value structures more slowly than do many individual members of the society, a condition described by anthropologists as "the dead hand of culture." But occasionally cultural changes take place swiftly. In Germany in the 1930s, the majority of the young people held pro-Nazi, prowar attitudes; by the early 1950s, after the Third Reich's defeat and the subsequent revelations of the war crimes trials, the pendulum swung almost to the opposite extreme and German youth adopted a strong passivistic outlook. American youth of the 1950s seemed mostly concerned with getting along, with not rocking the boat, with financial security and success; the young people of the late 1960s and early 1970s appear to be rejecting traditional materialistic values in favor of more socially oriented, humanistic values. Under some conditions, such a sudden shift in social direction might well lead to open rebellion. In explaining how the young rebels got that way, Richard Flacks offers hope that our society will undergo evolutionary rather than revolutionary change.

The scene might have been written by Genet; it was worthy of filming by Fellini. A young man, well clothed and well groomed but with his shirt collar open now, and his tie pulled down, shouted to the audience like an old-fashioned revivalist.

"Come up," he cried, "come up and confess. Put some money in the pot and be saved!"

And they came. The first youth, clutching the green pieces of paper in his hand, recited for all to hear: "My father is a newspaper editor. I give twenty-five dollars." His penitence brought cheers from the assembly. The sin of the next young man was a father who was assistant director of a government bureau. He gave forty dollars. "My dad is dean of a law school," confessed another, as he proffered fifty dollars for indulgence.

The occasion was not a rehearsal for the theater of the absurd but a convention of Students for a Democratic Society. The "sins" that the students confessed were the occupations or the social classes of their fathers. Their origins placed these students in the elite, the high-status group of any community, and yet here they were, exuberantly adopting a political stance and a style of life that they believed to be the very antithesis of those origins.

Why this should be so, frankly puzzled me and led to research that has confirmed and refined my earliest impression of the social make-up of today's youth in dissent. They are of the middle- and upper-middle class. They are the core of the student movement. They are the dissenters.

That the activist student movement is a small minority of the student population cannot be denied. But it is of great significance—partly because of the movement's social composition, partly because this movement is a phenomenon that was unforeseen by professional social scientists, and *mostly* because many of the themes and ideals of the movement are concurred in by a wide cross section of students.

Are students really in revolt? The simple fact may be that, on the contrary, today's students are tuned in to a developing cultural tradition in the United States, a tradition that has grown all but undetected because certain of our lingering assumptions about American society no longer prevail.

The phenomenon that has come to be called the student movement began in the late 1950s, when Northern white students responded to efforts by Southern Negro students to break down the barriers of segregation. However, as the protest has grown, it has broadened beyond the fight for civil liberties. Now, of course, it includes such issues as nuclear testing, the arms race, campus democracy, the educational quality of the university, and above all the undeclared war in Vietnam.

This evolution to active protest, and to action itself, began even as sociologists and social psychologists were despairing of political commitment among the young. University students of the 1950s were termed "the quiet generation," and experts predicted a button-down-minded generation. Polls showed that students were unconcerned with deep values; they were also complacent, status-oriented, and uncommitted. Conformity was much discussed, as were grey flannel suits, organization men, suburbia, status symbols, and security.

Then, suddenly, young people of the 1960s surprised everyone—they questioned everything and they protested most of the things that they questioned. Theorists were nonplussed, and conventional wisdom about the sources of radical action got a slap in the face.

We are not confronted with youths who are attracted to radicalism because they are economically deprived, or because their opportunities for mobility—or for anything else—are blocked. These highly advantaged youths are indifferent to, or repelled by, the best opportunities for high status and income. Yet these young people cannot be explained and understood as a generation in revolt. This is no effort to break free of the constricting, tradition-oriented, or obsolete values of parents. The parents of student protestors share with their offspring an unusual divergence from conventional religious, political, and social attitudes.

Most activists are recruited from a very special kind of middle- and upper middle-class family. In most of these families both mother and father are highly educated, the father is a professional, and the mother very often has a career as well. Many of these families are Jewish, but regardless of their denominational allegiance, both parents and children tend to be political liberals—there are very few Republicans among them. Activists say that their parents have been permissive and democratic, and the parents' description of themselves agrees.

Our studies indicate that activism, as well as other expressions of youth disaffection, are symptoms of the declining power of those values and goals that traditionally have given direction and meaning to the lives of the American middle class and direction to the American dream. Both students who are attracted to new radical politics and youths who experiment with new styles of Bohemianism—no matter how they may differ in personal history, personality, or perspective—repudiate mainstream middle-class values.

Moving parallel to the line of conventional middle-class values and the families that carry them, there appears to be emerging an alternative value system embodied in certain types of families. These variant families, intentionally or not, create dispositions in their children toward radical social action. This is a *result*, not *revolt*.

Dominant Values

There is a sociological consensus about the substance of middle-class values that derives from Weber's famous analysis of the Protestant ethic. Central in American life remains the value placed on achievement in an occupation.

This emphasis upon career demands a conception of self in terms of occupational status, so that the meaning of one's life centers around activity and achievement in a chosen profession. Thus, experience must be organized in terms of career patterns that demand a strongly future-oriented psychology—present experience is shaped to career requirements. And finally, in this conception, one's full potential for occupational achievement can be realized only to the extent that the emotional life is regulated and rationalized.

To the Weberian emphasis on achievement and self-control may be added the observation of Alexis de Tocqueville: Middle-class Americans are strongly concerned with the opinions of their peers. Increasingly, according to David Riesman and others, efforts to achieve group acceptance depend on one's skills as a consumer. Furthermore, according to Kenneth Keniston, absorption in consumption of material goods within the context of the family provides a much-needed balance to the discipline required in one's occupation.

Humanistic Values

Student activists and their parents are strongly characterized by humanistic values, whereas student nonactivists and their parents are characterized by dominant values. Two clusters of values can be identified within the humanistic subcultures. The first is a basic concern with individual development and self-expression, with a spontaneous response to the world. The free expression of emotions and feelings is viewed as essential to the development and integrity of the individual. Humanistic parents thus raise their children in an environment relatively free of constraints and favorable to experimentation, expressiveness, and spontaneity. They also stress the significance of autonomous and authentic behavior freely initiated by the individual and expressing his feelings and ideas.

Concern with self-development and expression also is reflected in this group's attitude toward aesthetic and intellectual capacities. Creativity in these areas is prized and encouraged in children, who also are given a feeling for their capacity for personal development.

The second group of values within the humanistic subcultures might be called ethical humanism. There is a sincere concern for the social condition of others. This strong humanitarian outlook results in socially and politically aware and active parents, who tend to share their views with their children.

Self-Expression Versus Self-Control

Humanistic values like aestheticism and intellectualism do not appear to be at odds with such dominant middle-class values as career achievement or materialism, but a basic conflict between the humanistic and the dominant attitudes can be seen in the contrast between self-expression and self-control.

In the dominant culture, behavior follows relatively fixed rules of conduct that represent objective authority and that secure the individual against unpredictable and possibly destructive impulses. The humanist, however, rejects such fixed rules. He is more flexible, and he sees the spontaneous flow of feelings and ideas as intrinsically good and necessary for personal growth.

Thus humanistic students are raised in a permissive and egalitarian family environment by parents who encourage them to be expressive and fill them with a sense of their own capacity for self-development. At school and at college these students first discover that the society at large expects them to be centrally motivated around goals and values that they cannot accept. Pursuit of status goals to them means hypocrisy and sacrifice of personal integrity.

In the eyes of humanistic youths, the public world is dominated by large authoritarian organizations, which severely regiment the individual. Subjection to impersonal authority is incompatible with their attitudes toward autonomy and authority. Many of these youths, suspecting that the policy of most organizations does not reflect their own ideals and principles, feel threatened.

Constraints on expression that exist in the world of work threaten youths who have been relatively unconstrained by parents. And they see the university as becoming just another impersonal institution—a big computer. Since so many plan university careers, they want to stop this trend.

Our original study of student activists and their parents, which led to the discovery of the humanistic subcultures, was made in 1965. The activist sample was matched with a control sample by type of college attended, neighborhood of parents' residence, sex, and religion. The interviews with both students and parents averaged about two hours and concerned political attitudes, broader values, and family life.

Parent and student values were not measured identically, although the definitions of values were the same in both cases. The aspirations that parents have for their children frequently were used to ascertain parent values. In most cases, the parents of activist students scored significantly higher on the values we have identified as part of the humanistic subcultures than did the parents of nonactivists. Parents of activists also scored much lower on most of the values we have identified as belonging to the dominant culture.

The values of activist and nonactivist students are very different. Youths active in the student movement have rejected the traditional middle-class values, which still direct the goals of the nonactivist students.

Romanticism, a humanistic value, was identified as a concern with beauty and a sensitivity toward the realm of feelings and emotions. The high romantic was likely to want to become a poet, musician, or artist. He frequently expressed a desire for experience and a love of wandering, an aversion to settling down, and a need to find a liberating social environment in which institutional constraints would be lessened. These themes are traditionally associated with Bohemianism, rather than with radical social action, but our study found them significantly related to student activism.

Parents of activists generally scored higher in romanticism than did parents of nonactivists—none in the latter group could be considered high romantics. Parents who were high romantics were vitally interested in the arts—and hoped their children would be, too. Only a few parents were professional artists; most of them were leisure-time aesthetes.

Intellectualism is high on the list of humanistic values. While romanticism and intellectualism often have been considered mutually incompatible, our data suggest that there is a strong positive relationship between them. Most of the students who scored highest in intellectualism expected to teach and write within a university. They read extensively, particularly in philosophy, the humanities, and the social sciences. The empirical relationship between intellectualism and activism proved to be very strong, as did the link between parent intellectualism and child participation in the student movement.

Parents who were highest scorers talked repeatedly about the importance of books in their own lives and how they had interested their children in books. Their reading interests were the same as their activist youths', and many reported a shared interest with their children in ideas, books, and intellectual discussions.

Authenticity was measured as acute sensitivity to hypocrisy, a wish for self-knowledge and understanding, concern that one's own personal potentialities—as well as those of others—be realized, rejection of imposed standards of behavior, and acceptance of situational ethics.

In appraising the American culture, students who scored highest in authenticity were critical of the political, social, moral, and religious hypocrisies characteristic of middle-class life. Our statistics clearly demonstrate that authenticity is strongly connected with activism and that scores of the children and their parents were closely related.

Parents who scored high on this value viewed their children as autonomous individuals who must have the chance to realize their potentialities. Children of these parents always had been encouraged to make their own decisions, even if they violated parental standards of morality. Like the students, but not to the same degree, these parents were sensitive to hypocrisy.

In student interviews, interpersonal intimacy was explored in terms of both friendship and love. Losing one's self in love and caring deeply were stressed by the highest scorers in this area. The idea of the I-thou relationship as developed by Martin Buber is the most fully elaborated expression of the possibilities felt to be inherent in depth relationships.

The range of interpersonal intimacy correlated less strongly with activism than any of the other humanistic values. But when this area was broken into the separate categories of love and friendship, it was found that concern with deep love was concentrated almost exclusively among the activist students; those concerned with continuous contact with friends were slightly more likely to be nonactivist students. Parents of activist students in turn were slightly more concerned than were nonactivist parents about open and frequent interaction with friends.

Humanitarianism is grounded in a compassion and sympathy for the suffering of others and an outrage at institutions that deprive individuals or groups at any level. In order to separate humanitarianism from activism, we excluded attitudes and actions that related specifically to political ideology or to organized political projects. (This area showed the strongest empirical relationship to activism.) The relationship between parent humanitarianism and activism of children was especially high in the case of fathers.

Occupational Success and Materialism

Occupational success is held up as a major value for boys in the dominant culture, yet difference between the two groups was not nearly as marked as one might expect. And the difference between activist and nonactivist girls is even less pronounced.

Activist and nonactivist males do aspire toward different kinds of careers, however. Nonactivists strive for careers in industry, law, or medicine, while activists lean toward politics, the arts, or the academic life. Only one activist male manifested a strong concern with success in a profession—a Harvard student whose goal is the Nobel prize in physics.

Activist parents consider career just as important as nonactivist parents do. Activist sons, however, tend to be a bit less concerned about a profession than nonactivist young men. Unlike their children, many parents

believe it is necessary to realize the dominant value of career in public life if one hopes to realize humanistic values in private life. The new generation either has not met the necessity for compromise, or *will* not.

Moralism and self-control were measured by studying implicit systems of morality, especially in the area of sexual and other forms of personal expression. Students who scored highest in this category indicated an adherence to a control-dominated moralism and an inflexible personal approach to morality centered around absolute right and wrong. The low-scoring end was for students who rejected conventional morality and who believed in free expression of impulses and emotions. Scores of nonactivist students, obviously, were much higher than those of the activists.

Parents who scored highest were deeply concerned lest the Protestant ethic break down through the weakening of discipline and authority in the institutional world. Low-scoring parents were convinced that traditional morality systems were hypocritical and repressive, and they supported a morality emphasizing expressiveness.

This rating is powerfully related to activism in students and appears to be at the core of value differences between the parents of activists and those of nonactivists. The strong correlation validates our thesis that the central conflict between dominant and humanistic cultures is the opposition between self-control and self-expression (see Figure 1).

In dealing with materialism and status, we explored the concern with making money and the enjoyment of a high level of material consumption, as well as the attainment of social prestige. Those who aspired toward material success included social prestige as an important goal, while those who rejected materialistic considerations were even more emphatic in their rejection of social status. The empirical relationship between materialism-status and student activism was a strongly negative one.

Although parents of student activists score somewhat lower on this scale than do the parents of nonactivist students, the relationship between the parents' material values and the students' activism is not statistically significant. Rather, this is often the major area of disagreement in the families of many students of both sorts. Students view their parents as rooted in an empty and ostentatious suburban life, and parents do not understand their children's rejection of comfort and advantages. Flagrant unorthodoxy in dress and personal appearance particularly disturbs parents. The haircut problem is acute.

Impact of Existentialism

As we tabulated the responses to our interviews, the possibility that existentialism has had a significant impact on the thinking of student activists became more pronounced. The writers who are important to students who scored highest on intellectualism were Dostoevsky,

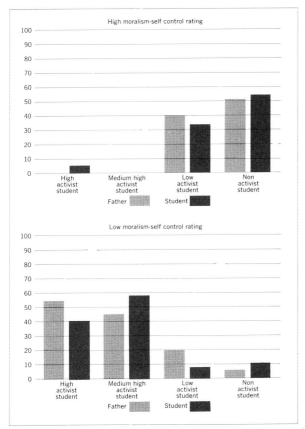

Figure 1. Correlation of activist and nonactivist students' and parents' ratings in terms of conventional morality and self-control versus free expression. The measurements were derived from the study of implicit systems of morality.

Nietzsche, Camus, and Sartre. An existential concern with authentic choice and action showed strongly on the authenticity rating.

In an attempt to discover whether activist students consciously identify with humanism and existentialism, we interviewed a second sample of student activists and again contrasted the sample with a control group. As a part of this interview, we gave students a list of twenty-two "isms" and asked them to list the three items with which they most identified (see Table 1).

The core of the current student movement consists of youths who are searching for an alternative to established middle-class values. And those who are engaged in this search come from families who are skeptical of conventional values. This tradition of skepticism and humanism is growing, and the families that identify with it are likely to increase rapidly in number.

Despite the apparent family roots of humanism and activism in the current student generation, it would be

an error to say that there is a one-to-one correspondence between parental and student values. It would be as great an error to say that parental influence is the sole factor in predisposing youth to radical politics. Children raised in the humanistic subcultures are potential recruits to a wide variety of student deviant, Bohemian, and drug subcultures.

Parental status, values, and practices indicate a predisposition toward humanist values and activist participation by students, but the degree or intensity of their involvement seems to depend on factors that are independent of family background. The college the student attends, the friends and teachers he meets in college, even the dormitory to which he is assigned his freshman year may affect his selection. Other strong influences include the impact of groups and organizations, of books and journeys, of historical events and how the individual experiences them, and of personal experiences such as long illnesses, living and working abroad, or time spent in jail.

The humanist family tradition has contributed a huge share of the initiators of the student movement, and a very large proportion of the most active participants continues to be recruited from middle-class humanistic subcultures.

TABLE 1

Impact of Humanism and Existentialism—Survey Results

Group	First choice (%)		Second choice (%)		Third choice (%)	
	Human.	Existen.	Human.	Existen.	Human.	Existen.
Activists (N = 61)	30	23	22	15	12	15
Nonactivists (N = 55)	16	11	16	5	11	4

Our parent-student research indicates strongly that the movement has a dynamic of its own, which is shaping student attitudes and their commitments. Our data show that the recent protest groups are made up, in part, of a central core of activists who come from humanistic subcultures and have a long history of active protest, and, in part, of a larger group of newly recruited students. Fascinatingly or alarmingly, depending on one's viewpoint, recent recruits more closely resemble the general student population. They come from widely diverse backgrounds, even from conservative and conventional parents. Protest appeals to an increasingly broader spectrum of students. The movement is spreading to the dominant culture.

Impulse, Aggression, and the Gun

Leonard Berkowitz

Almost all of us would agree that behavior is tremendously influenced by the environment in which the behavior takes place. Even innate action patterns are shaped by the stimuli that trigger off the instinctive acts. The male three-spined stickleback will show aggressive behavior toward any other male fish—or even toward a plastic model—that has a particular set of red markings on it; the male Siamese fighting fish will "flare" aggressively at its own image for days on end if you leave a mirror in its tank. In both these species of fish, the more opportunities the animal is given to aggress, the more likely it is that it will do so the next time the triggering stimulus is presented. In the following article, Leonard Berkowitz presents evidence that, in some respects, humans react to aggression-inducing stimuli such as guns in much the same fashion. The mere sight of a gun may invoke hostile actions on our part that would not occur if the gun had not been visible. As the noted Russian playwright Anton Chekhov put it, "If in the first act you hang a pistol on the wall, by the third act you must use it."

In November 1966, Robert Benjamin Smith, then eighteen years old, entered a beauty shop in Mesa, Arizona, and shot seven strangers, killing five of them. He said he had been planning the murder for three months, ever since his parents gave him a 22-caliber pistol for target practice. His original inspiration, he went on, was the preceding summer's mass killings in Chicago and Austin, Texas.

Almost everyone in the United States read about the murder of the eight Chicago nurses and about the massacre from the University of Texas tower, and millions of Americans own guns. But we cannot disregard Smith's remarks simply because they do not completely explain his behavior.

Now, more than ever before, there is need to answer the question: what effect *do* available weapons and vicarious experience with violence have on a person who is "ready" to commit an aggressive act?

Two series of experiments that my colleagues and I have performed on impulsive aggression bear directly on these questions. The first series indicates that even so small a matter as the casual sight of a gun can sometimes stimulate aggressive behavior. The second suggests that, contrary to what the so-called catharsis theory predicts, the sight of violence can increase the chance that a viewer will express aggression himself.

The Gun as Cue for Aggression

In experiments to test the effect of the presence of guns on aggressiveness, we observed the behavior of 100 students at the University of Wisconsin under different sets of circumstances. Some students were angry and some were not, some saw the guns and some did not. (We did not reveal the study's real purpose, claiming instead to be measuring the students' physiological reaction to stress.)

The stress, we informed them, would be a series of one or more mild electric shocks. We asked each student to make a list of ideas a publicity agent could use to improve the record sales and public image of a popular singer. Then we gave each student a "partner," ostensibly another experimental subject but actually an ally of the experimenter. The pretend partner's task was to evaluate the student's publicity ideas. If the partner thought the student's ideas were very good, he would give him one electric shock; if he thought the student's work was bad, he would administer up to ten shocks. Later, the student would be asked to evaluate a similar task of his partner's, and to convey his judgment in the same way.

By prearrangement with the experimenter, the partners gave one shock to half the students and seven shocks to the other half, regardless of the quality of the students' ideas. We assumed that the seven-shock students would feel physically uncomfortable and that they would feel humiliated as well. They were our angry group.

After each student had received the number of shocks allotted to him, the experimenter invited him to trade places with his partner and led him into the room containing the shock machine. The telegraph key that would send the shocks lay on a table at one end of the room. Sometimes the table was empty except for the key; at other times, badminton racquets and shuttlecocks (neutral objects) lay near the key. At still other times, the table held a 12-gauge shotgun and a snubnosed 38-caliber revolver.

The experimenter acted surprised at the sight of the guns and the racquets and explained that they had been "left over from another experiment." Matter-of-factly, he moved them aside. The students seemed to pay little or no attention to them. Later on, after the experiment was over, the experimenter asked each student what, if any, suspicions the student had felt. No doubts were voiced about the presence of the weapons.

Next, the experimenter showed the student his partner's "work" (actually prepared in advance and uniform for all partners). He reminded the student that he should use shocks to indicate his evaluation of his partner's work and he told the student that this was the last time shocks would be administered in the study.

As we suspected, the presence of the guns affected both the number of shocks the students gave their partners and how long they held the key down for each shock. Some differences between groups were less clearcut than others; from a statistical point of view, our most significant finding was that the angry men who saw the guns gave more shocks than any other group.

Both common sense and personality theory tend to neglect the "weapons effect" that this study demonstrates. Instead, they stress motives and, perhaps, psychological and social dislocations. What is often overlooked, perhaps because it is a frightening idea, is that much violence is *impulsive*. It is not primarily planned, purposeful activity; neither is it the "inevitable" result of internal drives or maladjustments. These things set the stage and help carry the action forward, but in many cases it is also important that there be a stimulus or immediate cue to trigger aggression.

It is quite conceivable that many hostile acts that supposedly stem from unconscious motivation really arise because of the operation of aggressive cues. The aggression can even be thought of as a conditioned response to the stimulus. If a gun can be that stimulus, then it is a double-barreled threat—an immediate cue that also presents the aggressor with a deadly *means* of aggression.

With our subjects, the guns did not enhance aggression unless the students were angry to begin with. But studies conducted at the University of Indiana show that, at least with young children, anger is not necessarily a factor. In these experiments, youngsters played with an older child whom the psychologist in charge had asked to behave in a friendly, neutral way. There was no quarreling. Then some of the children were given toy guns to play with while others chatted quietly with adults conducting the experiment.

After this preparation, each child was told that the older youngster he had played with earlier had built a structure of blocks on a play table in another room. "If you push this button on my desk, you'll shake the table and his blocks will fall down," the experimenter said. *More of the children who had played with guns pushed the button.*

Neither group of children was angry, but the guns had an effect. Guns did more than lower the children's restraints against aggression; they seemed to pull out aggressive reactions that would not otherwise have occurred.

Anger may not always be *necessary* in aggressive behavior, but it certainly facilitates it. And our society offers its citizens a wide array of anger-producing frustrations. It is not necessary to detail them here. It should be mentioned, though, that aggression is more likely to result from unrealized hopes than from deprivation alone. The deprived person who has no hope cannot really be said to be frustrated because he does not really have a goal he is trying to move toward. A person works harder to get something—whether it is food, a sexual object, or a new car—if he thinks he has a chance. Similarly, his frustration is most severe when he is blocked from a satisfaction he thinks should and could be his.

In social terms, this concept of frustration reveals

itself in "revolutions of rising expectations." Poverty-stricken groups are not frustrated merely because they have suffered severe deprivations; they are frustrated when they begin to hope. Privation is far less likely to cause violence than is the dashing of hopes.

Even given high frustration and an immediate cue, violence will not erupt unless there is a third factor as well: low inhibitions. The "normal" level of inhibitions to violence in our society is not particularly high. We take a lenient attitude toward what is sometimes called defensive aggression. It is quite permissible, even admirable, for a man to defend with vigor not only himself but his family, his home, and his country, and not only his physical safety but his principles of honor, law, and democracy. Even defensive aggression that is quite violent and smacks more of revenge than defense tends to be seen as an act of courage, a mark of manhood.

The air that hovers over Hollywood and New York (not to mention Washington) smells of the frontier, and one can detect a breeze from the Crusades as well. Nowhere is violence in the cause of good more consistently and more enthusiastically touted than in movies and on TV.

Fictional representations of violence are often defended, by people in the industries that sell them and also by many consumers, on the grounds that they serve a cathartic purpose. The theory, loosely derived from Aristotle's view of the function of tragedy, contends that violence that is indulged in vicariously drains a reservoir of accumulated hostility and releases tensions that might otherwise explode into actual violent behavior.

This theory receives additional support from the ideas and writings of the eminent ethologist Konrad Lorenz. Lorenz stresses the physiological rather than the psychological as a source of behavior: behavior results, he says, from the spontaneous accumulation of some excitation or substance in neural centers. He believes that "present-day civilized man suffers from insufficient discharge of his aggressive drive," and he recommends that society provide people with "safe" ways of venting their aggressive urge.

The question is, do vicarious or real-but-innocuous "outlets" in fact reduce the chances that aggressive behavior will occur? Although many psychologists continue to subscribe to the catharsis theory in some form, many others believe (and have demonstrated in experiments) that witnessed violence can stimulate actual violence and that a little aggression, like a snowball, can gather momentum and grow.

Viewed Violence

Let us examine the results of another series of studies. In this series, a group of students was made angry by ridicule and electric shock. Then, just before it was *their* turn to administer shocks, they were shown one of two movies. One was an exciting but nonviolent foot race between the first two men to run the mile in less than

four minutes. The other was a violent scene from *Champion*, the Kirk Douglas movie in which the prizefighter played by Douglas absorbs a brutal beating in the ring.

The students who saw this movie had been given two different plot summaries to prepare them for the scene. Half were led to regard the beating as justified: Douglas was a heel who had it coming. The other half heard a summary that was much more sympathetic to Douglas: it was clear that he did not deserve what he got.

The filmed violence was not cathartic; in fact, it had an opposite effect, at least on the students who thought the beating was justified. When given a chance to administer shocks to the partners who earlier had delivered shocks to them, these students responded with more aggression than any other group. Rather than feeling purged of their hostility, the students seemed to feel freer to express it. It was as if the justified aggression on the screen justified as well their own aggression against their tormenters.

These findings have been confirmed in five independent experiments, the most recent of which was conducted by James Hoyt and Percy Tannenbaum, now at the University of Pennsylvania. Hoyt and Tannenbaum presented the prizefight to some of the angry students as a grudge match. Douglas had behaved badly to his opponent, and now the opponent wanted revenge. These students gave more intense shocks than the other angry students, who had simply been reminded that violence was an inevitable part of prizefights.

Results like this present an awkward problem to TV and movie censorship agencies, and to producers who want to make violent films without encouraging real violence. The modern censorship agencies generally insist that crime and violence be used not just to entertain but to teach a lesson—"crime does not pay," for example. How the lesson should be taught is left vague; scriptwriters usually follow the maxim of "an eye for an eye."

But justified aggression is precisely the kind that seems likeliest to encourage the expression of aggression by members of the audience.

The effect is different if violence, though justified, seems excessive. If the punishment is badly out of proportion with the victim's crime, all aggression becomes less acceptable to the viewer, and his inhibitions rise. When some of the angry students who saw the boxing film were told that the fight had very serious results—Douglas was carried unconscious to his dressing room and died there—the scales that had been unbalanced by Douglas' villainy tipped the other way. These students gave fewer shocks to their experimental partners than those who were told the beating merely taught Douglas a lesson and induced him to reform.

In some ways, this is an encouraging finding. It means that viewed violence does not *necessarily* encourage actual violence. It can either lower inhibitions or raise them, depending on the viewer's interpretation of what he sees. Horror is an inhibiting emotion, and violence that strikes the viewer as disproportionate—as "too much" or "too real"—is likely to arouse horror. Many people who enjoyed *Champion* would not enjoy a front-row seat at a real prizefight in Madison Square Garden; many people who like war movies are extremely disturbed by photographs and news clips of the actual fighting in Vietnam.

However, the line between violence that is justified and unjustified, fictional and real, uninhibiting and inhibiting is anything but clear. To take just one example, the television screen itself puts distance between the viewer and what he sees. Watching a riot on television may be horrifying, but it is less horrifying than being there. The emotional effect of a ninety-minute documentary on riots is not so very different from the effect of a documentary-type movie about riots; the effect of a documentary-type movie is not so different from that of a "realistic drama"; and so it goes.

At some point on the continuum, viewed violence *stops* horrifying and *starts* exciting. Once this point has been reached, vicarious experience with aggressiveness begins to lower restraints against the real thing.

And it may begin to do something else as well. Like the guns in the experiment described earlier, witnessed violence can serve as a stimulus for the viewer, especially if he encounters someone he associates with the deserving victim in what he has just seen. At the beginning of the boxing film study, the partners of half the students were introduced as "Kirk," and the partners of the rest were called "Bob." The students who were led to believe that Kirk Douglas' beating was *justified* later gave more shocks to the "Kirks" than to the "Bobs."

In another experiment on this kind of mental association, students lost a chance to win a cash prize because (they thought) their partners had made a mistake. Soon afterward, the students were asked to evaluate two job applicants, one of whom had the same first name as the partner. The students consistently saw more bad qualities in the applicant who bore the partner's name.

Thus associations help determine the target of an aggressive attack—or, to put it another way, the stimulus properties of a possible target can affect the probability that an attack will occur.

In some cases, however, stimulus and target are not related—all that is required is that both be present. In a study conducted at the University of Iowa, C. A. Loew had college students speak either aggressive or neutral words aloud in what the students thought was the first step of a learning task. Later, when these students were given an opportunity to shock their partners for errors, the ones who had said the aggressive words gave stronger shocks than the others.

As for the snowball effect, when experimental subjects are given a number of opportunities to attack, the intensity of their attacks more often than not builds up.

By their own actions, the subjects—even if they are not emotionally aroused to begin with—provide their own aggressive stimuli and pull out further aggressive responses. Aggression stimulates more aggression.

Implications for Action

The social implications of the research I have described are clear, though they are much easier to recite than to act on. A society that wants fewer violent outbursts should reduce frustration, leave inhibitions intact, and remove immediate cues that can set off aggressive acts.

Reducing frustration in the United States, especially the frustration of social groups, is a long-term project that is receiving considerable attention. I will do no more here than recall the phrase "revolution of rising expectations" and mention that, for many people, expectations are likely to outstrip reality for a long time to come.

Leaving more of people's inhibitions against aggressiveness intact is, I think, a slightly less difficult matter.

Is it really necessary to use violence as a major source of entertainment? The catharsis theory does not hold up very well, and the frontier tradition may not be as strong as we think. Perhaps people enjoy violent books and movies more because they are absorbing than because they are violent. Books and movies in which violence plays a small part, or no part at all, are also absorbing; we might be able to arrange to have more of these.

The third possibility, reducing the number of aggressive stimuli people encounter from day to day, is probably the easiest one to effect, and the fastest. This may seem a surprising statement—deciding to remove aggressive stimuli from American life is a little like setting out to clean the Augean stable. But the task seems more manageable when one realizes that most aggressive stimuli fall into only a few large categories, one of the largest of which bears the label "Guns." Guns not only permit violence, they can stimulate it as well. The finger pulls the trigger, but the trigger may also be pulling the finger.

The Face of the Enemy

Jerome D. Frank

A gun hanging on the wall is a mild stimulus to aggression; a gun in the hands of one's known enemy stimulates us more than mildly. For enemies are real. They are not mere chimeras fabricated by clever propagandists. They exist; they kill. The very existence of a group that holds an ideology different from our own creates harsh anxiety in us, but our mental image of the enemy is shaped as much by our own inner psychological processes as by his reality. Once formed, this image is a strong stimulus to aggression on our part; but it is also a filter in our perception of our enemy. We shape information to fit the image we already have. We screen out what incoming data might blur or change that picture—that face of the enemy—so vivid in our mind's eye. As Jerome D. Frank tells us, we are often sadly, even tragically, unaware of this information filter—a lack of awareness that may well lead us to aggressive or hostile acts when none are called for.

An ingenious experiment by J. W. Bagby of New York's Roosevelt Hospital illustrates the phenomenon of perceptual filtering. This psychologist asked American and Mexican schoolteachers to look into a device that showed simultaneously a different picture to each eye. One eye saw a picture of a baseball player and the other saw a bullfighter.

An overwhelming proportion of the Americans "saw" the baseball player; the overwhelming proportion of Mexicans "saw" the bullfighter. What these teachers saw, of course, *was* mostly determined by their cultural filter.

No psychiatrist or psychologist would be so rash as to claim that one can make solid inferences about the behavior of nations from that of individuals, but it is startling how often similarities between the man and his country emerge when one starts looking carefully.

One psychological principle certainly is highly relevant to international affairs: a person's beliefs and his expectations largely determine how he thinks and how he behaves. Since citizens of a nation tend to share the same beliefs and expectations, this principle is impor-

tant if we are to understand how nations see each other and behave toward one another.

Russian and American Self-Images

Characteristic of each nation's self-image is the belief in national sovereignty, territorial rights, and national strength. Each nation believes in its right to pursue vital interests regardless of the effects on other nations.

The degree of fear in which one nation holds another nation depends upon perception of adversary ability and intent to harm. Whether the people of one nation perceive those of another as enemies depends primarily upon the nature of relations between the two countries. Thus it is when national interests clash and nations are in conflict that the enemy image begins to take its menacing shape. Because of the universal and innate distrust of strangers, a foreign power can easily arouse a sense of threat. Once the opinion-makers have singled out the threatening nation, this innate distrust is focused.

The Russian invasion of Czechoslovakia was portrayed by American mass media as an unprovoked rape of a country struggling toward freedom; the Russians justified it as necessary to forestall a takeover by anti-communist forces imperiling the security of the Warsaw Pact nations. With the United States invasion of the Dominican Republic, the shoe was on the other foot. To us, the action was necessary to remove a Communist threat to our security. To Russia, it was an unprovoked assault on the freedom of that little country.

Enemies create anxiety leading to a progressive simplification of their image in our eyes, and this results in formation of what has been called the mirror image of the enemy. These reciprocal images differ, of course, in the relative prominence of particular features. But to a surprising degree, enemies attribute the same virtues to themselves and the same vices to their opponents.

One excellent study of Russian and American self-images—as expressed in a selection of articles in both mass and elite publications of each nation—shows that virtually 100 percent of the articles described the adversary's goal as international domination or expansion.

Each nation's press portrayed the other nation as aggressive and treacherous, and neither Americans nor Russians accepted the idea that the other was motivated by self-preservation.

Americans tended to be more realistic about their own motives for offering foreign aid, with 42 percent of the articles in American periodicals indicating that the purpose of foreign aid was to strengthen their own side. But in Soviet Union publications, 95 percent of the articles claimed that their own foreign-aid programs were just to be helpful, or else to make it possible for the countries to maintain neutrality. The press on both sides was virtually unanimous in claiming that the *other* side offered foreign aid not to help but to strengthen a power position and to weaken that of their opponent.

The reciprocal images differed sharply in one respect —foreign policy. Some 69 percent of the Russian items regarded international events as predictable, while only 7 percent of the American items took this view. Strangely, this general view was contradicted by the way each side saw the other's specific behavior. The Russians described American foreign policy as a wild and unpredictable response to events, and the Americans tended to see Russian foreign policy as a masterful part of a deep-laid plot. Practically no articles in either American or Russian publications stated that national military measures would bring about the other's downfall, and so there was reinforcement for the peaceful self-image of each nation.

In addition, the press of both nations indicated belief that internal weaknesses and contradictions in the other's system would lead to its eventual downfall. This finding is supported by Urie Bronfenbrenner of Cornell, a Russian-speaking psychologist who did some informal but careful interviewing of people from different walks of life during a visit to the Soviet Union.

The Russians he interviewed believed that the people of the United States were being deluded and exploited, that they did not fully support the United States government, that American leaders could not be trusted, and that American foreign policy bordered on madness. (Many Americans reflect the flip side of the coin in their view of the Russians.)

Bronfenbrenner also found that nearly all of the Russians who came up to him and began a conversation expressed considerable discontent with life in the Soviet Union. On the other hand, more than 75 percent of the Russians who did not speak until he had initiated the conversation identified fully with the Soviet way of life and the Soviet Union's world view.

Another American scientist, Konrad Krauskopf of Stanford University, who visited the Soviet Union about the same time as Bronfenbrenner, had an opportunity for long, informal conversations with his Russian counterparts. He reported: "The Westerner regards the Russians as controlled for the most part without their knowledge, by an oligarchy of rapacious and malevolent men who seek constantly to foment world revolution. The Russian is equally convinced that the West (in Russian eyes, the West *is* the United States, and all other Western countries are American satellites) is victimized by a small group of profit-mad monopolists who pull the strings that control the government and the communications media, and who try to instigate wars in order to sell munitions . . . it was impossible to resolve this difference in viewpoint. Each of us was repeating what he had read in his own newspapers, and each was suspicious of the other's sources."

A striking feature of the enemy mirror that Americans and Russians hold is the perception that it is *leaders* who are the real villains, and that the general population of the other country is well disposed to one's own nation—or if they are not, it is because their leaders have misled them. Concomitant with this view is the belief that the masses in the other nation are discontented and would overthrow their leaders if only they could.

This combination is wonderfully consoling for citizens of both countries. It creates a positive image of one's own nation as a savior, and it simultaneously provides convenient, visualizable devils—the leaders— on whom to focus hostility and hate. This is illustrated by the Communists' monomania with "capitalists and monopolists" and with their intellectual concern for the "oppressed masses." And it is shown in the American tendency to focus on enemy leaders as targets—the Kaiser in World War I, Hitler in World War II, Stalin in the Cold War, and more recently Castro, Mao, and Ho Chi Minh.

Contributing to the formation of the mirror image of the enemy is the need men have to reduce cognitive dissonance, which creates anxiety. This accounts for many phenomena in human thinking and behavior, including the continual effort to make our world view emotionally consistent, even if it is not logically consistent.

In order to survive, every person must organize the flood of experiences pouring in on him so that he can predict the effects of his behavior both upon people and upon other things. This organizing process starts as soon as he is born, and it is guided by his experiences with his family and with other people in his society.

Image Reversal

In general, we filter and interpret incoming information to fit our preconceptions. Value systems are usually abstract enough so we can interpret events to fit beliefs, and also reinterpret our own behavior to make sure that it is consistent with those beliefs. The strain toward consistency tends, of course, to *reinforce* the enemy image.

But the same process also can help destroy the enemy image when a former enemy becomes a needed ally. This is illustrated by a long series of public opinion polls on how Americans characterize people in other countries. In polls, respondents often are asked to choose from a list of adjectives the ones that best describe the people of another nation. In 1942 the first five adjectives chosen to characterize the Germans and the Japanese included warlike, treacherous, and cruel. Not one of these adjectives was among the top three describing the Russians, but by 1966, all three adjectives had disappeared from American descriptions of the Germans and Japanese, and the Russians were seen as warlike and treacherous. Predictably, the Communist Chinese by 1966 had become "warlike" and "treacherous" and "cruel." (Interestingly, the characterization "hardworking" rates high among descriptions of all these countries, whether friends or foes. A hardworking enemy is more to be feared, and a hardworking ally is a greater source of strength.)

A change in the American view of the Germans and Japanese followed their *total* defeat. The enemy ceased to be dangerous, and our demand for consistency required that the enemy image be altered. A factor supporting the change was the American belief that these former enemy nations were needed to help combat the spread of Communism.

Thus, in the eyes of many Americans the "warlike, treacherous, cruel, slant-eyed, buck-toothed little Japs" of World War II have become a highly cultivated, industrious, charming, and thoroughly attractive people. The American image of the German people is even more remarkable—it has flipped four times in less than half a century. Americans admired the Germans before World War I for their industry, their culture, and their scientific know-how. Then, during the war, Germans became the hated "Huns." Next, the Germans of the Weimar Republic, a democracy, were regarded favorably. The Nazis changed that. Today Germans once more are staunch allies, even though many of the government officials are former Nazis.

By and large, the Germans today are the same people the Americans hated yesterday. Our change from hostility to friendliness has been made easier by the Germans' formal renunciation of Nazism. But it may be observed that if these individuals were true Nazis, their change is suspect; and if most were not true Nazis, then they did not warrant our earlier hatred.

The strain to develop a consistent world view may lead nations with contrasting ideologies to exaggerate the differences in their behavior, and this raises the hopeful possibility that national value systems need not actually change much in order to permit acceptance of coexistence.

A study of American and Russian value systems by R. K. White of George Washington University shows that the American capitalist system that Soviet citizens have been taught to fear is not actually so very different from the "Good Society" that the Russians themselves would like to see develop in the Soviet Union. Both systems are relatively modest variations on themes that seem to be among the common great aspirations of the human race.

In stressing how the group to which a person belongs determines his world view, I do not mean to imply that this view cannot be transcended by reflection and self-awareness. Today, human survival may depend on those individuals who can surmount a tribal outlook and appreciate the world views of people of other cultures.

Distorting the Enemy's Characteristics

There are studies that have attempted to relate personality attributes of individuals to their international attitudes, and most of these studies have dealt with an authoritarian character pattern whose dynamic core is the result of repressing strong hostility to parents and to other authority figures. The person with such a character pattern exaggerates the importance of power, of force, and of domination and submission in human affairs. He displaces his hostility to safer targets than the authority figures at home. He projects his internal psychological conflicts onto external enemies, and he expresses his bottled-up aggressive and sexual feelings indirectly by overconcern with the "immoral" behavior of foreigners and of the "out" groups in his own society.

People with authoritarian personalities score high on the F-Scale, which consists of a series of statements like: "What youth needs most is strict discipline, rugged determination and the will to work and fight for family and country"; "Most of our social problems would be solved if we could somehow get rid of the immoral, crooked and feeble-minded people"; "People can be divided into two classes, the weak and the strong." The greater the number of such statements a person agrees with, the higher his score, and a high F-score correlates positively with extreme nationalism.

Within each country, individuals differ in the degrees to which they see foreigners as enemies. At one extreme are those we might call xenophobic, those who hold a morbid dislike of foreigners; at the other extreme are the xenophiles, who display an excessive acceptance of protestation of peaceful intent on the part of a foreign power, as well as holding hostility toward the leaders of their own country. Both extremists are likely to be hostile toward authority figures, but the xenophobe displaces his aggression to a foreign group and the xenophile focuses on his own leaders.

To return to group determinants of the enemy image, a psychologically crucial part of the world view of any group is its ideology, and ideological differences contribute to the dehumanization of the enemy. Humans differ from other creatures primarily in the power to symbolize, so that we respond not only to physical violence but to psychological threats to our ideology.

Since nations cannot exist without ideologies, periodic "holy wars" may seem to be inevitable. But two factors mitigate this gloomy prospect. It is more satisfying psychologically to convert members of a rival belief system than to kill them. Conversion confirms superiority.

In addition, ideologies do not have to proclaim that they have exclusive possession of the truth. Some religions, such as Hinduism, declare that all religions have grasped some aspect of the truth, and some secular ideologies, such as the American one, value diversity of viewpoints in many areas. Adherents of world views like these can coexist with others indefinitely without resorting to armed conflict to protect their beliefs.

In the Vietnam war, ideological issues have become crucial. The North Vietnamese and the Viet Cong see themselves as fighting neocolonialism, as well as furthering the Communist ideology. From a strictly materialistic viewpoint, Vietnam is of minor strategic importance to the United States. The United States government sees its action in Vietnam as part of a worldwide commitment to prevent the spread of Communism. And the United States also is motivated by a determination to show the world that we are steadfast, that we stand by our commitments.

The Vietnam war has assumed the ideological characteristics of a holy war. Throughout history, such holy wars usually end in mutual exhaustion after tremendous carnage, and with the survivors on both sides still clinging to their beliefs. Psychologically speaking, the notion that making people suffer causes them to abandon their beliefs is a hangover from the days of the Crusades.

Nations at war could be said to resemble children, for whom punishment brings contrition only under certain conditions. As every parent knows, one can control behavior by punishment, but whether the punishment alters a basic attitude depends mainly on the child's belief that it was deserved.

Since every nation believes its own aims and actions to be righteous, it never sees punishment as deserved. As a result, peace has traditionally been the time between wars during which defeated nations prepared for revenge against the victors.

Since an enemy is seen as a threat to the survival of one's own nation, to change the enemy's image implies dropping one's guard. And the enemy's image has certain dynamic properties that make it resistant to change. First, an enemy mobilizes a nation's sense of solidarity and strength. He becomes a convenient scapegoat for internal problems. Second, the image that a nation holds of its enemy eventually will bring about behavior from the enemy that makes the image a reality.

The view that the actions of the other nation always are based on hostile motives may create a self-fulfilling prophecy. This term refers to the fact that a person's expectations lead him to act in such a way as to make them come true. A classic example of this is the international arms race. Each side anticipates that the other will add to its armament. In response to this expectation each increases its own arms, thereby fulfilling the expectations and convincing the other side that its fears are justified—which leads naturally to another round of arms increases.

Leaders on each side fear that their own people are so naive that they can easily be misled by enemy propaganda. The temptation to break off entirely or to restrict communication with the enemy is a strong one. Since the enemy is untrustworthy, if we communicate with him, he may trick us or learn something about us that we do not want him to know.

Another potential source of exaggeration of the enemy's unfavorable characteristics is what G. Icheiser called the "mote-beam phenomenon." People are especially sensitive to unacceptable traits in others that they fail to perceive in themselves. A person who tries to hide his own aggressiveness from himself is usually quick to spot aggression in others. In the same way, some Americans who turn a blind eye to the inequities in civil rights for blacks are very concerned about the restrictions of freedom in the Soviet Union.

Bronfenbrenner showed some American fifth and sixth graders photographs of Russian roads lined with young trees. When he asked why the Russians had planted trees along the road, two of the answers were: "So that people won't be able to see what is going on beyond the road" and "It's to make work for the prisoners." When he asked why American roads have trees planted along the side, the children said "for shade" and "to keep the dust down."

The distorted image of the enemy acts, finally, to block acceptance of his genuine conciliatory moves. An apparently friendly gesture tends to be seen as either evidence of the enemy's weakening, or an effort to create dissension within one's own ranks. These responses are apparent in the Vietnam war. The Viet

Cong interpret American gestures of peace as evidence of a weakening will to fight, while the American government sees the enemy's proposals as propaganda aimed at creating dissension in the United States.

The first step in contacting the enemy is psychologically the most difficult; it takes considerable courage to make contact with a distrusted adversary because this means exposure to dangers not only from the enemy but from one's own side. Here perhaps we can take advantage of what psychiatrists have learned about establishing communication with a frightened, angry, and suspicious person. The first step, we have found, is simply to show persistent willingness to listen, and to refuse to be discouraged by rebuffs. While you firmly defend yourself against physical attack, you ignore mere verbal abuse. It does not pay to be too friendly. The hostile person is convinced that you mean him no good, and so he is prone to interpret an overly friendly manner as an effort to deceive him. A firm and reserved but not unfriendly manner gets further in reaching out to him.

Communication is only the first step. From a psychological standpoint, a central long-term task is learning how to foster cooperative projects among nations.

Cooperative Activities to Reduce Conflict

An experiment done in a boys' camp by Muzafer Sherif of Pennsylvania State College some years ago suggests that activities requiring cooperation have a powerful effect in reducing antagonism between two hostile groups. When the boys arrived at camp, they were divided into two groups. Then the groups were made enemies through athletic competitions. In time, they became like two hostile nations. Members in each group chose friends only from among themselves, looked down on boys in the other group, and the two groups fought at every opportunity.

Once when a member of one group tried to act as a peacemaker, he was promptly ostracized by his fellows.

Then the camp director surreptitiously arranged events to force cooperation between the two groups. For example, he secretly arranged to have the camp water supply interrupted, and the whole camp had to work together to make necessary "repairs." A truck carrying food for an overnight hike "unaccountably" ran into a ditch. It took all the boys to pull it out with a towrope. A series of such events finally broke down hostility between the two groups, and friendly relations eventually were restored.

I would hesitate to generalize from boys in conflict to nations in conflict were it not for certain obvious parallels. In a sense, the nations of the world are in the same predicament today as the boys in that camp. Nations have to cooperate in order to survive, and the international scene contains many opportunities for cooperative activities, like those in the boys' camp, that can yield mutual benefits one nation alone cannot attain. The International Geophysical Year is a good example.

The chief danger of the distorted enemy image is that it makes false perceptions as hard to change as if they were true. Only by becoming highly aware of the psychological process that forms images can we hope to dispel the false aspects of an image. Otherwise, the difficulties in communicating with the enemy progressively harden our image of him. Fantasy fills the gaps left by insufficient information, and the face of the enemy reflects our own fears.

The Psychology of Police Confessions

Philip G. Zimbardo

The policeman has three major tasks: preventing violation of the law when possible, apprehending the violator if prevention is impossible, and gathering evidence to be used in court against the presumed criminal. The first two of these roles the policeman typically performs in public, sometimes under the scrutiny of a television camera. When gathering material to be used in a court trial, the policeman is less exposed to public view, and of all data likely to lead to a conviction, a confession on the part of the presumed criminal probably carries the most weight. Policemen are well aware of this fact and, once the suspect is safely incarcerated in the privacy of the precinct house, may go to great lengths to induce him to confess. According to Philip G. Zimbardo, some of the techniques the police employ are more compelling and coercive than is physical torture. The psychological ambience of the police interrogation was well depicted by Sartre in his study of Genet: "The fascination that the police have for the thief is manifested by the thief's temptation to confess when he is arrested. In the presence of the examining magistrate who questions him, he is seized with giddiness: the magistrate speaks gently to him, perhaps with kindness, explaining what is expected of him; practically nothing: an assent. If only once, just once, he did what was asked of him, if he uttered the "yes" that is requested, harmony of minds would be achieved. He would be told, "That's fine," perhaps he would be congratulated. It would be the end of hatred. The desire to confess is the mad dream of universal love; it is, as Genet himself says, the temptation of the human."

In recent times, the U.S. Supreme Court has invalidated many confessions obtained by psychological coercion and has laid down guidelines to protect the rights of the suspect. Zimbardo asks whether the courts have gone far enough.

PART I "Most defendants have, in effect, two trials. They are first tried by the police. If found guilty they are held for trial by the courts. If found innocent by the police, they are acquitted then and there. This procedure has no basis in law . . . but we know from practical experience that far more cases are disposed of in this manner than ever reach our courts." So wrote W. R. Kidd twenty-five years ago. Now the question of police interrogation procedure has become one of the most controversial and basic legal issues ever to face the nation.

Many recent Supreme Court rulings have concentrated on guaranteeing the protection of suspects under police interrogation. Suspects now have the right to counsel during questioning, and must be apprised of their rights under the Fifth Amendment. These rulings are particularly important because, according to police statistics, more than 80 percent of all criminal cases are solved by confession. A defendant seldom is acquitted once his confession is admitted as evidence during his trial. Thus, for a majority of defendants, trial is but a mere formality.

By what methods do police obtain such an unbelievable percentage of confessions? Perhaps a goodly number of these confessions are false, elicited only by unfair, illegal, or reprehensible methods of interrogation. But even if all the confessions were in fact true, would the loss of individual rights and freedom be worth the gain in police efficiency? These are basic issues with which every thoughtful citizen is deeply concerned.

We know from psychological studies of American prisoners of war in Communist interrogation camps in Korea that many good soldiers gave false confessions, incriminated themselves, and betrayed their fellow soldiers. In their study of Communist interrogation procedures, L. E. Hinkle and H. C. Wolfe reported that not only were men forced to confess to crimes they had not committed, but apparently they came "to believe in the truth of their confessions and to express sympathy and gratitude toward those who had imprisoned them." I am now convinced that the secret inquisitorial techniques of our police force are sometimes more highly developed, more psychologically sophisticated, and more effective than were those of the Chinese Communists.

What About the Supreme Court Rulings?

The new Supreme Court rulings do indeed represent an important safeguard of individual liberty and do, of course, clear up some of the legal inconsistencies and ambiguities surrounding police station confessions. But they leave a number of vital problems unsolved. First of all, there is no control over the way police tell a suspect what his rights are. "While a number of police departments have been issuing warnings," *The New York Times* said not long after the Supreme Court decisions, "the method probably has been cursory, with the words mumbled. Or, it has likely been done as a tactic to establish a rapport with the suspect."

A second unsolved problem involves the availability of legal advice. Some 60 percent of criminal suspects cannot afford to retain an attorney; some suspects distrust lawyers in general ("They are fast-talking shysters in it only for the money"); and some don't even know the name of a lawyer to call. Moreover, some police interrogators imply that requesting an attorney is a sign of guilt, or that an attorney is a stranger who will interfere with the "man-to-man" conversation between the suspect and his "friends" in the police station. The right to silence is countered by a police argument: "If you have nothing to hide, why are you afraid to talk?"

Psychology, Not Law

Many more legal problems remain—and perhaps some of them can be solved only by psychologists. How can a court assess the amount of psychological coercion, tell whether a confession was truly voluntary, or measure a man's ability to resist pressure? Central in defining and analyzing these questions is a knowledge of personality, behavior deviations, performance under stress and deprivation, the "social demand" implicit in a situation, persuadability, and the conditions for attitude change.

We know, for example, that innocent men have confessed to crimes they did not commit. What conditions could exercise so much control over a man that he would confess falsely to murder and sign a confession? If a prisoner later denies his confession, there are only two real sources of information—the accused and the accuser. And guess who usually wins. What we need are facts. Do judges really know what goes on in squad rooms? Does anyone?

Let us look at a frightening case in which a voluntary confession of murder was later proved false.

George Whitmore's Confession

In June 1964, Patrolman Frank Isola came to the aid of Mrs. Elba Borrero as she was being sexually assaulted in the Brownsville section of Brooklyn. The attacker fled. Mrs. Borrero described her assailant as a Negro, 5 feet 9 inches tall, pock marked, and weighing about 165 pounds. He had been wearing a raincoat from which she had torn a button as she fought him off. The button was the sole tangible piece of evidence in the attempted rape.

At eight o'clock the next morning Patrolman Isola and Detective Richard Aidala picked up George Whitmore, Jr., in the vicinity of the crime. He was a small man, just 5 feet 5 inches tall and he weighed only 140 pounds. But he *was* wearing a raincoat from which a button was missing, and he was a Negro. He was arrested because there was "a reasonable ground for suspicion supported by circumstances sufficiently strong in themselves."

Mrs. Borrero viewed him through a peephole and identified him as her attacker. By 10:30 that morning, Whitmore had confessed to the attempted rape of Mrs. Borrero. By noon he had confessed to the knife-slaying of a Mrs. Edwards.

In looking over Whitmore's belongings, E. S. F. Bulger, a homicide detective who had been called in to witness the murder confession, saw a photograph of a white girl. For eight months Bulger and many others had been working on the tragic double murder of two unusually talented young career girls, Janice Wylie and Emily Hoffert, who were knifed in their Manhattan apartment. Bulger recognized the girl as Janice Wylie, and Whitmore's interrogation was resumed with far greater intensity.

By 4 A.M. Whitmore "broke" and confessed to having murdered the two girls—his third confession during twenty hours of continuous questioning. Chief of Detectives (now Chief Inspector) L. J. McKearney announced: "We've got the right guy, no question about it."

Manhattan Assistant District Attorney Peter Koste, who was called in to witness the confession, reported that Whitmore was "composed" and "alert" at the end of the interrogation. Detective Bulger, the principal interrogator, swore that he had obtained the confession without "feeding" Whitmore information about the murders.

The confession was persuasive and convincing, and so

detailed that it was sixty-one typed pages long. It included drawings of the apartment where the girls had lived and died.

Two weeks later police discovered that the photograph was not a picture of Miss Wylie after all, and they turned their attentions toward proving that Whitmore had found it in the girls' apartment.

Meanwhile, Whitmore was tried and convicted of attempted rape. Brooklyn District Attorney S. A. Lichtman said in his summation to the jury: "We have nailed George Whitmore on the button, so to speak." (The prosecution suppressed the FBI laboratory report that the remaining buttons on Whitmore's coat were "different in size, design and construction" from the button Mrs. Borrero had torn off her attacker's coat.)

In October, a private citizen, Nathan Delaney, informed the police that his friend Richard Robles had admitted to murdering the two girls. Beginning to suspect the validity of the confession, the police began a new investigation.

Brilliantly, they matched the background of the photograph with a Wildwood, New Jersey, picnic area. They identified the girl in the photograph as Arlene Franco, who said she had thrown the picture away. Whitmore lived in Wildwood, and he had once said that he found the photograph there. After two witnesses swore that they had seen Whitmore in Wildwood the night the two girls were murdered in Manhattan, and after Robles confessed to the double slaying, George Whitmore finally was freed. An innocent man had spent eight months in jail. One police officer said: "It's an awful thing, but sooner or later things like this happen. I hate to say this but I'm sure that sometime in history we've sent innocent men to their deaths by unjust verdicts." And an assistant district attorney said: "If this had been what we so-called professionals call a run-of-the-mill murder, Whitmore might well have been slipped into the electric chair and killed for something he didn't do. Let's face it. We've had executions in the past based on nothing more than a dead body and a confession."

In New York State alone more than 500 appeals were made in 1965 by prisoners seeking to reopen cases based on confessions. One example of these appeals is the case of a Bronx factory worker who confessed to the murder of a woman and, after spending a year in jail, was found innocent by polygraph data that contradicted his confession. The accused, Santo Sanchez, a forty-year-old illiterate Puerto Rican father of six, went into the 41st Street Precinct in good physical condition, and after his indictment on December 21, 1964, was hospitalized for six weeks with cuts and bruises. (Incidentally, the major link to the crime was a photo of the accused that was found in the dead woman's apartment. But since they were relatives this does not seem so strange.)

Why did Whitmore confess? Why do any of them confess? "Call it what you want: brainwashing, hyp-nosis, fright. They made him give an untrue confession," said our assistant district attorney. Another said: "I am positive the police prepared the confession for Whitmore . . . I am also sure the police were the ones who gave Whitmore all the details of the killings that he recited to our office." Whitmore says he was beaten; the interrogator says he was not. The police claim his confession was voluntary, uncoerced, and freely given.

The squad room as portrayed in old movies—a dingy office, a light shining in the eyes of a suspect while a team of police shout questions and accusations—is long gone. Modern psychological methods have supplanted the old "third degree" because they are more effective. A popular police manual states that if the interrogator "has a layman's knowledge of practical psychology and uses the salesman's approach, he can . . . reach into a man's brain and pull out the facts he wants."

Police Interrogation Techniques

Though there is little direct evidence on what happens in the squad room, a secondary source of evidence comes from manuals used to train detectives and interrogators. Written chiefly by police officers, detectives, or former staff members of scientific crime laboratories, these manuals invariably include at least one chapter on interrogation techniques. The most recent manual, a 1962 revision of *Criminal Interrogation*, by F. E. Inbau and J. E. Reid, is devoted entirely to a discussion of the psychological tactics and techniques of effective interrogation of suspects.

The following paragraphs present a sampling of many of the approaches suggested in police manuals. I am convinced that these methods are psychologically coercive; that they deprive the individual of his human dignity and fundamental rights; and that they debase the police who use them even though the police are trying to be fair as well as efficient. Let the reader judge my contention that they do not serve justice.

Inbau and Reid claim that none of the tactics they suggest are "apt to induce an innocent man to confess," but they present no evidence except personal opinion to support this key generalization. Questions at issue are: How voluntary are confessions obtained by such techniques? What degree of coercion and psychological force is implied? And to what extent are our basic constitutional and human rights violated?

| DEMAND CHARACTERISTICS OF THE INTERROGATION | Modern psychology has alerted the police to the potential significance of every detail in the stimulus situation that can be manipulated and controlled, but police do not understand the implications of where such control may lead. In police questioning, an environment is created that minimizes sensory stimulation, maximally exposes the suspect's vulnerability, and provides for complete control and domination by the interrogator.

Police manuals generally agree that the suspect should never be interrogated in an environment familiar to him or in the presence of anyone he knows. The psychological support of a familiar environment should be withheld; the suspect must always feel that he is the "guest" of the police. Indeed, "By going to the police station the suspect has made the first act of yielding." (This and all quotations in the following paragraphs are taken from police manuals.) The police interrogation room should never resemble a jail or police department office. It should be private and free from distractions or unplanned interruptions. Preferably, it should have no windows. If there are windows and the usual bars, one manual suggests "Italian garden-gate" as a particularly suitable style for the ironwork. To keep attention properly focused on the business at hand, the room should be bare, with no pictures, only two chairs and perhaps a desk.

The suspect should be permitted no tension-relieving activities or objects (such as paper clips or ashtrays, which "represent a tacit invitation to smoke"). If there is a phone, one manual suggests a fake one that the interrogator can ring surreptitiously if he needs an excuse to leave the room.

"Since the subject should be deprived of every psychological advantage," the atmosphere should suggest the invincibility of the law. The suspect should be placed in an armless, straight-backed chair so that he cannot become too comfortable, and so that all his bodily movements can be observed.

Intensive questioning should be conducted by a single interrogator, alone with the suspect and standing or sitting as close to him as he can. "When a person is close to another physically, he is closer psychologically." He should bring "the full weight of his personality . . . to bear on the emotional situation."

To "command the respect his position requires," he should wear a conservative suit and avoid loud ties. No guns or police symbols should be evident. He must have no distracting mannerisms, and he should not distract the suspect by unpleasant breath, an item that should be checked by a fellow officer and remedied if necessary with mouthwash or "a chlorophyll mint." He must seize and maintain full control of the interview and never lose his composure. Small gestures that help establish his authority include directing the subject where to sit or telling him he cannot smoke.

The investigating officer is born, not made. "He must have a built-in psychology based on instinct and experience in which a man's weak points are exploited." Psychologist Hans Toch observed that citizens "meet police officers on an unequal basis, with punishment implicit in every encounter. Ultimately, the typical contact between police and public remains one in which there is essentially one-way communication against a backdrop of latent power." The suspect or potential witness is at a disadvantage, which is intensified in every way possible. In this setting the interrogator "breaks a man by intelligence."

| **PERCEPTUAL AND JUDGMENTAL DISTORTION** | Confes-sions are often obtained by minimizing the seriousness of the offense, by allowing the suspect a face-saving "out," or by misrepresenting and exaggerating the seriousness of the crime.

The interrogator may say that he does not think the suspect's indiscretion was so serious, that he has seen thousands of others in the same situation. He may talk of extenuating circumstances, the environment, or human weaknesses—any of which might lead someone to do what the suspect did. He may suggest a morally acceptable motive like self-defense, or a crime of passion; he may even infer it was an accident or a mistake. One manual recommends that to "open up" a suspect, good "bait" is to lay the blame for the crime on someone else: an accomplice, a fence, loan sharks, even the victim.

Inbau and Reid offer provocative examples of how experts use bait. A fifty-year-old man, accused of having taken "indecent liberties" with a ten-year-old girl, is told: "This girl is well developed for her age. She probably learned a lot about sex from the boys . . . and from movies and TV; . . . she may have deliberately tried to excite you to see what you would do." Or, the manual notes, in forcible rape cases "where circumstances permit, the suggestion might be offered that the rape victim acted like she might be a prostitute . . . that the police knew she had been engaged in acts of prostitution. . . ." If the suspect is married, his wife may be blamed: "When a fellow like you doesn't get it at home, he seeks it elsewhere."

Another manual advises that once the suspect is in a state of emotional confusion, "he is unable to think logically and clearly, since his sense of values has been disturbed and his imagination is distorting his perspective." The investigator can "obtain admission or even a confession from the suspect by further misrepresenting the picture."

This can take several forms. The *knowledge-bluff* is one. The interrogator reveals a few known items and pretends to know more; he may lie, saying that a suspect's fingerprints or blood were found at the scene of the crime. A suspect may even be shown falsified samples and records. Sometimes in a murder case, interrogators are instructed by police manuals to say that the victim is still alive. Misrepresentation may be used to intensify fear. It is suggested that in statutory rape cases the suspect might be told that the victim "has testified to being forcibly raped." In theft and embezzlement, the reported loss—and thus the consequences—can be increased. "To make it look more authentic," according to Inbau and Reid, "a letter typed on company stationery can be prepared, reporting the larger loss to the police and the insurance company."

Such police perjury may take even more extreme forms. In the *fixed line-up*, the interrogation is interrupted so that alleged witnesses, who are really "ringers," can point out the suspect as the guilty man. The interrogator then resumes questioning with an air of increased confidence. In the *reverse line-up*, the suspect is falsely accused (by fake witnesses) of a real or fictitious crime more serious than the one for which he is held. Confessing to burglary may seem the easy way out for a man accused of murder, rape, or kidnapping.

| SOCIAL-PSYCHOLOGICAL DISTORTIONS | Inbau and Reid urge the interrogator to role-play the position of the subject before the interrogation begins, and then respond to him "man to man, not as policeman to prisoner . . . It is a mistake to look upon the subject as an animal." The interrogator establishes a false relationship with the suspect by acting friendly, kind, sympathetic, understanding—by appearing like "a Dutch uncle," or an older brother. He can manipulate the suspect by bestowing social approval and status since "it is a basic human trait to seek and enjoy the approval of other persons."

Flattery is useful. The interrogator is advised to compliment a suspected get-away car driver on his maneuvering and cornering abilities. Teenagers are likened to a James Bond or a Willy Mays.

The white-collar first offender—the clerk, manager, cashier, or office worker—subscribes to orthodox ethical principles and moral standards, so the dignified approach of the physician is considered most effective. "The character of [such subjects] is weak and must be exploited fully," one manual says baldly.

To create rapport, the interrogator may pat the suspect on the shoulder, grip his hand, offer to get him a drink of water. "Gestures of this type . . . impart an attitude of understanding and sympathy better than words."

One of the most effective means by which the interrogator may gain a suspect's confidence is the *Mutt and Jeff* approach, reportedly used on George Whitmore. In this technique the arresting detective instills fear while the interrogating detective is being protective, supportive, and sympathetic. Records of Whitmore's case actually show that he believed Mutt was sincerely concerned about his welfare.

Jeff is typically big, cruel, relentless, and Mutt is the kind-hearted family man whose brother perhaps was once in a similar scrape. He asks Jeff to leave the prisoner alone and get out of the room. Then he confesses that he, too, detests Jeff's tactics (which unfortunately will get worse). The suspect's only hope is to cooperate quickly with his friend Mutt by confessing.

Face-saving is a variation of this technique that is used primarily with prostitutes who refuse to inform on clients, agents, or underworld connections. Jeff calls her vile names. Mutt throws Jeff out and apologizes for his behavior. Mutt tells the girl Jeff could lose his job for such behavior and that he will see what he can do about having Jeff disciplined if she discusses freely the case at hand. Once she complies, of course, that is the end of the matter.

When there are two suspects, police are able to play one off against the other. Such tactics almost always succeed. Both may be locked in the same cell and the weaker of the two removed almost immediately for an hour during which nothing happens to him—he isn't even questioned. When he gets back to the cell, he says this but his story doesn't sound right. The interrogator calls for the other prisoner and tells him that his partner has squealed.

If the suspects are father and son, some manuals advise questioning the father first and persuading him, no matter what he has told the police, to send a note to his son saying: "I have told the truth, you should do the same."

In a third method, one suspect of a pair is taken into the squad room, with the other left to sit just outside. Screaming and thumping sounds (which are faked) come from the room, and the man outside assumes his friend is getting the third degree and probably will talk. A similar tactic, *bluff-on-a-split-pair*, is quieter and considered more effective. One of the suspects is taken into the interrogation room, and the other hears muffled voices as he waits outside. Eventually a secretary is called on the intercom and told to come into the interrogation room—with her notebook. Later, she returns to her desk and begins typing, stopping now and then to ask the waiting suspect things like how to spell his name. When it is the second prisoner's turn, the interrogator waves a typed "confession" and says that it puts all the blame on him. Resentment toward the "squealie" can result in a confession to even the score.

These tactics and deceptions support Hugo Munsterberg's classic analysis of false confessions in his book *On the Witness Stand*. He writes that there are many motives that influence an accused person into making a voluntary false confession. Confronted with what seems overwhelmingly damaging circumstantial evidence, a man may make a false confession in the hope of receiving mercy. In a classic case, the brothers Boorn of Vermont confessed to murder in order to have the charge reduced from homicide to manslaughter—but the "corpse" turned up alive.

"Untrue confessions from hope or fear, through promises and threats, from cunning calculations and passive yielding shade off into others which are given with real conviction under the pressure of emotional excitement or under the spell of overpowering influences," Munsterberg says.

| THE CLINICAL-PSYCHOLOGICAL APPROACH | In Theodor Reik's brilliant analysis, *The Compulsion to Confess*, he focuses attention not only on the obviously mentally ill who flock to police stations with confessions after every major crime but on all of us who harbor deep-seated guilt feelings for our real or imagined transgressions during childhood. Since guilt can be relieved only by confession, punishment, and absolution, Reik holds that to at least some degree the need to confess is present in us all.

Part of "sizing-up" a suspect includes assessing his

personality and his strengths and weaknesses. Suspects who seem nervous are left alone to "sweat it out" for a long time. In handling "apparently guilty" subjects, the manuals say it may be necessary to offer justifications for their behavior before their guilt feelings are sufficiently reduced to enable them even to talk about their feelings and crimes.

When the suspect does not seem nervous, the interrogator is advised to point out that he is showing psychological and physiological symptoms of guilt. Calling attention to a part of the body or bodily process can cause the subject to react. Inbau and Reid suggest that attention should be directed to pulsation of the carotid artery in the neck, movement of the Adam's apple, dryness of the mouth, movement of the limbs, and a "peculiar feeling inside" caused by a troubled conscience. The authors urge the interrogator to be on the alert for "moments of indecision during which the suspect's struggle to avoid the consequences of his criminal act will be partially overcome by, or temporarily deadlocked with, his impulse to confess." This is the time to "move in."

If the suspect is a youngster, the interrogator may play on his feelings of guilt and shame by asking him how often he masturbates. This is so embarrassing to most youths that they will eagerly change the subject and can be led easily into talking about the crime of which they are accused. So says the manual. Basic innocence makes youth vulnerable to this tactic. But "intellectual type" men suspected of real sex offenses should be put off guard by reassuring reminders from the Kinsey reports: "Human and animal sex habits differ very little."

"Fear of the insane asylum" is discussed by W. R. Kidd. "We find some mentally affected persons who fear the asylum more than they do jail," he writes. "Threat of confinement in an asylum may secure a ready admission [of guilt]."

Police manuals remind interrogators to make use of all kinds of fears, including the common fear of lie detector tests. A suspect may be asked to take a lie detector test and told that refusal is an admission of guilt. Even nightmares are used. The interrogator may ask if a man ever dreamed of committing a crime like the one of which he is accused because "there is an obvious relationship between dreaming and acting out the crime."

| SEMANTIC AND VERBAL DISTORTION | Most manuals deal at length with the art of phrasing questions and of tailoring the vocabulary to fit each suspect. These recommendations help neophyte interrogators develop sensitivity to the power of language.

Some subjects can be classified readily, and for them the rules of procedure are specific. "Mother" is the magic word for most juveniles, and the effect of the crime on her should be emphasized. The big shot should be put down by using his first name, but the uneducated person should be flattered by being called "Mister." Inbau and Reid say that the culturally deprived "should be interrogated on a psychological level comparable to that usually employed in questioning a child." An adulteress should be called by her first name because the word "Mrs." may make her feel guilty. A homosexual should never be called a "pervert" or a "queer." That only causes resentment and lack of cooperation. And one manual insists that an elderly female suspect should never be called an "old whore." Even the interrogator's tone of voice is important. Inbau and Reid say: "Care must be exercised as to tone of voice, because a very soft voice seems to lull the subject into a state of tranquility."

Justice

Recent theory and research on public compliance and attitudes assuredly come into play with the suggestion that the interrogator should discourage a suspect's denial of guilt, since the more often any man repeats a lie the harder it becomes for him to tell the truth.

PART II It is my professional opinion as a psychologist concerned with the experimental modification of attitudes and behavior that current police techniques represent a highly sophisticated application of psychological principles that for many people are more compelling and coercive than physical torture. These techniques involve confusing the suspect, lying, cheating, faking, distorting the facts, and manipulating a suspect's social values and personal needs.

Not only are police methods likely to make a guilty man incriminate himself against his will, but I am convinced that they also can lead to false confessions by the innocent and to voluntary and unintentional false testimony by witnesses. Any catalogue of current interrogation techniques would show a debasement of human nature and stands as a disgraceful slur on the American system of justice.

I am on the side of the individual; society's major function is safeguarding his rights—your rights. Such a position seems to conflict with today's police concepts of "efficiency" and "necessity." F. E. Inbau and J. E. Reid declare in their popular police manual that they "approve of such psychological tactics and techniques as trickery and deceit that are not only helpful but frequently necessary in order to secure incriminating information. . . ." These authors are not alone in their conviction. A former American Bar Association president, L. F. Powell, Jr., has said, "The pendulum may have swung too far in affording rights which are abused and misused by criminals." Many other experts are of the same opinion, and in fairness to their position, it must be noted that crime is increasing at a phenomenal rate in America, as in most countries. Since 1958, serious crime in the United States has increased by 60 percent, six times the population increase. The public is justifiably afraid, and police have responded to public pressure for action. Both the public and the police must remember, however, that the police are the enforcers of law. They do not make laws, nor should they be the judges of those who have broken the law.

Recently, many critics have questioned the need for police reliance on confessions. Certainly over-reliance on the effectiveness of interrogation lessens the use of other good crime detection methods. Back in 1872, the framers of the India Evidence Act said it for all time: "It is far easier to sit comfortably in the shade rubbing pepper into a poor devil's eyes than go out in the sun hunting up evidence." Confessions do absolve the individual of his guilt feelings, for both real and imaginary transgressions; in addition, they absolve police of the responsibility for court convictions that mean prison or death for fellow human beings.

But do confessions really aid law enforcement as much as we have been led to believe? Washington, D.C., Police Chief Robert Murphy complained that new Supreme Court rulings reinforcing the rights of suspects "will result in a complete breakdown in law enforcement in the District of Columbia." Actually, Washington long has operated under Federal regulations, which are protective of the individual. In comparable neighboring areas of Virginia and Maryland, there had been no such hampering of police efficiency. Felony crime rates in the nation's capital increased one percent from 1950 to 1960; in the surrounding areas, felony crime rose 69 percent during the same period. Protection of suspects' rights would seem, at least in this case, to serve the law well.

Chief Circuit Judge David L. Bazelon of the U.S. Court of Appeals has said: "We must deter not only crime but also the debasement of the individual." This imperative should include both the suspected criminal and the police interrogator. Tearing the cloak of secrecy from police interrogation, therefore, is of primary importance. Giving suspects the right to immediate arraignment would be one sure way to do this. With proper and workable procedure, suspects or witnesses could be brought at any hour to a central point, where a magistrate, defense attorneys, and even interpreters for the non-English speaking would be available during questioning or arraignment. Such a centralized system would make video tape recordings feasible, and such records would be valuable safeguards for both the police and their suspects. (Detroit, which has come a long way toward effective and impeccable police work, is the first city to schedule video tapes for confession identification.)

Other effective ways to meet the challenge of justice in this era of misused and misunderstood psychology might include: working with police academies to put to the empirical test many conclusions developed from the common-sense psychology of police manuals; serious study of the Supreme Court's criteria for invalidating a "coerced" confession; a study of public awareness of the legal rights of the individual; a before-and-after study of emotional and physiological responses of suspects during actual interrogations; and a large-scale study of various interrogation techniques on groups of subjects who vary in major personality traits, to see if there is a relationship between confession and character or personality. Central in determining the validity of confessions are the psychological criteria of coercion, free will, and the ability to resist. Psychologists have played no role in such determinations; they have not been involved professionally with this problem and do not have specific relevant empirical research findings to offer the courts.

Greater knowledge of the dangers involved in police attempts to coerce confessions is vital to our society. In our attempts to understand, the study of Carnegie Tech's Daryl Bem in inducing belief in false confessions is a landmark, as well as a model laboratory experiment. The self-persuasion factor in confessions is a major area of consideration if police interrogation is to serve justice well. Bem demonstrated that cues normally associated with telling the truth can cause us to recall the truth less accurately or to believe in our false confessions.

The United States is at a critical stage of development, and the rights of the individual to protest are being challenged all the way from Washington to Sacramento. Thus, responsible citizens must be alert, more than ever, to the malleability of man in order to safeguard his real freedom and human rights.

IV
Social Deviancy: Drugs and Sex

The Quiet Revolution

Leonard and Elizabeth Uhr

During the past decade, American society has opened up in many ways that would have seemed almost impossible to most of us even as late as the 1950s. Taboo topics, such as drug taking and sexual activity, are discussed openly even in polite society. Stories so explicitly sexual in content that their publication would have led to the publisher's being jailed in 1950 appear routinely today even in family magazines. LSD and marijuana, once used only by ghetto groups and jazz musicians, have been adopted by millions of college students and now are being "taken up" by high school populations. Behaviors considered extremely deviant at the mid-century mark are rapidly becoming socially acceptable. How has this process of change come about and how far will it go, particularly in the twin cases of drug use and sexual behavior? Leonard and Elizabeth Uhr begin this section with a thoughtful and provocative description of the quiet revolution in drug taking.

During the last eight years, and especially since 1963, a quiet revolution has been generating from college campuses throughout the United States. It is a strange revolution in which people are not trying to change society—just themselves. This is a revolution in which the individual chooses to go his own way, to make forays into the world of altered consciousness. And it is just this quiet revolution that is raising disquieting questions about society's role in protecting the individual against possible psychological damage.

The focus of this quiet revolution is a group of chemical compounds known as the psychedelic or "consciousness-expanding" drugs. Many people who try these drugs feel that they have undergone a profound, beautiful, self-revelatory experience. But there are clinical reports that the drug experience can produce anxiety, depression, and psychotic episodes. It is clear that the more powerful psychedelic drugs—LSD, psilocybin, mescaline, dimethyltryptamine, among others—are the agents for prodigious experience, and that their effects are far more pervasive than those of alcohol in freeing the individual from the usual controls of his conscious ego. No one knows how many Americans have used the psychedelics in the last few years, but for marijuana it must be millions, and for LSD, thousands, or hundreds of thousands.

Marijuana merits special attention because, though not strictly speaking a psychedelic drug, it occupies a central place in the quiet revolution. Marijuana is widely used throughout the country by people who are convinced that the effects are innocuous, the dangers nil, and the total impact good. However, marijuana is classified legally with heroin and other strong opiates because, it is claimed, its use leads to major crime, sex perversion, addiction, and mental illness. Punishment for sale or possession of marijuana is severe.

Because there has been almost no controlled experimentation with marijuana, it is difficult to make positive statements about the drug's effects. The consensus of scientists who have examined the literature, however, is that marijuana appears to be less psychologically addicting than alcohol, less likely to release aggressive and antisocial behavior, and far less likely to produce a hangover. Marijuana seems to make people calmly happy, loving and friendly, and imbued with a feeling of goodness—in contrast to the anger, hostility, and maudlin behavior so often triggered by alcohol.

Responsible research should begin as soon as possible.

If the facts show that marijuana is dangerous, effective and reasonable laws should be written to control its use. If it is not dangerous, the use and possession of marijuana should be removed from the list of criminal acts.

When Should a Drug Be Outlawed?

Most laws are instituted to protect society, or to protect the individual. Laws concerning drugs fit into this legal framework. For example, narcotics are outlawed because their continued use can cause physical and mental debilitation of the individual and lead to crime against society. Obviously, society must have laws governing the distribution and use of dangerous drugs, but are marijuana and the psychedelics really dangerous, or are they scapegoats in society's retaliation against the quiet revolution? Perhaps society is protecting itself against those who are using drugs as a weapon to expose the fraying fabric of a "phony society." On the other hand, society may be acting rationally in restricting the use of drugs about which too little is known. If the latter is true, is this cautiousness interfering with the basic right of the individual to pursue his happiness—in whatever form he views happiness—as long as he does not harm others? Can a society really legislate against psychological damage?

What if these drugs, despite their possible damaging effects, hold out a hope for enriching our lives? What kind of society would blindly suppress their use? And why should it limit scientific inquiry into their positive and negative effects? Legitimate research on marijuana has been cut off for years, and research on the psychedelic drugs has all but stopped, partly because of public caution and partly because scientists are reluctant to become involved in such a highly charged subject.

Thus we—the objective researchers—find ourselves in the embarrassing position of knowing less than the students who are taking the drugs in their sub rosa activity. The student who is intrigued by the effects of LSD, who feels that it has given him a fresh view of the world, new understanding of himself, and a new warmth of compassion is behaving much more in the great tradition of Western civilization's search for the truth, the principles of the universe, and the meaning of existence than is the more passive, well-adjusted individual who accepts the nontruths of official culture. On the other hand, when students—as happened recently at the University of California at Santa Barbara—search for spiritual meaning by lying on their backs marveling at the sun and come out of an LSD trance with damaged retinas from the sun's rays, we must do something to help them. But instead we make ignorant and hypocritical statements that help no one.

Subjective Drug Effects

The variety of psychological effects produced by psyche-

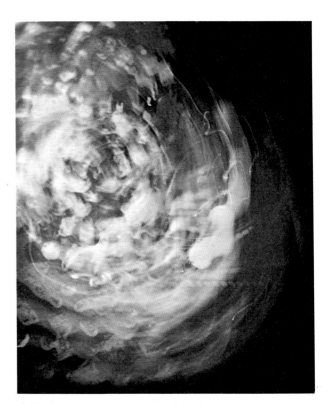

delic drugs is legion, and subjective descriptions have been eloquently and ubiquitously expressed for years in books and in the press. Briefly, commonly occurring effects include: nausea, brilliantly colored visions of dancing lights, losses and variations in perceptual constancies, synesthesia (reaction to one sensory stimulus as though it were another—"seeing" bees buzz), loss of connection with one's body, increased sensitivity to other people, a deep feeling of oneness and empathy, profound philosophical and religious feelings, and swift flights of fancy. Any of these sensations may be accompanied by a profound emotional state, ranging from extreme anxiety or depression to an almost transcendent elation or euphoria.

Drug takers believe that they see the world in a new way, a true and valid way that deepens their understanding of sensuous reality. Often the freshness of early childhood becomes crystallized in a simple color tone or vibrant pattern. A homely object like a leaf, a crack in the ceiling, a grain of sand, anything—can be the departure point for journeys into new worlds of beauty and revelation. It is common to feel a calm and objective detachment from everyday anxieties, and to believe that life's true meanings are being understood from a higher and more mature plane. In these and many other ways, the drug experience has been described as profound, memorable, and enlightening.

The drug state is subtle, precarious, and easily manipulable. Probably the most important psychological component of psychedelic drugs is the freeing of the mind so that perceptions, thoughts, and emotions may

wander unrestrained. The number of possible reactions is probably as large as the number of possible states of the normal human being, but each state is often enormously exaggerated. The effect of the drug experience seems to depend upon the total frame of mind of the taker, and upon all of his potentialities for experience. The effects further depend upon the subject's momentary mood, fears, and expectations—and upon conditions under which the drug is given, size of the dose, and physical and social environment.

Objective Drug Effects

There have been a number of attempts to explore the effects of the hallucinogenic drugs by controlling one or more variables, or by means of objective tests that measure the subject's intellectual or sensory functioning while under the influence of a drug. Unfortunately, scientific research has not been much more successful than "lay" research in pinning down the psychological effects of the psychedelics. More research is needed in which several groups of matched subjects are exposed to differences in setting, suggestion, drug dosage, and other relevant factors. Such studies are probably impossible until the current suppression of drug research is lifted and more rational attitudes prevail. Some important research has indicated, however, the crucial role that suggestion plays in the drug experience.

In Canada, psychotherapists who administered LSD to patients as part of a ritual involving white robes, burning candles, and crucifixions, reported a lot of Dante-esque religious content. The various groups cen-

tered on Aldous Huxley, Alan Watts, Timothy Leary, and Richard Alpert have similarly stressed mystical-religious experience but with a Buddhist orientation—and have reported experiences resembling those described by Eastern mystics. In conventional psychiatric experiments conducted in hospitals or prisons, patients typically became extremely anxious when drugged, particularly if they were warned of the dangers of drug-taking.

This is not to say that "setting the stage" has been found to control drug effects completely; on the contrary, there are many other factors that might well determine an individual's reactions. To eliminate the effects of suggestion, J. Pollard and Leonard Uhr conducted an experiment in which drugs were administered in a bland and neutral setting. The aim was to eliminate any extraneous influences that an emotionally charged setting might contribute to the drug's effects per se.

We had been struck by the reports that Mexican Indians and San Francisco beatniks were experiencing wonderful effects from these drugs, whereas experimental subjects participating in scientific investigations experienced extreme anxiety. Fortunately, in 1960 when we ran our experiment (as part of a large-scale continuing study of various psychoactive drugs), people had not yet been exposed to predisposing information or misinformation in the press, so it was possible to eliminate almost all of the suggestive factors surrounding drug taking. Our results were in striking contrast to the previous scientific reports that the psychedelic drugs produced anxiety. Most of our subjects enjoyed the experience and found it interesting, but their reactions were far less profound, revelatory, and earth shattering than those now reported in the press.

Objective studies of psychological functioning during the drug experience have produced solidly based and reproducible results, but all too often they have examined aspects of behavior that are extraneous to our understanding of psychedelic phenomena. Moreover, confidence even in these results must be tempered, because reports convey the impression that when the experimenter intrudes into the drug-induced state, the subject regards what he is asked to do as being totally irrelevant and nonsensical—rather like being at a party, half-drunk, dancing with someone exciting, and having the host tap your shoulder and ask you to work out a series of problems in mental arithmetic.

In general, experiments on human subjects have shown that psychedelic drugs impair simple perceptual and cognitive functions, and that the impairment increases with the size of the dose. Performance scores go down in tests measuring ability in mental arithmetic, memorizing strings of numbers, word naming, and verbal comprehension. Motor coordination may be less affected by psychedelic drugs than are sensory and mental functions.

There have been many subjective reports that psychedelic drugs greatly increase perceptual acuity, but objective tests suggest the opposite: Perceptual acuity is worse under the drug's influence. In a study of the effects of mescaline, LSD-25, and psilocybin, Hartman and Hollister found that color perception, as judged by ability to discriminate between hues, decreased, and subjects responded more slowly to visual stimuli. These researchers concluded, "The experience appears to be more subjective than related to increased sensitivity."

A commonly reported drug effect is a conviction of attaining profound insight into the reality of things. But here again, objective studies have failed to demonstrate any increase in understanding. On the contrary, McKellar reports, "After administration of mescaline the subject's intellectual standards begin to exhibit deterioration. His thinking becomes more loose and slipshod. There is a weakening of the forces of control which direct his thought toward logic and evidence. . . ." Such observations may, of course, merely show a lack of communication between the drugged subject and the experimenter, or the subject may be captivated by thoughts and sensations quite alien to mundane intellectual procedures. During one of our experiments, an intelligent student participant made the following sequence of statements: "I still feel like I'm being whizzed through outer space. Some high velocity. I wish I could listen to the Tiger game on the radio. . . . They might win. I don't know. I'm hungry." McKellar suggests that "Mescaline and other hallucinogenic drugs may alert people to notice things that are going on all the time in normal mental life. Typical human thinking is less characterized either by realistic assessment of evidence, or by sustained acts of logical inference than is often supposed."

Psychedelic Psychotherapy

The most enthusiastic advocates of the psychedelic drugs are the handful of psychotherapists who make use of them in treatment. Unfortunately, there is little evidence that psychedelic drug therapy works. (But then again, there isn't any scientific evidence that psychotherapy of any kind—from psychoanalysis to shock treatment—works.)

In psychedelic psychotherapy, the administration of psilocybin has often been used as part of the diagnostic procedure, since some therapists hold that when the patient is drugged, "The outline of the underlying psychosis or neurosis is revealed or exaggerated as in a caricature by the induced psychological alterations, thus facilitating its identification." However, no firm conclusions can be drawn from such therapeutic studies because there is a lack of scientific rigor: no control groups, no valid criteria for improvement, and no adequate follow-up procedures.

Psychedelic drugs have been used alone or in conjunction with traditional psychotherapeutic sessions. Though some incredible successes have been reported, it

should be borne in mind that clinical results are always hard to evaluate. Too often in the past, we have witnessed overenthusiasm for therapeutic methods whose value (if any) could not be demonstrated in scientific terms. Nevertheless, and in spite of negative or inconclusive reports, there seems to be more and more evidence that psychedelic drugs may have a place in treating a wide range of psychoneurotic, psychopathic, and near-psychotic disorders.

However, even in the most positively structured environment, psychedelic drugs may produce occasional bad effects ranging all the way from temporary anxiety, during the few hours under the drug's influence, to days or even months of psychosis. When such psychotic episodes do occur, one doesn't know whether they were triggered by the drug per se or whether they would have occurred anyway—without the drug's influence. The incidence of such episodes, as reported in the literature, ranges from 3 in 100 to 1 in 1,000. Unfortunately, it is hard to know whether such rates are low or high. However, other studies have shown that people who volunteer to participate in drug experiments tend to be more unstable than the average and are therefore likely in the first place to be predisposed to such breaks. This is probably even more true of those who take drugs illicitly, in the face of social and legal pressures; thus, in addition to their irrational fears, they are subjected to rational fears that would exacerbate their anxiety.

What Must Be Done

Overenthusiastic and irresponsible proponents of expanded consciousness and mystico-religious experience have conducted their propaganda in such a way as to harden opinion against psychedelic drugs, and appreciably reduce the possibility that disinterested research can or will be conducted. Equally reprehensible has been the timidity of the academic and research establishment, which has tended to prohibit socially disapproved inquiry, to avoid controversy and publicity, and instead has turned quietly away to other, safer problems.

Good science and art are dedicated to the exploration of the unknown. There are far too many attempts, especially in psychology and the social sciences, to apply the results of scientific inquiry before there are any results, and to debase science into serving as propaganda for what society would like to believe. The fact is, the facts are not there. We do not know enough about psychedelic drugs. We can learn only through free, enlightened, probing research.

But in the meantime psychedelic drugs are readily available, considered important by many, and widely used (and they are sure to be even more widely used in the future). If scientific experiments were to demonstrate that these drugs are dangerous, their use would drop precipitously, for it is not based upon addiction, and it is chiefly found among educated, scientifically responsive people.

In the meantime, we must devise some effective way to control their present use. Further laws and increased legal restrictions will simply make matters worse (recall the days of Prohibition). Only a few users would be caught and they would be excessively punished. The number of responsible users might be reduced somewhat, but the number of thrill seekers would increase.

However, until we have discovered and demonstrated that we can use them safely, we cannot let people buy these drugs over the counter. Control over their use should be put in the hands of people who understand and respect the drugs' possible potential for artistic creativity, self-fulfillment, and self-understanding, but who are *not* committed to any particular religious, medical, psychotherapeutic, or social dogma.

One possible way of accomplishing this—of institutionalizing the use of psychedelic drugs—would be to administer them to volunteers at research-study centers. People could then be screened psychologically and physically, and supported when necessary during the drug experience. Screening should be carried out by medical and psychological professionals who would be available to handle any untoward incidents. The research setting should be structured to offer a variety of pleasant surroundings and promote pleasant experiences. Such study centers should be run by responsible people—be they bankers, psychologists, journalists, lawyers, physicists, artists, or neurologists—who wish to explore psychedelic phenomena.

Such centers could also serve the crucial scientific purpose of data collection. Valuable information about the incidence of anxiety, about psychotic episodes and other negative effects could easily be obtained if the centers were staffed properly. Such institutions would: (1) restore to responsible citizenship the intelligent students and professional people who have become interested in these drugs; (2) make far less dangerous the drug experience; (3) change the general climate of ignorance, hostility, and titillation; and (4) initiate an era of calm, constructive research.

Daytop Village

Alexander Bassin

All revolutions have their victims. In the case of the quiet revolution in drug taking described by the Uhrs, the victims too often are young people who get hooked not on such mild drugs as marijuana but on the hard narcotics, such as heroin. Because use of heroin leads to physiological changes that make the body dependent upon a constant supply of the drug, the heroin habit is extremely difficult to break. The "cold turkey" approach typically used in the past, in which the drug was withdrawn all at once and the patient tossed back into the world when his withdrawal symptoms had vanished, simply does not work. Drugs are more a psychosocial problem than a physiological hang-up, and we are beginning to see that the addict needs social support more than physiological treatment if he is to have a successful cure. In the following article, Alexander Bassin describes the approach used at Daytop Village, a halfway house where drug addicts learn to help themselves back from deviancy.

A pretty coed from nearby Wagner College, fulfilling a class requirement for *Sociology 416*, "Social Problems in Modern America," visits Daytop Village on New York's Staten Island during a Saturday night open house party. Soon she is in deep conversation with a young man who might pass as a college senior—except that he is neatly dressed, wears coat and necktie, and his hair is short and combed.

"What is Daytop all about? What do you do?"

"I'll tell you right up front. We take a guy, say twenty-five years old, who's been a waste all his life. He's been stealing and robbing, and is in and out of jail. He's a thief and a parasite who would con his own mother out of her food money to buy some crap to shoot into his veins. And do you know what we do with him?"

"No, what? What do you do?"

"In a matter of a year and a half to two years, we transform him into an honest, decent, responsible human being who has a new set of values, who has some interests beyond the bang-bang on the boob tube, who knows a little something about art, music, literature, and the war in Vietnam. In other words, we, like, take

an order of scrambled eggs that has been spoiled and smells, and we change it into a sweet and cool lime Jello pudding."

"Gosh," murmurs the collegiate miss, "you Daytop people are wonderful."

The message gets through to the coed very well indeed. As well it might. The drug addict the young man is talking about is *himself*.

The psychological basis for treating drug addicts at Daytop Village differs radically from conventional methods. Neither punishing the addict by jailing him for extended periods nor slobbering over him with sympathy and pity has shown any great rehabilitative value. Nor has it helped to regard the addict as a sick person, a "medical problem," as some well-meaning folk put it. The Daytop philosophy is to consider the addict as an adult acting like a baby: childishly immature, full of demands, empty of offerings.

The addict sees nothing as his fault—not his addiction, not his degradation, nor his desperation. He is convinced he has been thrown into life without the armor and weapons that others have. Heroin enables him to escape from the unfair battle. It deadens his desire for friends, for achievement, for wealth, for strength, for sex, and even for food. The satisfactions sought so relentlessly by other people, the junkie obtains, for a short time anyway, with a five-dollar deck of heroin.

In pursuit of heroin, the addict is able to muster extraordinary cunning, shrewdness, gall, and acting ability. Usually, he is untouched by normal psychotherapeutic approaches. For him treatment is a game of upmanship, an arena for practicing his confidence-man skills.

Conventional methods of treating drug addicts have been grossly ineffective. For example, follow-up studies of addicts treated in the U.S. Public Health Service hospitals in Lexington, Kentucky, and in Fort Worth, Texas, reveal that more than 90 percent of released patients relapse into drug addiction within a few years. And many of the addicts treated at these excellent medical facilities do not show even the simple respect for their $50-per-day treatment of waiting forty-eight hours after release before taking a shot of heroin.

The change agent most likely to be effective with the junkie is another addict who has made a commitment to change himself, one who is prepared to use himself as a role model and become *involved* with his "brother." When a professional therapist attempts to communicate with the addict, he is simply turned off with: "This dumb bastard doesn't know what he's talking about. He doesn't know the scene. He's never been there."

Who Gets In

The Daytop intake process is organized to challenge the applicant's sincerity in wanting to break his habit. Thus, when a kind-hearted social worker, psychologist, psychiatrist, judge, probation or parole officer telephones Daytop in an effort to smooth the admission of a "worthy" case, he is politely advised it would be best if the addict applied for himself or herself. The applicant should be over sixteen years of age and not a pillhead. When withdrawal takes place outside the hospital, Daytop personnel consider the barbiturate, amphetamine, and methadrine addict to be in far greater danger than the heroin addict. In any case, the addict himself must telephone to arrange for admission to Daytop.

When the addict does call he is told that Daytop is crowded, many addicts are clamoring to get in, and space is limited. But if he is really interested in getting in, if he wants to make an "investment to save your life," he may call again tomorrow at 2:30 sharp. If he "forgets" and calls a day late, he is told, "I guess you're not very serious about helping yourself. So we are putting you at the bottom of the list." When he calls at the designated time, he is commended for his interest and told to call again a day later. If this commitment is kept, he is invited to present himself at Daytop Village, clean of drugs for at least twenty-four hours, with his

parents and family if possible. Some applicants go through a half-dozen telephone calls before they receive an invitation.

What is the rationale for this apparently heartless system?

Few addicts are motivated for therapy and change. Treatment is usually the lesser of two evils to the junkie. He comes to Daytop because he thinks it is "easier time" than jail, or because there is a panic in the streets and no drugs are around anyway, or because the heat is on and he needs a hideout, because he has been kicked out of the house by his wife, because he wants to dry out for a while and is tired of finding ways to pay for his expensive habit. But permanently give up the use of junk? Impossible! Once a junkie, always a junkie. So the addict reasons with himself about the prospect of going straight.

Every step of the Daytop intake procedure is designed to shock the addict into realizing that this place is basically different from the social agencies he has learned how to manipulate. Here he will not be indulged like a spoiled child, here his usual con games will not work.

When the addict arrives at Daytop on the scheduled date and on time, he is admitted to the reception area and told to sit on the "prospect's chair" and wait until he is called. Meanwhile, his parents and relatives are ushered next door and given counsel that makes their jaws drop as tears come to their eyes.

"Mama, here at Daytop we don't blame parents for the misdeeds of their children. We know you never encouraged him to use dope but he's always tried to make you think it was all your fault. He's stolen money from you, lied to you, abused and cursed you, made your life a hell on earth. How do we know all this? Did we read it in some book or in *Life* magazine? No, mama, we are all ex-junkies, just like your Johnny, and that is what we did to our own parents."

Members of the interviewing team then give the relatives thumbnail autobiographical sketches of themselves. Next, each extols the near-miraculous benefits of a year or two at Daytop.

Finally, the parents are given some astonishing advice: Make yourselves as cold, as hostile, and rejecting as you can toward Johnny. If he telephones, hang up! If he sneaks out a letter, return it unopened to Daytop. And if he suddenly turns up at home and turns on the woebegone, contrite mannerisms the addict puts on so well, if he tries to melt your hearts with tales of the abuse he suffered at the Village, then grit your teeth and tell him, "Go back to Daytop, get lost." And slam the door in his face.

Meantime, back at the reception desk, the prospect has been going through a nerve-shattering experience. He sits facing a wall. Behind him is the open door—and freedom. By now, he has cased the setup and notes that there are no bars anywhere, that the windows are at ground level—and wide open. All about him is the hustle and bustle of a happy family household rather than the aseptic silence of a hospital or of a prison. Nobody is walking around in hospital pajamas or prison uniforms; there are no doctors with stethoscopes hanging out of their pockets, no nurses in white uniforms, no uniformed security personnel.

Then he sees a blood brother, a crony with whom he had shot up only a short time ago in alleyways and public toilets—sharing the same spike. But instead of the warm welcome he would have received in any prison or hospital in the country, his former pal looks through him as though he were invisible and doesn't respond to Johnny's big hello.

Momentarily uneasy, Johnny relaxes with the thought that junkies will be junkies. They must have a supply stashed away someplace, and once he gets into the swing of things, he will be able to cut himself into the action. For the third time in twenty minutes, he asks when he will be interviewed. His frustration tolerance is low, and he has never willingly waited for anyone.

"We are very busy here, as you can see, and you will have to wait until the interviewers can see you," the receptionist answers coldly. The implication is clear; if he doesn't like it, he can beat it. No one is keeping him. He may wait from forty-five minutes to four hours before being called for the interview. If he does not flee through the open door, he passes another initiation rite for admission to the Daytop fraternity.

The interview room is cozy, homelike, a room without desk, or diplomas, or any of the accouterments of the professional office. Three clean-cut, conventionally dressed young men politely ask Johnny to come in, apologize for the delay, and start questioning him in a kindly, sympathetic manner. What did he want from Daytop? What was the problem? What neighborhood did he come from?

Within a few minutes, Johnny has sized up the situation. These cats are obviously social workers and he can con them out of their bank accounts if he really tries. He talks to them about his hard and sad life, about his fears and anxieties, his unresolved conflicts, his determination to be cured of the horrors of drug addiction and to make himself over into something better.

Suddenly, one of the interviewers jolts Johnny:

"Hey, stop this garbage! Who the hell do you think you're talking to?"

Two of the interviewers talk to each other: "Did you ever hear such bullshit in your life?"

"This crazy dope fiend thinks he's inside another joint."

"Maybe he didn't get enough luff from his mudder and fodder!"

The interviewers curl up with laughter and poke one another in the ribs as they mimic the addict's words and expressions. After a few minutes, they turn serious and

begin a "cleanup" operation. No, they are not social workers, psychologists, intake workers, or whatever he thought they were, but street junkies just like him.

Right now they can tell him just what is going through his mind because junkies are pretty much alike. They are under the impression the world owes them a living because they are hooked on dope, and they dare anybody to cure them. But here at Daytop you learn "there ain't no free lunch."

They tell Johnny that despite his physical size and age, he is a baby in terms of maturity, responsibility, and judgment. So he will be treated like a three-year-old who is told what to do because at this point he simply does not have enough sense to keep from getting killed.

"You'll see a lot of things you don't understand. Don't waste time asking a lot of fool questions. Your brain is not strong enough for that kind of exercise just yet. Maybe in a few weeks or months you will understand. But for the time being, you must *act as if* you understood, *act as if* you are a man, *act as if* you want to do the right thing, *act as if* you care about other people, *act as if* you are a mature human being."

At Daytop, Johnny is told, we don't spend valuable time trying to find the essential *cause* of his addiction. That whole process would be exploited by the addict to avoid the responsibility for his behavior. At Daytop we *know* why somebody is a dope fiend—because he chooses to act STUPID! That's the only acceptable explanation for addiction: stupidity.

At the end of the interview, the "noodle-head" is told there are only two cardinal rules of the house:

1. No chemicals or drugs or alcohol may be used.
2. No violence or even the threat of violence.

No excuse is accepted for breaking either of these two basic rules. If he does, he will be kicked out, exiled.

Daytop Methods

The interviewers now become affable. They say that Daytop is one place where the people really care for one another, treat each other like brother and sister. Everybody tries to live as openly and honestly as possible. No con games, manipulations, lying, or cheating. Everybody in the house, from the director to that girl at the reception desk, is a junkie. There's no "we versus they" business here. Everybody is a member of the staff, and there's no job he can't aim for—even director.

Johnny is assigned a low-status job at once. He cleans the toilets, washes pots and pans, or mops floors. He is introduced to his three roommates, who have been trained to welcome him to their midst and to assume responsibility for the welfare of their new brother.

If he is experiencing any withdrawal symptoms, no big fuss is made about it. He goes through the withdrawal on a couch in the living room with residents all about him, laughing, playing cards, listening to music, dancing. He is too ashamed to put on the expected exhibition of wall climbing and swinging from chandeliers. He knows that these people will not be impressed by his performance. He knows there will be no payoff for his histrionics from these wise, hard-nosed critics. And somewhat to his own surprise, he kicks the remnants of his habit in record time with no more discomfort than the average guy with a mild case of flu.

One of the principal methods for achieving self-image and behavioral change at Daytop is the three times a week *group encounter* therapy.

During the encounter, at which attendance is compulsory, the building echoes with ear-piercing screams, curses, oaths, blasphemy, shouts, tears, and laughter. The vehemence is hard to believe. Gutter language and four-letter epithets explode from the rooms. One member after another is assigned to the "hot seat," where he is attacked and criticized for failing to adhere to the basic precepts of Daytop, for being less than 100 percent honest and open, for being insensitive to the feelings of others.

The encounter is called a *pressure cooker* by David Deitch, the thirty-five-year-old director of Daytop Village. "It is a safety valve to relieve the tensions that have built up during the previous day. The Daytop resident cannot use profanity at any time except during the encounter. He cannot act moody or irritable or be overcome with self-pity between encounters. He has to *act as if* and wait until the encounter to get the garbage out of his system. The encounter is a gut-level teaching device that speeds up personality alteration, just as a pressure cooker speeds the preparation of food."

Many professionals are abashed and frightened by the fierceness of the attack therapy. But Dr. Lewis Yablonsky, research consultant to Synanon, after his first twenty-five sessions, found that the group "attack" was an act of love in which was entwined the assumption: "If we did not care about you or have concern for you, we would not bother to point out something that might reduce your psychic pain or clarify something for you that might save your life."

Every day but Sunday, at one o'clock, the Daytop membership assembles in the auditorium. Before them, on a blackboard, they see a quotation, perhaps from Emerson, or from Einstein. It may be a Biblical quotation or a poem by Emily Dickinson.

A different leader is appointed for each seminar. He asks: "Who wants to say something about this?" Before the words are out of his mouth, a dozen hands are waving in the air. The leader points and a member rises, nervous and uneasy. He mumbles a few words, and sits down to a broadside of friendly applause. For an hour, the performance is repeated with speakers of differing degrees of fluency.

Other seminars feature free choice sessions, in which residents talk spontaneously about a designated topic, or mock speaking engagements, in which members act as if they are appearing before an outside community group.

A visitor to Daytop sees signs and slogans prominently hung in the kitchen, dining room, offices, and hallways. Typical slogans are:

> There is no free lunch.
> Honesty *is* the best policy.
> Hang tough! (Don't give up.)
> Seek and assume responsibility!
> Be careful of what you ask for.
> You may just get it!

Every resident seems to incorporate these shorthand behavioral prescriptions into his speech repertoire. You hear them spoken at encounters, seminars, and while "rapping with the squares" (talking to nonaddicts) at the Saturday night open house party.

If a Daytop resident commits the heinous offense of "splitting" (leaving without permission), an emergency Fireplace meeting might be called when he returns, even if it requires routing everybody out of bed at three in the morning. He is placed on the hot seat and must beg at the top of his voice to be readmitted into the house. Sometimes he is subjected to a "haircut," a severe verbal reprimand. And if his offense is serious, his hair is actually cropped to the skull while house members boo and jeer.

John Ruocco, director of Daytop at Staten Island, once told me: "An errant member submits to a haircut to show he is sincerely sorry for the stupid thing he did and that he wants to make a solid investment in his recovery. His bald head helps him remember not to act stupid and irresponsible in the future."

Banishment is the most serious sanction at Daytop Village. But it is reserved for a flagrant violation of the house rules. Exile is considered equivalent to a death sentence—an all too frequent fate of the junkie, who can end up at the city morgue, dead of an overdose.

The greatest number of dropouts in the Daytop program occur during the first thirty days. About 8 percent of the addicts who come through the front door leave immediately or within a month. The great majority remain for three months, when another critical period is reached. Approximately 17 percent will split after ninety days. According to Dr. Daniel Casriel, medical psychiatric director of Daytop, the addict who remains three months has better than a 75 percent chance of completing the program and emerging as a new vibrant human being.

Dave Deitch, on the other hand, adamantly refuses to become involved in a numbers game about the success rate of Daytop. He notes that besides the several hundred residents of Daytop who are leading lives free of drugs and crime, there are more than sixty who have met Daytop's extraordinarily high standards for personal transformation and are leading active and self-supporting lives in outside communities.

Every three months or so, a marathon encounter led by specially trained staff members is held. Basically, the

The Concept, a hit off-Broadway play, is one of Daytop's proudest achievements. Hailed by drama critics as truly outstanding theater, the play is an improvisation by ex-narcotic addicts from Daytop about one person's drug addiction and recovery. This photograph and the one on page 122 are from a performance of the play.

marathon is an extension of the floor encounter for a period of twenty-four to forty-eight hours. The meeting is continuous except for a few hours of sleep. In many cases, there are experiences of rebirth and personality alteration that have no exact parallel in psychiatric literature.

Twice a year, Daytop closes its doors, unhooks the telephone, calls in all members, and engages in a week-long retreat. It is a time of self-criticism, meditation, institutional assessment, and charting new directions.

On Saturday night, Daytop Village is open to visitors. A phone call will reserve a place but frequently every opening is filled weeks in advance. This open house has become a favorite field-trip assignment for professors of psychology, sociology, and education. There are some speeches followed by music and dancing, but the best part, most visitors agree, is the opportunity to talk with a remarkable group of intelligent, alert, healthy minded young people.

History of the Approach

About seven years ago, a team consisting of the late Professor Herbert Bloch, criminologist at Brooklyn College, Dr. Daniel Casriel, a psychiatrist with many years' experience in treating addicts, Joseph A. Shelly, chief probation officer of the Brooklyn Supreme Court, and myself visited and evaluated the leading narcotic treatment centers in all parts of the United States. Nothing very exciting turned up until we came to a little-known converted armory located on the beach at Santa Monica, California. Here our psychiatrist was surprised to find several former patients of his whom he had dismissed as being hopeless. But here they were healthy and happy, and most important of all, they were free of drugs!

The place was Synanon, and its founder, Chuck Dederich, assured us that it was destined to become one of the most significant developments in treating not only drug addicts but all forms of deviant behavior, even chronic criminals and the so-called psychopath.

In a gravel-tone voice, our bull-necked host explained his approach in anthropological terms: "We attempt to create an extended family of the type found in preliterate tribes which usually have a strong, almost autocratic, father-figure, who dispenses firm justice combined with warm concern, who is a model extolling inner-directed convictions about the old-fashioned virtues of honesty, sobriety, education and hard work."

Our mission experience resulted in a proposal to the National Institute of Mental Health for the establishment of a halfway house for drug addicts on probation, who would be treated along the lines we observed at Synanon, except that they would be regularly tested for traces of heroin. On April 15, 1963, we were informed that NIMH had awarded us $390,000 for a five-year study.

For a name we selected the acronym *Daytop* (Drug Addicts Treated on Probation) and *Lodge*, to avoid the unfortunate semantic associations with orthodox treatment centers.

Our first manager was driven to the verge of a nervous breakdown by the antics of the residents and the problems of setting up a pioneering experiment

under the aegis of a court bureaucracy. In the first year the project chewed up half a dozen managers. At the same time, residents of the local community protested against the presence of Daytop with picket lines, law suits, and angry letters in the local newspaper.

The turbulent development of Daytop was stabilized with the acquisition of a new manager, David Deitch, a native of Chicago with a history of some fourteen years of addiction. He curbed his habit at Synanon, rose to a position of leadership there, but left after two years because of some differences with Dederich.

Although conditions at Daytop improved under Deitch's leadership, a plateau was reached that called for a reevaluation of methods and goals. Up to this time, only male addicts had been admitted. It was decided that the small initial group of thirty males did not provide the diversity of personality types required to operate the dynamics of a therapeutic community. According to Deitch, "The junkie needs new faces on whom to try out his recently acquired skills. It is necessary to create a community of men, women and children who live and work and love together if our people are to grow into mature responsible citizens."

NIMH agreed to permit the original research plan to be expanded and the inclusion of females. The name of the project was changed from Daytop Lodge to Daytop Village.

Its Present and Future

Today, Daytop is operating a 100-residence facility at Staten Island, and another with a capacity of 200 at Swan Lake in the Catskill Mountains, about 120 miles from New York City, and a third at New Haven, Connecticut, in joint sponsorship with Yale University.

Methods developed at Daytop are being applied to new fields. For professionals, such as psychologists, social workers, and clergymen, Daytop has conducted several hundred Intensive Training Institutes at its center in the Catskill Mountains. Participants become members of the Daytop community and experience the encounter process. They come to grips with their own emotional and social problems. Almost all emerge with the comment: "This has been one of the most meaningful experiences of my life."

Daytop has established three storefront centers called SPAN, which are designed to induce the street addict to sample the Daytop approach. These centers also work directly with people in the ghettos to improve their community.

Abraham Maslow, president of the American Psychological Association, and O. Hobart Mowrer, a former president, both have proclaimed Daytop as one of the great therapeutic community developments of our time. Mowrer is now writing a book on Daytop, *The Daytop Dynamic*.

Daytop is optimistic about its future. The leading force in the organization of Daytop, Monsignor William B. O'Brien, sees the principles and methods developed there as useful not only for the rehabilitation of narcotic addicts but also for the training and revitalization of teachers, psychologists, psychiatrists, social workers, businessmen, and government officials.

"The Daytop approach can be used in prisons, penitentiaries and reform schools," he says. "As a fellow priest once remarked to me after spending a month at the Village: 'God is not dead, He lives at Daytop!' People in all helping professions can learn from Daytop how man can be taught to help himself."

Epilogue

After five years of exciting existence, Daytop reached the ultimate crisis of its being when the Board of Directors recommended that David Deitch be retired. The stormy events leading to this decision are difficult to chronicle in an altogether dispassionate manner, but in essence the Board felt that Deitch was establishing a cult of personality and infallibility. He flatly refused to consider a relaxation of his rule excommunicating any member who "split," regardless of extenuating circumstances or subsequent patent success of the Daytopper in dealing with the strains and stresses of the outside community. He also refused to consider the proposal that Daytop affirm the goal (set at the time of its establishment under NIMH and Brooklyn Supreme Court auspices) of returning the residents to their homes and communities after one to one and a half years. In trying to dissuade Dave, board members pointed to the evidence that most of the splittees were making it reasonably well in the street, so why not recognize the remarkable impact of the Daytop experience in changing basic attitudes and behavior and strive to become a short-term therapeutic center rather than an institution requiring a lifetime of residence and a monastic type of existence? But Dave would not be moved.

Many members of the board were convinced that it was Deitch's personality, the force of his leadership, that accounted for Daytop's success, and they were afraid that without him, the institution would disintegrate. The board's dilemma was resolved by those who argued that if Daytop was primarily interested in establishing a *treatment methodology,* a philosophy, and set of techniques with interchangeable parts, it could not depend on one person for its viability.

After the decision, Deitch threatened to barricade the premises and fight eviction with force. But at the last moment he heeded a court order and departed, taking with him almost the entire leadership corps and the majority of residents. Board members Monsignor O'Brien, Dr. Casriel, and Mortimer Levitt promptly reorganized the management of Daytop and stepped back to see whether the Daytop approach possessed the inner vitality and creative force to survive as an institution and treatment procedure. Eight months after the departure of Deitch the verdict is in. *Daytop is alive and doing better than ever.*

Questions
for the Global Conscience
Arthur J. Dyck

Problem: There are too many people in the world today, and the population is growing faster than the food supply. Solution: There are many effective forms of contraceptives, if only people would use them. Problem: The very people who (from society's point of view) need to use contraceptives the most are the least likely to do so. Solution: Education, both factual and ethical, seems the best answer. Problem: What rights does a member of society have as far as his own life and death are concerned; are we morally justified in making suicide and some types of abortion illegal? Solution: According to Arthur J. Dyck, we must find new ways of making moral decisions about life, death, and sexuality.

Kant once spoke of being aroused from his "dogmatic slumbers." Recently a group of Radcliffe college girls woke me up to certain central moral issues that had lain dormant in my thinking about my own work at Harvard on moral problems associated with the rapid growth of the world's population. During a seminar discussion of population problems, student questions turned abruptly, and with great intensity, to the question of suicide.

Why, these very intelligent, concerned young women asked, should we cling to our traditional scruples about suicide when they are but vestiges of outmoded and outworn religious dogma? Why doesn't every person have the right to dispose of himself or herself as he or she chooses? If a right to free speech is generally acknowledged as such, why not the right to commit suicide as well?

I was totally unprepared both for the intense interest in suicide and for the view of it that the students espoused. Why should such able, promising youths who readily and morally condemned the daily sacrifice of human lives in Vietnam and the human suffering in the ghettos wish so fervently to have the right—free from legal restraint and moral censure—to take their own lives? At first, it made no sense to me at all. Gradually, however, I think I have come to see the critical issues that are at stake and to understand some of the implica-

tions of my own line of argumentation developed in reply to them that night.

Suicide and Self-Determination

Suicide has been seen often as the ultimate expression of self-control and of the determination of one's own fate. Some scholars and laymen even see suicide as the paradigm case of human freedom. In thinking of suicide as a *right* comparable to freedom of speech, the Radcliffe students were emphasizing their desire, in principle, to be free of social coercion and control in considering whether they should live or die. But suicide is a paradoxical phenomenon. It does represent the ultimate form of self-control, but at the same time it is also the ultimate loss of self-control and self-determination. By this act, one relinquishes any personal contribution to one's own earthly fate and the future destiny of mankind. And it is precisely at this point that the act of suicide becomes morally questionable. (Suicide, of course, also has a dimension of hostility the students did not discuss. Behavioral scientists have learned that violence directed toward one's self and violence directed toward *others* are closely linked. The man who commits suicide may, indeed, be trying to "kill off" someone else.)

To commit suicide is to opt out in the most final way from further contributions to the life and welfare of one's community and of the human race. In deciding to commit suicide, one decides that one will not be available to one's fellows, that one will not even be of potential benefit or service to the human community. This is the critical difference between taking one's life and giving it. Giving one's life is heroic and morally laudatory, when it is done for someone's benefit or for the sake of humanity generally. Taking one's life is pathetic and morally blameworthy when it is a form of withdrawal from the web of one's existence and from the human community.

Suicide, then, is hardly comparable to the right of free speech. The free expression of opinion is, as John Stuart Mill observed in his essay on liberty, essential to the development of a democratic society and to the maturation of its citizens; taking one's own life is not a contribution to one's community except under very special circumstances as in wartime, and then it would not be seen as suicide, but as a form of giving one's life for another or others.

Why were the students, in arguing their case, inattentive to this difference between freedom of speech and a "right" to commit suicide? It is not that they were focused simply upon the right to self-control and the control over their own destinies. Rather they were focused upon the kind of social and moral coercion exerted by society at large from which they wanted to be free. The community here is seen to have something of the oppressive and repressive quality of what in contemporary rhetoric has often been called the Establishment.

The importance of this focus and perception can be illustrated by attention to arguments over the control of drugs. Both those who want increasing legal and other forms of control over the use of drugs and those who want less are concerned with maintaining the powers of self-control and self-determination. One group sees the use of certain drugs as contributing to the loss of self-control, especially when the drug in question is habit-forming or otherwise mentally debilitating. This loss of self-control can, in some instances, be harmful not only to the user but also to other innocent persons who may be victimized by the user. Those who emphasize more freedom with respect to drug use point to the harsh and restrictive nature of many of the laws governing drug use and to the general repression associated with making laws to regulate individual, private behavior. Of course, one's views concerning the moral and legal status of drug usage depend very much upon the specific drug in question and the amount of accurate knowledge available about the drug's immediate and long-run physical and psychological effects. Nevertheless, one's view of the human community and its relation to self-determination are very much involved in this and a whole host of critical social issues, from suicide, to drug use, to sexual behavior and population control.

It is not surprising, then, to find that the problem of relating the demands of self-control to the demands of the larger community also arise in moral deliberations over the use and control of reproductive behavior and sexual responses generally. There are those who emphasize the private character of sexual conduct and who tend to see legal and social restraints as repressive and unnecessary; there are those who emphasize the social and institutional character of sexual conduct and who see legal and social restraints upon it as appropriate and essential.

With the rapid growth of the world's population, and with the very real threat that such growth rates will bring about extensive human suffering within the next two decades, the control of reproductive behavior is no idle issue. It is essential that we achieve control.

Forces for change are at work everywhere, including among contemporary Roman Catholics. Acting out of the fervent desire to realize blessings of God, in the form of health, education, and general well-being for their offspring, increasing numbers of Catholics sanction and practice the methods of birth control, so recently condemned by Pope Paul VI.

It appears that the majority of Catholics, certainly in the West, see the Pope on the wrong side of this issue. In the choice between Papal concern for right doctrine and God's concern for human welfare, God wins out over the Pope. Religious change is going past the Pope, and so the problem of the viability of this kind of church structure is heightened.

Sexuality and Survival of the Species

Ultimately, given the upper limits of air and water pollution and the limitation of sheer space, the survival of the human species is at stake. Roger Revelle, director of Harvard's Center for the Study of World Population Problems, has stated the need for controlling our reproductive behavior in the form of a poignant question: "Can man domesticate himself?"

Assuming, then, that something must be done to reduce birth rates (increasing death rates is surely a morally unsatisfactory way of reducing population growth rates), we must ask how this is to be accomplished. To this question, there are a wide variety of responses that are considered to be morally acceptable and/or practically feasible. Suicide is not one of the answers.

We can divide these responses into three very broad groups: (1) those who oppose the conscious control over the number of their offspring; (2) those who favor family limitation as a voluntary decision on the part of the individual couples or family; (3) those who favor various forms of governmental control directly aimed at the control of reproductive behavior. From the viewpoints or "strategies" found within these broad groupings, let us look at those that differ most notably from one another.

There are two rather distinct viewpoints among those people who oppose self-conscious control over the number of their offspring. Some people do not wish to exercise the kind of forethought, interference, and control over sexual behavior necessary if one is predictably to plan to avoid or to have children as a result of intercourse. Self-determination here is seen as keeping sexual expression as unfettered and spontaneous as possible. It has been found, for example, that some American college women play a kind of "Russian roulette" by deliberately refusing to use contraceptives, claiming that thereby they obtain an "authentic sexual experience." James Beshers characterizes such young women as "short-run hedonists."

Another group, while expressing a willingness to limit and restrain sexual behavior in various ways, does not consider it entirely proper to consciously limit the size of the family. For some, this stems from their belief concerning God's active sphere of dominion and participation in human reproductive processes.

Beliefs in the will of God do indeed find their expression in folk piety. Rural Moslems speak of having as many children as God wills, and they sharply restrict the use of contraceptives. Hinduism and Buddhism have doctrines of *ahimsa*, noninjury, and of the cycle of *karma*, the law of cause and effect—or of sowing and reaping—in human affairs. Thus, the conscious endeavor to prevent a conception or a birth other than by abstinence often has been interpreted as injury to life and as an interference in natural and morally inviolable cosmic processes.

Interesting parallels to these religious beliefs can be found in certain subcultures. The gauchos of South America who work on ranches as cowboys consider it unmanly to take rational forethought. For them, rational forethought is cowardly, a failure to face what "life" or "fate" has in store for each of us. Among working-class wives in the United States, described by Lee Rainwater, there is a tendency to be skeptical of thinking and planning ahead.

The styles and beliefs of these various groups would, if generally followed, give us little hope that birth rates around the world could predictably be lowered and controlled by leaving the decision to families.

But there are groups, like the Population Council, who believe that such groups are small enough now or will through the press of circumstances diminish enough so that they pose no barrier to the eventual success of voluntary family planning as a strategy for reducing birth rates to the necessary and desired levels.

Many governments, including our own, along with various planned parenthood organizations, share this viewpoint. Thus, policy consists in making effective contraceptives and contraceptive information readily available and in communicating the alleged advantages of keeping one's family small, but this has not been found to be the most effective approach. Voluntary family planning is thus taken to be at once morally desirable and practically feasible.

But others who agree that voluntary family planning is morally desirable do not share the belief in its practical feasibility unless certain other phenomena connected with reproductive behavior are changed.

We shall look at two such strategies for controlling birth rates that differ so much in magnitude as to constitute, in their long-range consequences, quite different policies.

On the basis of intensive research over a period of seven years in the Punjab region of India, John Gordon and John Wyon of Harvard have hypothesized that people in such an area would be motivated to reduce their birth rates if: mortality rates for infants and children were sharply decreased; local social units were stimulated to measure their own population dynamics and to draw inferences from them concerning their own welfare and aspirations; and efficient methods of birth control were introduced. Introducing these conditions would substantially increase the opportunities of each family unit to reduce family size without undue fear, to assess in a more exact, realistic way *how* fertility goals would affect themselves and their community, and to plan with more realistic hopes for success in attaining their goals. Whether birth rates would be markedly lowered by bringing about these conditions alone would depend not simply upon the extent to which people in that region stand to benefit from such a reduction but also upon the extent to which they actually perceive such benefits—both social and economic—and believe that they are attainable.

The gathering of vital statistics is, therefore, a crucial aspect of this proposal. Not until statistics were introduced did the first vaccine against disease gain general acceptance in the West. Without accurate information, a sense of group responsibility cannot exist on a rational basis, and will have no perceptible dividend to the individual members. The proposal of Gordon and Wyon for the Punjab assumes that rational and purposeful behavior exists already to some degree and can be intensified by modifications in the environment that make the intensification of such behavior more beneficial and more attainable.

Roger Revelle explicitly agrees that it is essential to do the very things that Gordon and Wyon suggest. Looking, however, at the total ecological context within which arise population problems, especially of undernourishment and starvation, he is certain that nothing less than substantial technological changes will be effective. These changes, which he sees as quite indigenous *and* locally controlled, could spawn highly industrialized, urbanized countries with scientific market agriculture throughout the globe. Such an environment certainly has, in the demographic history of the West, been associated with sharp declines in birth rates. The kind of setting within which these birth declines occur more or less adequately provides the incentives and the means to control the population growth of the world and the material resources for the sustenance and gratification of its human inhabitants.

But Kingsley Davis is convinced that any reliance upon voluntary planning by individual families is doomed to fail. Pointing to the necessity for achieving *zero* growth rates, he points out that many highly industrialized countries have not attained such rates and, given the average number of children desired, show no prospect of doing so. He urges government policies explicitly designed to alter the institutional arrangements that reward present reproductive behavior and ideals. He calls for policies that would encourage and reward the single life, childlessness, late marriage, small families, and activities for women that would have the effect of curbing their preoccupation with childbearing and child-rearing.

For Davis, only direct intervention and planning by government is practically feasible and, in the light of his dark picture of the problems of population growth, morally acceptable. His strategy includes governmental efforts to change our current values—values he believes stand in the way of preventing otherwise inevitable disaster.

A more directly coercive role is assigned to the state by the Communist government of China. Restrictions upon reproductive behavior include such measures as mandatory late marriages (men must be thirty, women twenty-five) and severe economic and vocational sanctions against couples having more than two children. None of these policies are justified as attempts to control birth rates. (A socialist state is supposed to provide for everyone; "overpopulation" is a problem for capitalist countries.) But they are, of course, forms of population control, though presented as measures to protect women and children, to improve the education of the rising generation, to contribute to the health and prosperity of the nation, and to honor the need to devote more energy to the development of the state.

How shall we assess the moral desirability and acceptability of these various responses to the control of reproductive behavior? Within ethical theory there are two very basic sets of criteria to help judge what is morally justifiable: the *normative*, and the *meta-ethical*.

Broadly stated, rapid population growth and the possibility of ultimate overpopulation on the earth becomes a normative issue because of the human misery and death that come from rapid population growth and the threat to human extinction that inevitably follows overpopulation. If, as seems evident, birth rates must be extensively reduced and therefore in some way controlled, responses that hinder or block control are, in this respect, morally blameworthy. Conversely, those responses that facilitate and bring about the desired end are morally praiseworthy.

But human responses, certainly strategies or policies for action, tend to be morally complex, and usually possess a number of right- or wrong-making characteristics. There are some very significant and closely related sets of moral values connected with sexual and procreative activities.

Human sexuality is an important expression of our individuality and a source of intensely gratifying pleasure. Any strategy for controlling human behavior will certainly tend to be *right* or *wrong* to the degree that it enhances or diminishes the extent to which we find self-fulfilling freedom and joy as sexual beings. One can think of this freedom and joy as a human right.

But sexuality, like life itself, is at once a right that belongs to us as individuals and a gift that each of us receives from others—his parents most immediately, but also from the wider human community. Indeed, it is a gift *from* the human species *to* the human species. We owe, therefore, some considerable debt of gratitude to these sources of our unique genetic and social individuality for the very possibility of experiencing sexual pleasure and for the considerable rewards of childbearing and child-rearing.

We incur, then, as those who have been chosen to live, an awesome but joyous obligation to see to it that this gift of life, sexual expression, procreation, and child-rearing has a future. Our obligation to the larger human community is particularly vital insofar as each of us has unique genetic endowments and unique talents to offer and to perpetuate. No one else can give to the species what we bring to it. That is why committing suicide is such a threat to the human community and represents a profound failure to participate in our own self-determination and in the destiny of the human community.

Sexual and procreative behavior is at once individual and communal, joyous and creative, a right and an obligation. One of the difficulties in inducing the reduction of birth rates has to do with the necessity of making people aware that the survival of the species does not now depend upon a large number of births; indeed, it depends upon *some* births, but not too many. The need for a new sophisticated awareness of species responsibilities has been brought about by our success in reducing death rates and extending life expectancies. Failure to reproduce, like taking one's own life, requires special justification if it is to be morally responsible vis-à-vis our obligations to others. But this same moral responsibility to our species requires us also to limit the number of our offspring under prevailing conditions. If we do not cultivate and assert this responsibility, we are threatened by the loss of self-determination and will be increasingly assailed by those who would advocate harsh and repressive means to save the species.

Justification of Moral Judgments

What about the meta-ethical criteria? Meta-ethics is concerned with the meaning and justification of moral statements. In its investigations there is growing agreement that the rationality of moral claims can be judged by the extent to which they exhibit the following criteria: (1) knowledge of facts; (2) vivid imagination of how others are affected by our actions; (3) universal loyalties with respect to both our interests and our passions so that what obtains for one person obtains for another and for ourselves as well. Strategies designed to cope with population problems will more nearly satisfy our considered moral judgments as they approximate these rational processes.

Applying these normative and meta-ethical criteria, we can see quite readily that opposition to the self-conscious control of the number of one's offspring is not a very viable moral option. The short-run hedonists may enjoy a certain kind of freedom and pleasure, but both of these—if sufficiently generalized—would be disastrous to the species and would not, for long, satisfy any of the specified criteria. Those who will not, for pious reasons, specifically determine the number of children they will have also fall short on all counts, but with this major difference: Given their loyalty to God, these people are highly susceptible to new knowledge and circumstances that would permit them to see that their health and welfare, which God would have them act to secure, can best be served by reducing birth rates.

For this last reason, both the Revelle and the Wyon strategies are morally superior to plans that simply provide contraceptives and contraceptive information to facilitate family planning. Indeed, the Wyon and Revelle proposals move further in the direction of realizing and facilitating what is demanded by the normative and meta-ethical criteria than any of the other policies or proposals.

One might object, as does Davis, that their strategies will not succeed in *sufficiently* reducing birth rates. Certainly further research and trial is needed, but given the assault on human values and the threat to a "sacrosanct" sphere of human freedom, the practicality of the governmental coercion Davis advocates is at best doubtful. Thus any widespread attempt to implement birth-control policies like those of the mainland Chinese government undoubtedly will meet with resistance and be shown as impractical.

Another subtle flaw in turning to governmental coercion in reproductive matters is that such a move already represents at least a partial acceptance of the notion that the great masses of men cannot or will not learn what is in their best interest. Policies predicated on this premise will tend increasingly to rely on coercion rather than upon the processes of rational persuasion and the creation of conditions conducive to successful communication.

People and nations must find a morally justifiable form of population control in which they will contribute to human survival. Strategies like those of Wyon and Revelle commend themselves insofar as they enhance human freedom and encourage responsible community behavior. Wyon's proposal has the advantage of introducing a minimum of disruption into a culture. It may, by the same token, be inadequate to induce the requisite behavior without further transformations of the social and economic lot of the people involved. Revelle's policy has the advantage of a total ecological vision seeking to bring about the conditions that presumably maximize the technical possibilities for controlling the whole web of existence for man's benefit. (Herein lies its potential weakness as well. Not only do we have no assurance that technical advances ultimately will provide this control but, more importantly, we cannot ascertain what losses mankind suffers when entire cultures are transformed into the Western technological and industrial mold.)

One last observation: To be rational, moral judgments must rest on universal loyalties. The problem of overpopulation makes this criterion concretely explicit. The preservation of the species demands loyalty, not simply to one's own family and one's own immediate community and nation, but to mankind, and beyond that, to the total ecological environment upon which man's life depends. The assassinations of Martin Luther King and Robert Francis Kennedy reveal the demonic and evil character of acting out of partial loyalties to racial or political groups when seeking to do what one may consider right or justifiable. We should not underestimate the powerful force of the religious symbol of one God to nurture universal loyalties of the sort we now desperately need. Love for all of our fellows is not now, if it ever was, a moral luxury. The survival of our species depends upon enlightened, impartial love.

Sex and American Society

William Simon

Sexual behavior can be viewed from many different angles. One can look at sex as a purely biological function and assume that anything that organisms do is perforce "natural." One can look at sex as being concerned chiefly with procreation, hence view it chiefly as a problem in population planning. One can assume, as does analytic theory, that sex is a strong biosocial drive that must be channeled or controlled somehow in order to achieve good mental health; "abnormal" sexual behavior (however defined) therefore becomes a psychiatric problem. Sexuality may be seen as being primarily a religious, a moral, or even a legal subject of discourse and study. Whatever the case, perhaps the most interesting aspect of sex in modern American society is the fact that it can be studied, that it can be talked about openly in quite factual and unemotional terms. And this new state of affairs, as William Simon points out, may well be what most of us mean when we speak of the current "sex revolution."

In less than half a century sex in American life has rocketed from the unmentionable to a topic of almost obsessive public concern. The management of sexual activity, either as a social or personal phenomenon, has become a high-priority preoccupation for vast segments of our society. The major theme of preoccupation that emerges from this many-voiced choir is the question: What has changed in American sexual styles and behavior?

In earlier periods the silence kept everyone at a distance from the question itself. Because of pluralistic ignorance—no one had any idea what anybody else was doing or feeling—it was possible to hang onto a vague sense of some natural order of things in sex. And despite all that we have learned about sexual matters—and it is not nearly enough—this notion of the natural order of things persists; it is a major theme whenever the sexual dimension of man is considered. We should also note that our increase in knowledge about sex has won acceptance largely because the researchers worked under the rubric of the natural sciences—the zoological commitment of Kinsey, the medical context of Masters and Johnson. Thus, we began to talk aloud about sex, and a many-sided public dialogue continues. Some see this increased sexual knowledge as a rare opportunity for personal growth and maturity. Others see it as a portent of a crumbling society. The only agreement seems to be that we are in the process of change, and that the change is possibly profound.

This agreement that there are profound changes, even though the changes are often vaguely defined, has led to the clamor about the so-called sex revolution. The very ability to embrace a concept of sex revolution may in itself be truly revolutionary. Yet, to talk about sexual revolution in purely sexual terms makes as little sense as talking about political revolutions in exclusively political terms. There is one promising facet of the preoccupation with sex: it may help us consider the sexual dimension in the context of on-going social and psychological life. This would certainly be an improvement over most of our past, in which the specter of sexuality was an isolated figure in a denuded social and psychological landscape or, at best, was accompanied by the gray figure of orthodox morality. The point is that for the first time we have an opportunity to pursue this subject in breadth.

There is, however, a dual aspect of sexuality that generates complexity in both sexual activity and social regulation of it. The sexual dimension links man to his evolution and gives him a sense of participation in species life and species survival. The sexual component also remains a powerful reminder of the mediating and limit-setting functions of the body. But perhaps most important, man's sexuality can be an equally powerful reminder of how unnatural and unprogrammed the human experience is. We need only look across cultures or through the histories of single cultures to see the impressive variety of adaptations and meanings that are possible. For in acting upon his sexuality, man simultaneously celebrates one of his most universal aspects and his utter dependence upon the sociocultural moment. What, after all, is more unnatural to most of our contemporaries than the nude human body in a sexual posture?

Public Sexual Representations

Changes in the definition or representation of the sexual dimension in American cultural life since World War II have proceeded at a gallop. In looking at them, it is important to differentiate between the public and private faces of sex. The changes in the public face of sexuality are easy to discern. The hard part is to find the implications of these public changes for the private face of sexuality.

With nation-wide media systems, we are surrounded by sexual imagery more explicitly erotic than any we have had before in our society. This erotic environment may be seen in two distinct dimensions. The first involves the limits of permissible public or quasi-public representation of the sexual. This boundary has shifted markedly, particularly in the last decade. Some part of this growing permissiveness is a direct result of the federal judiciary's handling of a number of major cases involving erotic materials. The courts may be somewhat ahead of the social consensus in this permissiveness, but there are substantial continuities involved in both the production and consumption of culture in our society. Both the popular and the more traditional arts are living in closer collaboration with what had previously been their underground. In fact, the underground itself becomes increasingly a special part of our public culture. To indicate how far and how quickly we have come, it might be noted that in 1948 *The New York Times* refused to carry the publisher's conservative, medical-textbook advertising for the first Kinsey report. By the mid-1960s the *Times* was carrying, without apparent reluctance, rather lurid ads for books that were previously almost unavailable except in the locked library cases of Kinsey's Institute for Sex Research.

What is publicly permissible, however, only suggests what is available to the society. Contrary to the would-be censors' predictions, permissiveness did not attract massive portions of the population to the new erotic frontiers. Relatively few people in our society are gourmets of the extremely and/or exclusively erotic.

In fact, the second dimension of the new erotic environment may be even more important; it is the extent to which the sexual is included in conventional public discourse, without new images or language. Here we can see a profound increase in concern for the sexual. Consumer advertising, the popular arts, the middle-range sources of information such as women's magazines and television documentaries—all provide occasion and language for both thinking and talking about sex in social situations. Educators appear almost but not quite ready to admit that there may be more to sex education than studies in reproductive biology and

social etiquette. The new liberal theologies—particularly those infected with the new morality—find in the sexual an imagery that achieves a kind of instant salience. All at once we find sex at center stage instead of on the fringes of self-awareness.

The result is that we now live in a relatively lush erotic landscape, and it is increasingly difficult to separate that which is expressive of disturbed fantasies and aroused anxieties from that which is descriptive of the present and/or prototypical of the future. There is almost a shift from the question of the legitimacy of what one is doing and wants to do to the question of what more should one do or want to do.

The sexual images we are now offered are confused and frequently contradictory. In the wake of Masters and Johnson's powerful study, the ladies' magazines appear to have established the legitimacy, if not the necessity, of female orgasm almost before they have established the necessity of sexual intercourse. Thus we can talk about orgasm easier than we can talk about intercourse. Wife-swapping, for example, is talked about in ways that define it rather curiously as a social problem. One is all at once unsure of what is an appropriate response; one senses, however, that there is more talk about wife-swapping than there is actual swapping, and that participation is extremely marginal. Much the

same is true of what the young are reputed to be doing sexually.

A point to remember is that, often, significant social change does not come about merely because behavior patterns change. The point of change may be simply the point at which given forms of behavior appear plausible. An example of this phenomenon is the current status of homosexuality as a public topic. There is no evidence of recent growth in the proportion of our population that has homosexual preferences. Of course, the number of such persons has increased along with the total population. But, aside from relatively localized situations, little has changed in the life situation of the homosexual. He must still face both the risks of arrest, conviction, and imprisonment and the frequently more feared risk of rejection by family, friends, and employers.

Nevertheless, in recent years homosexuality has become part of the standard fare on the frontiers of cultural consumption. The subject is the pivotal theme in an increasing number of novels, plays, and motion pictures. It is covered by television, newspapers, and magazines. This implies that ultimately society will respond more rationally to the homosexual. Even more important is the implication for the future status of heterosexuality. Our thinking about homosexuality conditions our thinking about heterosexuality and sexuality in general.

All these changes in the public representation of the sexual—be it of the homosexual, the alleged youthful vanguard of the sexual revolution, the female doubly liberated by the pill and the language of the multiple orgasm—could represent a watershed where both the status and content of sexuality are transformed. Unless one sees the sexual as a nearly immutable evolutionary inheritance, one must assess the complex process in which the idea of the sexual is formed and transformed, the process in which—one might say—it is invented.

Sex and Gender Role

The author sees sexual behavior as dominated by sociocultural factors. This view is supported by cross-cultural research and by study of data restricted to the United States. The individual can learn sexual behavior as he learns other behavior—through the interaction of complex social and psychological factors and not as the result of some masked primordial drive. This means that sexual behavior can often express and serve nonsexual motives. For most people, including most of the young, a heightened awareness of the sexual dimension need not be followed by an ability to incorporate this awareness into their own sexual commitments.

It is not uncommon for those who view the sexual component as a high-order biological constant to see it as pressing against the layers of experiences and adopted roles that describe the individual. These layers of experience, in this view, may provide an authentic expression of the sexual. The contrary perspective describes these layers of experience and role incumbency as essentially creating the sexual or at least forming the frameworks within which our respective sexual scripts are formed and evolve. It is not surprising that the notion of the high-order biological constant has achieved such great currency—because for all but a very few individuals in our society, a sense of the sexual self is typically experienced as something discontinuous with other —more public—senses of self. Despite the seeming remoteness of the sexual, the very capacity to be sexual appears to be linked to larger senses of self and linked in very fundamental ways. To understand possible changes in the sexual dimension, then, we must first understand something of these other aspects of identity.

The sex act is obviously more than the joining of sex organs. A crucial sense of gender not only shapes the performance but also may be a necessary precondition for something sexual to happen in the first place. Consistent with this is the finding reported by Kagan and Moss that the most powerful predictor of adult sexual commitment may be the quality of the nonsexual sex-role learning during the later years of childhood—ages six to ten. The importance of the gender role for sexual activity has two dimensions. One, what kinds of acts are consistent with what kinds of commitments to concepts of masculinity and femininity? And, two, what kinds of sex-role characteristics make it possible for one to see another person as potentially erotic? As these crucial gender roles undergo change, we may begin to expect changes in sexual patterns far more dramatic than those presumed to be prompted by the pill or sexy movies. Major shifts in just these social definitions of gender roles may be now in process. There is far less data on this topic than its significance requires.

Impressionistically, there appears to be a growing tendency toward greater and greater tolerance for deviation from narrow, stereotypic definitions of appropriate male and female behavior. There always was more such tolerance at the higher socioeconomic levels, and this apparent shift may reflect only a widespread affluence. The people in higher socioeconomic levels have an outsize role in creating public images of private life, in determining the modalities of self-image. The middle-class urban young who are mixing gender symbols freely with hair and dress may be expressing just this kind of shift of gender role learning. And our current crop of young appear to have an earlier and possibly greater capacity for heterosociality, which is likely to have an effect on their capacity for heterosexuality. Their sexual style will probably continue to be expressive of the assimilation of these changing gender roles. But one's sexual style need not be a test of one's gender commitment, as it is for so many adults today.

Implications of Public Trends for Private Behavior

There is, to be sure, a great deal of continuity as well as change. For many, including many of the young, sex continues to be a fearful test that must confirm what it can confirm only provisionally. For males the fear of sociosexual inadequacy and incompetence and for females the double fear of being too little sexual and too much sexual will keep the sexual game precisely that: a game in which the costs of losing often outweigh the rewards of victory. But the trends we have noted earlier do represent a new countervailance and the prospect for a cooler attitude.

The trends need not have immediate implications for what people do or the frequency with which they do it. The important changes may be in the attitude with which they approach sex. Instead of acting out of need (the need for social psychological validation rather than a response to inarticulate strivings of the body), people may develop a heightened ability to act out of desire. This in turn suggests that a casualness might affect both style and frequency. But such a change does not necessarily mean stepped-up sexuality. On the contrary, it might produce a marked lessening among those to whom sexual commitment was an imperative, a test or ordeal.

For the time being, however, new patterns will strain for accommodation with older patterns. Adolescent boys will continue to make strong commitments to their own sexuality by masturbating and by spinning complex fantasies. For most of them, masturbation, as commitment and rehearsal, will continue to be organized around fantasy themes that feed directly from their own sense of emerging masculinity. This sense of masculinity will tend to be aggressive and direct in ways that will almost never find expression in heterosocial communication. But there will also be strong pulls toward engagement in sociosexual activity as success on this level wins social support and social award.

For girls, on the other hand, there is little reason to expect an immediate or marked shift to increased sexual activity, either masturbatory or sociosexual, during the early or even the middle years of adolescence. They will continue learning how to appear sexual and will receive social support and rewards for success at it. But there will be no rewards for sexual activity as such.

This cosmetic sexuality will form in a rhetorical atmosphere of social competence and competence in the managing of emotional relations, abilities that make sociosexual activity legitimate. Until now the legitimating conditions for sexual activity for most females have been tied to family formation or courtship in very fundamental ways.

Many of the facets of sexuality that we have considered are related to major shifts in the life styles and public values of the American middle class. In a situation where decisions that commit the total society—such as the tragedy of Vietnam or even factors that affect the immediate quality of community life—appear remote to most people, the sexual takes on a significance and power beyond that which is intrinsic to it. Nowadays one strives for competence and self-actualization, which, as goals, are far more flexible than the achievement that one sought before. In fact, the so-called new morality involves a shift from the morality of significant acts to the morality of personal competence. Sexuality gives the individual at least the sense of making moral decisions. Not only may his sense of personal effectiveness thus be enhanced, but his focus is shifted from the act to the quality of his motives, in the form of personal competence. Management of sexuality, as a consequence, becomes significant in self-identity. The negative is that sexuality increasingly must demonstrate achievement and competence. Whether a relatively limited sexual capacity can sustain such additional burdens is questionable; we still cannot put that very private capacity into the competition for social reward and validation.

The constant affluence experienced by the American middle class since World War II also creates certain pressures on sexuality. The young, who have only the most abstract notions about nonaffluence, increasingly demand that the landscape on the other side of traditional achievement be described in terms that make sense as experience. Affluence generates a kind of anomie all its own. The ease and abundance with which certain goals are achieved trivialize the goals. One response to the anomie of affluence, as seen long ago by Durkheim, is a quest for new, more intense experience. Something of this phenomenon can be seen in the pursuit of drug experience by many middle-class young people. Sexuality obviously is a key way station in the pursuit of intense experience.

In the long run both of these trends—for personal competence and for intense experience—should encourage all of society, young and not-so-young, to become even more concerned with sex, more sexually active, and possibly more sexually experimental. This suggests not only a narrowing of gender distinctions but quite possibly a narrowing of generational distinctions. Parents and children might increasingly share sexual style and commitment as the young become sexual earlier and the old remain sexual longer. Generational difference could erode considerably and, in fact, may already have begun to do so.

Although exotic and marginal sex is at center stage, most sexual activity still is aimed at family formation and maintenance. But as the imagery of sex changes, there are changes in the character of the family and in its relation to the larger society. Students of family life have for some time commented upon the narrowing of family control and the shift of socializing functions among the young to places outside the home.

Along with these changes, new weight has been given to interpersonal attachments—as against external constraints—in the maintenance of a viable family life. Here again, sexuality is taking new relevance; it may have to serve as both content and visible proof of enduring attachment. This is reflected in the emphasis we now place upon sexual competence in marriage, one that borders on sexual athleticism.

This poses a difficulty. One still finds it hard to get social recognition and support for his sexual competence in marriage. For many, making competent conversation about sex becomes a bid for this social recognition. This is reflected in the growing demand for technical and pseudotechnical information. The results are mixed. Some find reassurance in their verbal performance. Yet, the more one talks sex, the more detail one has against which to compare his direct sexual experience. This does not always enhance one's sense of competence or even one's identity.

In general, the sexual dimension in our society comprises a limited biological capacity that is harnessed and amplified by varied social uses. Within that context we have sketched possible uses and modes of amplification. We have emphasized that the expression of the sexual component is the celebration of a social and psychological drama rather than a natural response. We have suggested that there may be substantial change in this social drama. In the past the drama has been a silent charade. Now we appear to be giving the drama a sound track and inviting the audience to participate. Competence increasingly replaces guilt as the major source for amplifying complexity. Guilt had the power of endowing limited behavior with enduring emotions. Competence may require an enlargement of the scope of the behavior. Keynes may have to replace Adam Smith as the metaphorical cartographer for our sexual style. Whether the principle of "the more you spend the more you have" can apply to the body any more effectively than it applies to the economy is questionable. For while physiology may not be our destinies, it can still be a major source of their frustration.

Homosexuality and Social Evil

Martin Hoffman

The term "abnormal" has so many meanings that the word may well be almost useless from a scientific point of view. Regular attendance at church or synagogue is abnormal in a statistical sense, in that there are more people in the United States who do not attend religious services regularly than who do. If a highly religious person seeks psychiatric help, we do not automatically assume that his religious behavior is at the root of his problem, nor do we conclude from the small percentage of such disturbed individuals that all church-goers are deviants whose behavior merits psychiatric treatment or legal prosecution. Homosexual behavior is likewise abnormal in a statistical sense, yet in this case most of us automatically assume that its practitioners are mentally or emotionally ill and in need of psychological assistance or legal punishment. Perhaps, as Martin Hoffman reminds us, our view of homosexuality is distorted both by outmoded morality and by the fact that we tend to see only those homosexuals who are, indeed, badly adjusted, and we then unwisely generalize from this limited sample to the entire population.

Every occupation has its hazards. One hazard of theoretical work in psychology and psychiatry is psychologism: overemphasis on psychological factors in explaining puzzling phenomena. Psychologism plagues the study of homosexuality. All the phenomena of this complex sexual orientation have been explained by the psychoanalytic theory of homosexuality—a brilliant but nevertheless incomplete analysis.

This theory is set forth clearly and economically in Otto Fenichel's classic work, *The Psychoanalytic Theory of Neurosis*, which dazzles with its profound insights into what most of us regard as a very mysterious kind of behavior. Unfortunately, we link his study with another idea: the disease concept of homosexuality. This concept holds that homosexuality, by its very nature, is always either a mental illness or a symptom of such an illness. I immediately reject this idea as too sweeping a generalization. Emotional disturbance causes many men and women to become homosexual. But a number of studies now show that there are many homosexual men who are not emotionally disturbed.

Because my own research and clinical practice has been almost entirely with male homosexuals, I am not going to discuss female homosexuality, except to mention a few differences between the two groups in order to make a theoretical point. This article is on male homosexuality; I even use the term homosexuality to refer to male homosexuality alone.

The Hooker Study

Evelyn Hooker, psychologist at the University of California at Los Angeles, made the classic study that refuted the disease concept of homosexuality. She found thirty homosexuals, not in treatment, whom she felt to be reasonably well adjusted. She then matched thirty heterosexual men with the homosexuals for age, education, and IQ. Hooker then gave these sixty men a battery of psychological tests and obtained considerable information on their life histories. Several of her most skilled clinical colleagues then analyzed the material. . They did not know which of the tests had been given to the homosexual men and which to the heterosexuals; they analyzed the tests blind. Hooker concluded from their analyses that there is no inherent connection between homosexual orientation and clinical symptoms of mental illness. She stated: "Homosexuality as a clinical entity does not exist. Its forms are as varied as are those of heterosexuality. Homosexuality may be a deviation in sexual pattern that is in the normal range, psychologically." This conclusion is based on the fact that the clinicians were unable to distinguish between the two groups. Nor was there any evidence that the homosexual group had a higher degree of pathology than the heterosexual group.

A number of more impressionistic studies, based on psychiatric interviewing, support Dr. Hooker's conclusions. Two London psychiatrists, Desmond Curran and Denis Parr, reported in the *British Medical Journal* in 1957 that of 100 homosexual men seen in psychiatric consultation, only 49 percent had any significant psychiatric abnormalities. In late 1966, the Homosexual Law Reform Society, based in Philadelphia, wrote to a number of distinguished behavioral scientists, asking their opinions on the relation of homosexuality to psychopathology. The responses to the society from some of the country's most eminent scientists supported the position that Dr. Hooker and I hold: that homosexuals are not necessarily mentally ill.

Let me quote a few of the responses.

Paul H. Gebhard, Ph.D., director, Institute of Sex Research, Indiana University (founded by the late Alfred C. Kinsey): "the collective opinion of the members of the Institute for Sex Research . . . based on extensive interviewing and other data is as follows . . . homosexuality is not a pathology in itself nor necessarily a symptom of some other pathology."

Norman Reider, M.D., training analyst, San Francisco Psychoanalytic Institute, and recently visiting professor of psychiatry at the Albert Einstein College of Medicine in New York: "Homosexuality per se is no evidence of psychopathology."

John L. Hampson, M.D., associate professor of psychiatry, University of Washington: "In most instances the homosexual life-style is the product of certain complex early learning influences and should not be thought of as a 'mental illness' or 'psychopathology' . . ."

Fallacies in the Disease Concept

One could go on with further quotations refuting the fallacy that homosexuality is necessarily connected with mental or behavioral disorder. There is, to be sure, opinion on both sides. It seems to me, however, that the opposing view—that homosexuals are all sick—arises from two main sources. First, since the concept of sin is no longer in fashion in Western thought, we do not know how to label behavior when we disapprove of it on moral grounds. Second, psychiatrists who assert that homosexuality is an illness generally know homosexuals only as patients. Since psychiatric patients are disturbed, therapists conclude that they represent the general homosexual population when, in fact, they are

but a small fraction of it. As Dr. Judd Marmor, analyst and editor of the book *Sexual Inversion* wrote: "If the judgments of psychoanalysts about heterosexuals were based only on those they see as patients, would they not have the same skewed impression of heterosexuals as a group?"

This issue made me want to conduct a nonclinical, ethnographic field study of the male homosexual population in the San Francisco Bay area. I reported on this study in my book, *The Gay World: Male Homosexuality and the Social Creation of Evil.* As a clinical psychiatrist, I was seeing only disturbed homosexuals, and I wanted to find out what kinds of lives other members of that group were living. So, I interviewed many homosexual men to learn whether they suffered from mental disorder. I examined them as psychiatrists usually do, asking about their doubts, anxieties, possible phobias, depressions, and the like. Large numbers of them showed no clinical signs of mental disturbance. I am convinced, after talking to these men, most of whom had never sought psychiatric treatment, that one of the most important causes of the currently fashionable disease concept of homosexuality is that clinicians do not see a representative sample of homosexuals. If they did, they would be hard put to maintain their dogmatism about *all* homosexuals.

An example of the dogmatism is a magazine article called "A Way Out for Homosexuals," by Philadelphia psychiatrist Samuel B. Hadden. (Group therapy is the "way out.") Hadden says, "In my observation, homosexuals are deeply troubled people" (again the clinician's fallacy), "their numbers are increasing" (he gives no evidence for this, and there is none), homosexuality is "a grave social problem" (yes it is, but hardly in the manner Hadden thinks it to be), "from earliest childhood none of the homosexuals I have known have been truly psychologically healthy individuals" (one would hardly expect this from a psychiatric patient population!).

Hadden implies that homosexuals are abnormally prone to violence. This is utterly fallacious. In the most recent Institute for Sex Research report, which deals specifically with sex offenders, no categories were needed to describe homosexual acts that might involve force. In contrast, categories involving force (for example, rape) were needed to analyze the data on heterosexual acts. As the report states, "the use of force is rare in homosexual activity."

Finally, consider this statement by Hadden: "In my view, we should treat homosexuality as a handicapping disorder. *And I further believe that society has a right to expect those afflicted to seek treatment . . .*" (my italics). He clearly implies that those homosexuals—the vast majority—who do not wish to become heterosexual should be forced into psychiatric treatment. Let us be quite aware that Hadden's pronouncement borders on frank totalitarianism. Should all individuals who deviate from current social norms be forced to conform, whether or not their behavior harms others? Is psychotherapy to operate in an atmosphere in which the patient has the ultimate right to make up his own mind about what he will do with his private life, or is psychotherapy to become an agent of social control?

In the light of Hadden's remarks, we may do well to note the attitude of Communist China toward deviants. Some Chinese prisons for brainwashing are called "hospitals for ideological reform." And Mao Tse-tung has said, "our object in exposing errors and criticizing shortcomings is like that of a doctor in curing a disease. . . ." Robert Jay Lifton, who quotes this line in *Thought Reform and the Psychology of Totalism*, goes on to say, "In all of this it is most important to realize that what we see as a set of *coercive maneuvers, the Chinese Communists view as a morally uplifting, harmonizing, and scientifically therapeutic experience.*"

Assuming, then, that the disease concept of homosexuality is a gross oversimplification that carries dangerous implications, are there, nonetheless, any connections at all between homosexuality and psychopathology? Yes, there are a number that we can group into two general categories: psychological and sociological.

Psychodynamic Explanations

The psychological factors are well covered in the psychoanalytic theory of homosexuality. Reaction-formation, or the defensive substitution of one feeling for another that is unbearable, can lead to homosexuality. For example, a boy may hate his father or brother

and also may be unable to express his hostility. So he changes hate into love by that substitutive magic that is the hallmark of defense mechanisms. If the love becomes sexualized, it may lead to a homosexual object-choice. Another explanation for homosexuality involves incorporative wishes toward the male, the penis, or masculinity. The homosexual may feel chronic emasculation. He may be able to achieve some sense of reparation only by taking the penis of his partner into his own body. In this way he thinks he has incorporated some of the imputed masculinity of the other man into his own deficient organism.

These psychodynamic explanations are very striking and highly appealing. I am sure they are true for a number of homosexual men. There exists no good evidence that they or any other psychoanalytic constructs explain all homosexual behavior. In fact, we do not know very much about the relation between sexual arousal and the symbolic triggers that act on the central nervous system, leading to the complex sets of behaviors that form the various stages or types of sexual arousal. Until we know about the mechanisms of sexual arousal in the central nervous system and how learning factors can set the triggering devices for these mechanisms, we cannot have a satisfactory theory of homosexual behavior.

We must point out that *hetero*sexual behavior is as much of a scientific puzzle as homosexual behavior. Why, for example, is a particular man aroused by a large-bosomed brunette on a movie screen? Reflection reveals that we really do not have a satisfactory answer, and until we do we cannot answer analogous questions about homosexual arousal. We assume that heterosexual arousal is somehow natural and needs no explanation. I suggest that to call it natural and thereby to dismiss it is to evade the whole issue; it is as if we said it is natural for the sun to come up in the morning and left it at that. Is it possible that we know less about human sexuality than the medieval astrologers knew about the stars?

Psychoanalytic theories postulate that if an individual's sexuality is formed as described above, it must run a pathological course throughout his life, inasmuch as his sexual behavior is merely the acting out of unresolved childhood conflicts and problems. Such a viewpoint is attractive, for it seems to explain some very problematic homosexual behavior.

Promiscuity

One of the characteristics of homosexual interaction in the public places of the gay world—bars, beaches, parks, streets, and steam baths—is that sex is anonymous and promiscuous, not typically associated with affection or even, often, with identifiable individuals. John Rechy's novel *City of Night* describes such pick-up places and their way of life, as does my own book. Very often, in these places, one man is simply meeting or having sex with another of a certain physical type and does not want to know anything about his partner. Superficial acquaintanceships do spring from these meetings, and not infrequently the men repeat the sexual encounter. What is striking about these acquaintanceships, and even about many of the love affairs that last for several weeks to several months, is their shallowness. These people use each other in an instrumental, narcissistic way to gratify their own fantasies. Their partner is not really a lover, though he is often called by that label, but rather a necessary aid to acting out of the sexual (and nonsexual) fantasies that analysts believe originate in childhood. The man with a compulsion to fellate one individual after another until his conquests run into the hundreds may simply be vainly trying to replenish his masculinity. The two lovers who had had a stormy, tempestuous six-month relationship before one finally moves out may be acting out a sadomasochistic game in which the reaction-formation against hostility toward other males can be functional for only a time. During periods when it does not repress that hostility, there may be terribly long bouts of friction, punctuated by episodes of sexual activity.

Of course, such descriptions could easily fit many heterosexual couples; homosexuals have no monopoly on problematic relationships. But what is so striking about male homosexual alliances, in contrast to both heterosexual and female homosexual alliances, is their fragility, their tendency to be transitory, and the all-pervading promiscuity that characterizes the public places of gay life. Lesbians, who would perhaps be expected from a psychoanalytic point of view to have the same instability in their relationships, actually have much longer-lasting ones and do not in any way use public places for anonymous sexual contact, as homosexual men do. They do not cruise streets or parks and do not use lesbian bars—which are much less numerous—the way males use their gay bars. Lesbian bars are more like social clubs, where they go with their lovers to meet friends. Homosexual men also make some such use of bars, but cruising for an anonymous partner is specific to the male and not to the female homosexual.

Which ought to lead one to ask the so often unasked question: Just how much of male homosexual behavior can be explained by the fact—and this fact alone—that such relationships involve two *males?* The question at first sounds like a tautology, but I hope it will be seen that it is far from that. For I think it can be said that much of what seems to the observer as pathologic in male homosexual behavior is merely the result of having two men in a sexual situation. Most of what has been said, only partly in jest, about males being promiscuous by nature and females being the stable member of the heterosexual pair is true. Without the stabilizing female the dyad tends to break up. When two females interact, as in lesbian relationships, the dyad tends to be more stable.

Psychological Effects of Social Condemnation

I have saved for last what I regard as the most significant cause of unhappiness and psychopathology in the

gay world: society's attitude toward homosexuality. I regard this as so significant both because social attitudes have been so little discussed in psychological writings on the subject and because they are, at least in theory, the most correctable and therefore the most pertinent for our immediate consideration.

Society has not only regarded the homosexual with the most abusive scorn; it has also preferred to think (until very recently) that homosexuality does not even exist, that is, is *unthinkable*—in spite of the fact that there are literally millions of Americans who are exclusively or predominantly homosexual. The ramifications of this attitude on the life of the homosexual are subtle and far reaching. A great deal of the anonymous promiscuity in the gay world can be understood only if we consider that the homosexual *cannot* be open about himself and his identity. His anonymity is forced upon him by the very society that, partly by means of the disease concept of homosexuality, condemns him for its consequences. His promiscuity results, in part, from the social attitudes that prevent him from living with another man in dignity and openness.

One of the critical ways that this pressure operates is by means of the social sanctions that would be visited upon the homosexual if his sexual orientation were known. The treatment accorded homosexuals by their employers, their acquaintances, their families, and by government agencies—especially the military—constitutes a continuing hidden scandal in the moral life of our nation. In a more subtle and terrible way, social condemnation acts directly on the homosexual's conception of himself. A well-known fact in the study of oppressed minorities is that they, tragically, adopt toward themselves the degrading view that the larger society has of them. The homosexual accepts this stigma. He views himself as queer, bad, dirty, something a little less than human. And he views his partner in the same way. Paul Goodman, describing some of his own homosexual encounters, says of some of his partners, "since they disapprove of what they are doing, they are not supposed to like the partner in it." How, then, can we expect them to have any kind of stable, meaningful relationship after the initial sexual thrill is over? (James Baldwin's novel *Giovanni's Room* describes what happens to a homosexual relationship as a result of such self-definitions.)

Self-condemnation pervades the homosexual world and, in concert with the psychodynamic and biological factors that lead toward promiscuity, makes stable relationships a terrible problem. In spite of the fact that so many homosexual men are lonely and alone, they cannot seem to find someone with whom to share even part of their lives. This dilemma is the core problem of the gay world and stems in large measure from the adverse self-definitions that society imprints on the homosexual mind. Until we can change these ancient attitudes, many men—including some of our own brothers, sons, friends, colleagues, and children yet unborn—will live out their lives in the quiet desperation of the sad gay world.

The Long Weekend

Frederick H. Stoller

In recent years, there has been a growing dissatisfaction with traditional forms of psychotherapy. Perhaps it all began with Hans Eysenck's report in 1952 that patients in British hospitals given no psychotherapy at all showed a greater improvement than did patients given analytic or eclectic therapy; perhaps it stems more directly from Moreno's work with psychodrama or from Carl Rogers' writings on client-centered therapy. Whatever the case, a great many scientists are now convinced that mental illness is primarily a social phenomenon and must be attacked in the social environment that caused it. According to this viewpoint, the individual therapist-cum-father-figure who "cures" his patients by listening to them can often be replaced by a group of individuals all of whom undergo a meaningful emotional experience together. In the following article, Frederick H. Stoller describes one such approach—the marathon encounter group.

A young Mexican-American, imprisoned for drug addiction, inarticulate, fearful, and sullen, becomes a forceful dormitory leader.

A Greek-Jewish survivor of a Nazi concentration camp, having vegetated for seven silent and inactive years in a state mental hospital, suddenly decides he wants to leave, begins work in the hospital laboratory, and earns his discharge within a few months.

A clinical psychologist whose sole aim has been competence as a technician begins to function as a recognized innovator in his field.

The drug addict, the concentration camp survivor, and the psychologist are linked by a common bond. Each, within a relatively brief time, made use of personal resources whose existence had been totally unrecognized by himself and by others. And each participated in an intense group experience that changed his view of himself, his world, and his future.

These three people did not undergo traditional group therapy. They were members of a different kind of group, one of the new intense encounter groups whose goal was exploration rather than cure, and whose orientation was self-education rather than the amelioration of psychopathology. Many techniques of the new group are not dissimilar from traditional psychotherapy,

but the assumption made about the members is that they are *not* sick. This is true even when some or all group members are disturbed. But it is not necessary to feel that one "needs therapy" to join a group, for it appears that everyone can benefit from experimentation with new ways of behavior and new social arrangements, and the most effective groups are made up of "chronic undifferentiated people." These new groups are explosive because they concentrate on immediate behavior within the group, not on explanations of past behavior—that tempting search for a scapegoat. They are also unpredictable, because each participant is encouraged to scrutinize himself and his relationship to the world without the shackles of normal role expectations.

When a person is labeled—neurotic, psychotic, executive, teacher, salesman, psychologist—either by himself or by others, he restricts his behavior to the role and even may rely upon the role for security. This diminishes the kind of experience he is likely to have. Indeed, it is groups whose members have a shared label—be it schizophrenic or executive—that are hardest to help move into intimate contact.

The importance of avoiding labels is shown by the experience of a young bachelor, who was urged by myself and other group members to stop frittering away his time at the YMCA when he should be involved in the heterosexual world. By the last day of the marathon he walked like a tiger—his growth was impressive. Then I discovered he was a former mental patient. Had I known this earlier, I would have thought, "Your adjustment is pretty good, considering where you've been." I never would have responded to him so directly. And his marked behavioral change would have been blunted.

During group sessions, exclusive reliance on a narrow range of roles is broken down. The chronically hospitalized patient who helps another patient, or the juvenile delinquent who persuades a boy not to run away, sees himself in a new and liberating light. It is this opportunity to shift freely from the role of patient to that of therapist or observer that is the unique feature of group therapy.

Since the essence of the new group movement is flexibility and experimentation, new techniques and procedures constantly are being tried. Experiments with the length of sessions resulted in the marathon group; experiments with technological innovations resulted in the use of video tape to capture behavior; experiments with group makeup resulted in the family workshop.

The 300-Year Weekend

As its name implies, the marathon group, which grew out of my experiences in a sensitivity-training laboratory in 1963, is a continuous session. My first attempt to use the marathon—with a group of psychotics—was both rewarding and exciting. The model finally developed by George Bach, one of the pioneers in group psychotherapy, and myself lasts from twenty-four to thirty hours, often without a break for sleep—a distinct departure from the precisely scheduled "fifty-minute hour" of traditional psychotherapy. The marathon group represents a radical alteration in the quality of the psychotherapeutic experience. It assumes that people are capable of coping with undiluted, intense experience and do not require carefully measured exposure to therapy; it has been called a "pressure cooker" because of the tension it builds up. And like a pressure cooker, it also can compress the amount of time required to do its work. The development is infinitely more rapid than under conventional therapy and the progress can be startling. The marathon uniquely maximizes and legitimizes people's readiness for change.

The marathon group is more than an exercise in massive confrontation and involvement. It is an educational experience primarily useful for what *follows* the conflict—crisis, anxiety, and reaching out for contact.

And in order for what follows to be meaningful, it is essential that group members neither avoid nor dilute their discomfort. The tension must rise. Members of the group are asked to react to each other, immediately and spontaneously, at all times; these immediate reactions—the "feedback"—inform the recipient in un-

mistakable terms of just what impact he has on others in the group. Thus, ground rules for the marathon specify that the group remain together throughout the session; they outlaw psychological or psychiatric jargon of any school; and they call for authentic, honest, and direct reactions.

The group leader's role is quite different from his role in traditional therapy. He deliberately refrains from gathering case histories about the marathon group participants. The leader must build up his impression of participants exactly as other members of the group do, and he must share the impact of each participant. For, in a marathon group, being *understood* is not what is essential; the importance is in being *reacted* to.

The group leader sets the experience in motion so that the pressure gauge will begin to rise. His position is clear and unmistakable, but he does not remain the traditional, aloof clinician—he is also a group member, a distinct human being. For this reason, I frequently hold marathon groups in my home, and my wife participates.

Marathons run a fairly predictable course. In the first phase, participants tell their "stories." Basically, they present themselves as they wish the world to see them: they describe their frustrations or their life circumstances, with careful attention to the response they hope to evoke. They may anticipate solutions to their problems or look for support of their actions or attitudes. Inevitably they encounter static from the group—unexpected reactions that they find difficult to accept. Thus they meet their first crisis: feedback that is different from what they intended or wanted, or expected. And learning begins early. One man said that he felt—for the first time—that someone knew him well enough to tell him more about himself than he already knew.

Most people have learned that the best way to handle a crisis is to run away. However, the marathon does not offer that option. For one thing, retreat is against the rules. For another, each group member contributes to the crises of the other participants at the same time as he is experiencing his own, so that he is drawn closer to the very people with whom he is in conflict. A counterpoint between the urge to retreat and the necessity to become more involved characterizes the second phase of the marathon.

Tears and Threats

During this middle phase the group members, not surprisingly, learn a considerable amount about each other. They also learn to react more directly and honestly. Their ways of moving through the world become more and more apparent. They sense that their approach to others is limited and tentative, and so their awareness of other possibilities grows. No clear-cut solutions emerge, but the struggles at this point are intense. It is the most explosive period of the session. Dramatic, frightening, moving interchanges are likely to occur. Tears and threats are not uncommon.

It was at this point that I once had an extreme confrontation with a young man whose religious fanaticism made it impossible for him to have a relationship with anyone who did not share his feelings. As the marathon progressed, I found his insistent intrusion of religious dogma abrasive and, after making it clear that I did not operate within a religious framework, demanded that he specify his reactions to me. He was thrown into conflict between his usual stance and his feeling for me. Suddenly he cried and talked about his concern for hypocrisy he saw within his church.

Another young man, who had been observing quietly, also began to cry. He was so deeply moved by the religious man's struggle that tears coursed down his cheeks. He said it was the first time in his life that he had found himself touched by another human being. Now he realized how distantly he had conducted his life. And he wept. The change in this silent observer was as profound as that in the young man who was the temporary focus of the group. This "spectator therapy" is a group phenomenon that is accentuated by the marathon experience.

As the session nears its end, there is in any marathon group a new sense of intimacy among all the members, and positive feelings emerge in a spontaneous and deeply felt fashion. This phase has been called a "love feast," because participants reach out to one another with unguarded intimacy. They now permit themselves to experience more—more fear, more love, more empathy, and more excitement. A Negro youth, following a marathon experience, wrote: "It seemed to get me out of that fake shield that I had been hiding behind practically all of my life."

Solutions and alternatives begin to emerge, usually through the realization by the group member that he can reveal more of himself than he thought safe.

Taking part in a marathon is like watching oneself through the wrong end of a telescope: everything is sharp, concentrated, miniaturized. It becomes clear in this microcosm that one's life is, to a considerable degree, something one creates and something for which one is responsible. Gradually, the inhabitants of the small world learn to act upon their environment as well as to be acted upon. It becomes apparent that the larger world can be altered in similar fashion. This is my deep belief.

Mirror, Mirror on the Wall

One function of a group is to show its members the effect they have upon one another. Responding to other people develops one's ability to communicate perceptions directly and honestly; receiving responses increases one's self-knowledge. But it is hard to sit still and listen to information about one's self that may be unpleasant, and it is hard to assimilate what one is told in mere

words. This is why I turned to a new medium, which some therapists since have adopted and which others question.

Video-tape equipment makes it possible for group members to see themselves in action, which they find highly informative as well as fascinating. In one group, a wife had spent considerable time complaining bitterly that her husband "behaved like a child" with her. On video tape, I was able to show her that she used many of the mannerisms of a scolding mother with him—she would glare, shake her finger, and, when pleased, pat his head. "I couldn't believe it," she said. "It was worth a thousand words."

Contrary to what one might expect, placing a television camera in the midst of a group does not seem to affect behavior. Television camera and video-tape machine become part of the group circle. The camera may be manned by a co-therapist or even by the group members themselves. This arrangement gives them a chance to observe the group from an unusual and therefore useful point of view. Their choice of what appears on the tape is in itself a commentary—on the action and on the cameraman as well.

Unless responses are observed soon after behavior, they have little value. So when Lee Myerhoff and I began to use video tape during marathons, I decided to interrupt the group from time to time and replay the tape. This did not break the continuity of group interaction. Instead, group members would react to themselves on the television monitor, and other members would react to this reaction. Consequently, the viewing usually was followed by fuller concentration than before on immediate group behavior and events.

Focused Feedback

Video tape shares one unfortunate characteristic with life: It contains too much information. It is necessary to select what relates to the goals of the group and to focus the attention of the group members on it. A rationale for focused feedback can be found in the works of George Herbert Mead, who preceded the technical reality of video tape by many decades. Essentially a social psychologist, Mead developed a theory of personality development that stressed the social environment within which man becomes human. Among Mead's speculations was the theory that preceding each act, people rehearse that act in their minds and anticipate the response others will give to it. On the basis of the anticipated response, the act is initiated; on the basis of the actual response, behavior is modified. An act consists of a range of gestures, some of which (such as speech) can be monitored by the initiator, and some of which (such as facial expressions) cannot.

Video tape shows the group member—sometimes all too clearly—the relationship between an anticipated and an actual response. Often the two correspond; at critical times they often do not. In either case, comparing them is extremely useful for the group member. Tape also makes clear the discrepancy between a person's inner state and what he communicates to others. Most people are surprised to discover how much effort they invest in hiding their true responses, as if life were a poker game.

The pictures on the video tape are added to the verbal pictures painted of each group member by himself and others. And on the screen, for the first time, the participant confronts himself instead of having to interpret information filtered through the mind of another individual. He also sees himself, on tape, in each of the three major group roles: the patient role, when he is the focus of attention; the therapist role, when he attempts to extend help to others; and the observer role, when he is an inactive witness to the struggles of others.

Recent studies by Margaret Robinson, conducted at Camarillo State Hospital for her doctoral research at the University of Southern California, tend to confirm my observation that after seeing himself on video tape, a group member often changes his behavior before incorporating the change into his self-concept. After four sessions of focused feedback, there was a marked drop in the incidence of specific behavior units that were the objects of the feedback, but the self-concept— as measured on self-rating tests—remained unchanged. When behavior first changes, there is a period of awkwardness, then an improved level of behavior. The changed behavior elicits new responses from other people, perhaps initiating a chain reaction.

Games Families Play

In our family workshops, developed in collaboration with Ann Dreyfuss, of Western Behavioral Sciences Institute, three or four families remain together for several days, generally for a weekend. At first, the scene is chaotic—children are everywhere, in constant motion. Because of their short attention span, young children sometimes are segregated from the main group from time to time during the weekend, but a rule of the family workshop is that *all* members participate, and no one is talked about when he is not present.

Parents are quite devious with their children, and they teach their children to be devious with them—beginning when the children still are at the preverbal level. And this is complicated by the fact that the family as a unit puts on an act before outsiders.

Families come to the workshop with ready-made relationships, but they have not learned to talk about them. As initial shyness and family chauvinism wear off, the interplay begins. Even very young children pick up the emotional tone of the workshop and seem to be aware that a struggle is taking place.

There are rules: Regardless of which family they belong to, group members are expected to respond to each other directly, and to express their perceptions as clearly as possible. As families get to know one another, they become aware of the implicit contractual arrangements that determine their behavior. The workshop, like the marathon, is a microcosm of the difficulties that families encounter at home; experimenting with new and more fruitful ways of dealing with these problems is a major goal of the session.

Early in our sessions, each family in turn is given a large piece of paper and pastels. The family is asked to draw a design together for five minutes, without speaking. Mothers are more likely to be uncomfortable in this situation than are fathers. Interestingly, most families will fight for space; each member will try to use the whole sheet and to invade others' territory.

After the picture is completed, the family members discuss their reactions, and then the rest of the group talks about how they perceived the family. During the discussion, family members tend to draw parallels between the ways they behaved in this situation and the ways they behave at home.

The picture exercise takes the workshop out of the realm of words and removes the advantage from the parent and gives it to the child. The art game actually helps teach youngsters to give feedback, and they soon warm to the task (see Figures 1 and 2).

On other occasions, a box is placed in the center of a family group. They are told that something terrible is inside the box and asked to imagine what it might be. Typical guesses range from "a little dinosaur" to "a creeping hand" or "something soft and gooey and icky." This game represents an attempt by the family to share their fears.

Sometimes we ask the chosen family to pass sticks in a circle according to a specified pattern, or to perform rhythmical handclapping "dances." The purpose of these games, which usually come late in the workshop, is to give the family a chance to have fun together, to cooperate under the easy conditions of play without the restrictions of the usual family roles. In other words, a mother is invited for a moment to stop functioning as a mother and to become instead a playmate with responsibilities no greater than her child's. Some mothers do this well and enjoy it, others do not—in either case, the results are informative.

If parents complain, as they often do, that their children never listen to them at home, the family may be asked to talk together for fifteen or twenty minutes, perhaps about their reasons for coming to the workshop. The rest of the group comments on this; their response is supplemented by a replay of video tape.

The family workshop has wider implications. The current American family is becoming increasingly unique in that it sees itself as an independent unit, operating without reliance on the extended family— grandparents, uncles, aunts, cousins. This is an impossible task. As families are brought up in isolation, social agencies move into the vacuum created by the dissolution of the extended family. And as the family influence diminishes, there is an accompanying growth in the strength of the adolescent culture.

The intimate relationships developed during the workshop can be the nucleus from which to explore and experiment with new social arrangements. An intimate network of families who had shared workshop experiences could be created. These families would provide the help and emotional support originally supplied by the clan or the extended family.

A powerful group experience permits the individual to explore his own resources, those of the people with whom he finds himself, and those of the world about him. Group experiments provide experiences, not intellectual exercises—and experiences have the power to reshape us. Perhaps we need to establish "colleges for growth." Just as a student is not stupid because he goes to college to learn, so a person is not sick because he seeks group therapy or encounter experience to help him grow.

Figure 1. One family drawing. The mother tended to hang back, seemingly unhappy about the lack of structure inherent in the exercise. The father made more attempts to participate but these were largely toward the edge of the paper. The older girl worked in a neat fashion but the young boy began to fill the paper with his scribbling. Finally, there was an attempt on the part of the parents to involve the children in a tick-tack-toe game, which ultimately was scribbled over by the boy (including the tear in the paper). The mother complained that the boy inhibited her by his hyperactivity, but she could be seen as inviting him to fill space by her reluctance to act without structure.

Figure 2. The family's product.

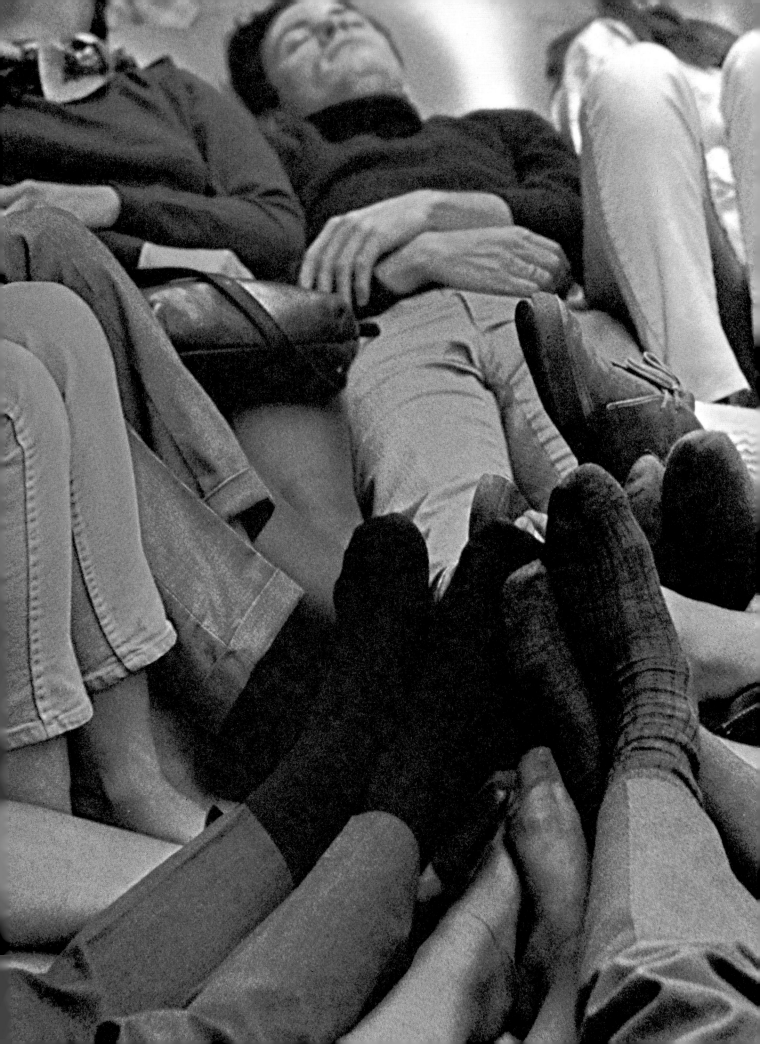

Esalen

Michael Murphy

The more highly developed a society becomes, the more complex and the more mechanical it seems to be. Machines give man freedom from many distasteful chores, but man-machine interactions have a kind of impersonality that many people fear may have dehumanizing consequences for all members of our culture. Machines are needed, for they give us the great luxury of free time that we never had before. We must use that great gift wisely, according to Michael Murphy, to learn more about ourselves and about our fellow man, to explore the very essence of being human. And that is what Esalen is all about.

We conceive Esalen Institute as primarily a forum for theories and practices concerned with evoking positive human potentials that have been neglected in our culture. In our programs we draw on the arts, religion (ancient and modern, Eastern and Western), from psychotherapy and the behavioral sciences in general, from psychosomatic medicine and other fields.

A weekend seminar with B. F. Skinner, the developer of operant conditioning, will be followed by a series of workshops with a Protestant theologian, a Carmelite monk, an existential psychotherapist, a historian, an authority on ESP, a Zen scholar, an architect, or a Hindu mystic. Skinner, Harvey Cox, Alan Watts, Father William McNamara, Rollo May, Abraham Maslow, Arnold Toynbee, Gardner Murphy, Shunryu Suzuki, Buckminster Fuller, and Haridas Chauduri all have participated in the work of Esalen. Part of the excitement at Big Sur comes from the force of encountering the leading exponents of varied points of view and divergent disciplines.

Most of our workshops are experimental and experiential. They are conducted in an atmosphere with few institutional restrictions, where social scientists may "do their thing." Our primary concern is the affective domain—the senses and feelings, though we certainly are

interested in the cognitive. We hope to educate people, if only for a weekend, in what Aldous Huxley called the "nonverbal humanities"—long neglected in our culture because of the heavy emphasis that is placed on the verbal-rational aspect of man.

That man is capable of heightened functioning in *all* fields is proved every day. Wine tasters and perfume smellers sharpen their senses; the skin diver, the mountain climber, the skydiver, the miler who keeps cutting seconds off his time—all push the limits of human functioning. And people in the fields of dance, the arts, and physical education are devising ways to extend the human potential.

Esalen is, perhaps, a product of the times. Along with the trend toward life-long education has come a rise of popular interest in the existential philosophy of the here and now. We find more and more Americans who want to experience the present, to contact their feelings, to communicate intimately with others. At Esalen, as at Esalen-inspired institutes like Kairos in Southern California and Shalal in Vancouver, we try to expand human consciousness and help people "turn on" without drugs or alcohol.

The experiential methods used at Esalen have been developed primarily by our associates in residence, whose techniques demand the total involvement of participants and, like the experiences of an LSD trip, are intensely personal, and extremely difficult to describe in conventional language.

On a walk around the grounds and through our redwood buildings clustered on a high bluff above the Pacific Ocean, one might see a blindfolded person led about silently in a group leader's effort to restore the individual's sense of touch and to give the experience of dependency. Or one might watch people "converse" with their bodies and eyes, cutting through society's excessive verbalism to authentic feelings, or one might find six or eight people lying side by side in a "sandwich" or rolling over one another to sense the presence of others, and to learn it's all right to touch each other.

Married couples whose physical relationship has become mere repetition are resensitized to each other. Eyes shut, they pat each other's faces and open their eyes to see a different person. They are taught new ways of body massage and brought into closer contact. Our body-awareness workshops include a series of simple procedures to increase sensitivity, to quiet the mind, and to achieve an optimal *tonus* between being too tense and being too relaxed.

Frederick Perls, the seventy-six-year-old founder of Gestalt therapy, works with a group structure in his institutes but leads each person individually to his impasse point and, hopefully, beyond. Nothing is too small to escape examination in his groups. He pays strict attention to physical manifestations of inner conflicts, making the "patient" aware of the sound of his own voice, his breathing, and his posture.

A psychologist who also was trained by Max Reinhardt as a theater director, Perls relies on props and on his uncanny sense of seeing a person's basic stance in the world. The props include a "hot seat" in which patients sit, a vacant chair that serves as a "screen" for the patient's projections and a focal point for his dialogue with other parts of his own body, and videotape equipment for feedback. In a typical session, Perls may ask a patient to verbalize and to act out a dream or fantasy, telling him to play all parts of the dream in the present tense. At one point, he may shift a dialogue between the patient and that part of his dream "sitting" in the vacant chair into a conversation between the patient's right and left hands.

Such dialogues call attention to basic polarities in the patient's personality and usually, after the patient has carried out his dialogue, bring him to the impasse point at which the dialogue ceases and he is in a panic-stricken whirl, unable to leave what Perls calls "the merry-go-round of compulsive repetition." Now the patient is stuck, unable to crack through his self-defeating ego games. Not every person can break through his impasse, but in a Gestalt session, most do reach or approach an understanding of their own polarities.

Perls was influenced by Freud in Germany but abandoned traditional psychoanalysis in favor of his own Gestalt technique many years ago. Today, his theories are similar to those of existential psychiatry, but he goes further in concentrating on sensory behavior and in declaiming the intellect as fantasy—"the rehearsal stage on which we prepare for the roles we want."

The basic theory of Gestalt therapy is that maturation is a continuous growth process in which environmental support is transformed into self-support. In healthy development, the infant mobilizes and learns to use his own resources. A neurosis develops in an environment that does not facilitate the maturation process. Development is perverted into patterns designed to control the environment by manipulation. At the core of the neurosis is an existential "impasse," a situation in which no environmental support is forthcoming, and the individual clings to the status quo, held back by a "catastrophic expectation" that prevents risk taking.

Virginia Satir, one of our directors and a founder of the Mental Research Institute in Palo Alto, California, conducts our family-therapy programs and workshops for couples. In her experiential sessions, she seeks four results from participants: heightened individual self-esteem; improved communication, particularly of a nonverbal nature, between couples and their children; an understanding of the couple or family as a system with a set of expectations; and a developed potential for new growth in any relationship.

A series of exercises—including "eye-alogues," where feelings are expressed to another solely with the eyes—art expression, encounter methods, and role-playing are used in their workshops to achieve what Virginia Satir considers a "creative marriage." In her conjoint family therapy, for example, she may ask family members to take each other's roles and thereby experience various points of view. She urges participants toward full understanding and expression of their feelings and a resolution of the conflict between intimacy and autonomy. She puts it like this: "In every marriage there is a 'me,' a 'you,' and an 'us.' Once people fully realize this, they can begin to think of totally new ways of self- and other-validation."

William Schutz, who was the director of the Group Process Section of the Albert Einstein School of Medicine before joining Esalen, is a specialist in interpersonal behavior. His encounter groups cover many methods of exploring the human potential, including fantasy, body awareness, and psychodrama. In one exercise, for example, group members link arms in a circle and one person tries to break out of the ring, experiencing frustration and anger when he fails to do so. The group then may hold a person and throw him into the air to help him feel his passivity, or a pair may engage in an arm-wrestling contest. In another exercise, the members of a group lie on the floor in a circle, their heads together, to create a giant dandelion. Schutz gives them a situation, and they form a train of fantasy together.

Afterwards they talk together about the fantasy and what it reveals. Schutz's goal is to amplify feelings and to help turn suspicious, hostile, or dull individuals into trusting and aware people capable of more meaningful lives.

We have grown since our first tentative programs in the Fall of 1962; 5,000 people come to the Institute at Big Sur every year now, and our new San Francisco center attracted over 10,000 people during its first year of operation.

In September of 1966, we began our first residential program, an attempt to combine elements of seminar programs into a unified nine months' curriculum. In 1967 twenty-one resident fellows—who included the curriculum expert from an eastern state university, a Duke graduate student preparing a doctoral thesis on meditation, and a theologian from a Jesuit college—began our second residential program in self-awareness under the direction of Schutz and Edward Maupin, formerly on the staff of the Neuropsychiatric Institute at UCLA. This program has now been shortened to four and a half months; two such sessions are run each year, led by associates in residence John Heider, Steve Stroud, Schutz, and Maupin. It remains to be seen whether the moments of healing and moments of illumination that occur regularly in weekend workshops can be sustained on a long-term basis.

Richard Price, cofounder of Esalen, is working with Julian Silverman and others on a center for the treatment of schizophrenia. It appears that some acute schizophrenic breaks are relatively short and are followed by a reintegrative process, so that the individual returns from his "trip" more integrated and fully functioning than he was at the beginning. We hope to find new ways to make such breaks valuable, function-heightening experiences. This project will also explore ways in which an individual's neurophysiological make-up might affect the outcome of his psychosis, and ways in which varying treatment programs affect different kinds of individuals.

During the 1967–68 school year Esalen conducted a project for elementary- and secondary-school teachers with the assistance of a grant from the Ford Foundation's Fund for the Advancement of Education. The project was directed by Dr. George I. Brown of the School of Education, University of California at Santa Barbara, and included a staff of elementary and secondary school teachers drawn from various schools in the Santa Barbara and San Francisco Bay areas. The project explored ways to provide in the school curriculum experiences in the affective domain, such as those explored in our regular seminar programs. The object was to integrate the affective and cognitive domains so as to provide richer and more relevant classroom learning. A large number of approaches were used with much success. A comprehensive report, entitled "Now, the Human Dimension," was assembled by Dr. Brown and his colleagues. Plans are now underway to extend the project.

Another project underway is bringing theologians and other religious professionals into our workshops so that they might experience the work being done there and then reflect upon its significance from a theological perspective. Participating theologians and philosophers all share in the contemporary effort to ground theology and philosophy in the human experience; the revolutionary and growth-promoting experiences that our workshops so often facilitate are significant for their theological-philosophical inquiry. And our increasing experimentation with human potential may benefit greatly from their reflection upon crucial experiences of change and growth. Sam Keen, Harvey Cox, Michael Novak, Bishop James Pike, Gordon Kaufman, John Cobb, William Hamilton, Richard Rubenstein, Brother Antoninus, Maurice Friedman, Bishop John A. T. Robinson, and John Maguire and Andrew Young of the Southern Christian Leadership Conference are among the theologians and philosophers who have participated or will participate in this series. The periods of reflection have been tape recorded by the Human Development Institute of Atlanta, Georgia, and will be turned into an educational program for churches and other religious groups by the Institute.

This series has led to a residential program for theologians to be directed by Sam Keen. This more extended program is designed to give religious professionals an opportunity to sample a wide variety of growth-facilitating experiences and to reflect upon their theological significance. Participants will join in a frontier effort to formulate a type of theological reflection based upon direct experience. The methodology of this experiment will involve a continual interplay between experiential exploration and reflection. The National Council of Churches, through its division of Church Life and Mission, is cosponsoring the seminar series on Theological Reflection and will collaborate with us on the residential program.

It is hard for us at Esalen to assess our impact on the scientific community. We are aware that Esalen is controversial. While many people respect what we are doing, and some might agree with Abraham Maslow, who called Esalen "in *potential*, the most important educational institution in the world," many others consider us little more than kooks and cultists.

There are risks in an organization like Esalen, but we prefer risks to the status quo. Some of our approaches will hold up with the passage of time; others will be discarded as foolish or useless. In any case, we intend to be on the cutting edge.

AKE a walk in the garden where the action is—the swinging, sensuous "Garden of the Human Potential," which grew in our artist's mind as Michael Murphy, president of Esalen Institute, talked about who he thinks is doing what and going where along the way toward the expansion of the mind of man.

DRUGS

Aldous Huxley (1894-1963), novelist and critic, who became interested in the effects of drugs and in Indian mysticism. His drug experiences were described in *The Doors of Perception.*

Humphrey Osmond invented the word "psychedelic"; introduced Aldous Huxley to mescaline.

Alan Watts, a popularizer of Zen Buddhism, who is working to unify science, philosophy, and religion. Advocates the use of LSD.

Timothy Leary, formerly of the Department of Psychology at Harvard University, has turned on and dropped out. Advocates the use of marijuana and LSD.

Hippies, members of a subculture in opposition to the dominant U.S. culture, characterized by dress, drugs, and communal living.

Freebies, the newest group on the scene; they are an extension of the hippies.

ESP (Extra-sensory Perception)

British Society for Psychical Research, founded in 1882 to conduct research into the fields of parapsychology.

American Society for Psychical Research, founded in 1888 and modeled after the British society.

Cross-correspondences, this attempt to communicate with the dead through mediums and by messages pre-arranged before death flourished especially from 1910-1930.

J. B. Rhine, the father of parapsychology, was connected with Duke University for many years. Since his retirement he has been director of The Foundation for Research on the Nature of Man and The Institute for Parapsychology.

Gardner Murphy, director of research at the Menninger Foundation, is the author of *Challenge of Psychical Research: a Primer of Parapsychology.*

Stanley Krippner, director of research, Dept. of Psychiatry, Moses Maimonides Hospital, New York. Conducts research on ESP during dream sleep.

Montague Ullman, on the staff at Moses Maimonides Hospital, New York. Conducts research on ESP during dream sleep.

Ian Stevenson, research psychiatrist, University of Virginia Medical School. Deals with cases suggestive of reincarnation.

J. G. Pratt, at University of Virginia Medical School. Has been a co-worker with J. B. Rhine in the field of parapsychology.

Charles Tart, at School of Medicine, University of Virginia. Interested in dreams, hypnosis, and personality.

HYPNOSIS

Franz Mesmer (1734-1815), Austrian physician, who developed the theory of animal magnetism, later known as Mesmerism.

Pierre Janet (1859-1947), French psychologist, a student — as was Sigmund Freud — of J. M. Charcot, who studied the disordered personality.

Sigmund Freud See below, PSYCHOANALYSIS.

Josef Breuer (1842-1925), Austrian physician and psychologist. A forerunner of psychoanalysis who used hypnosis in treating patients.

Bernard Aaronson, at School of Education, Rutgers University. Interested in verbal behavior, neural correlates of behavior, and psychotherapy.

Milton Erickson, a psychiatrist from Phoenix, whose fields are hypnotherapy, clinical psychotherapy, and training hypnosis.

Leslie LeCron, psychologist and hypnotherapist from Carmel, who does research in hypnosis and the alteration of consciousness.

MYSTICISM

William James (1842-1910), American psychologist and philosopher who delved into religion and mysticism in *The Varieties of Religious Experience.*

Gerald Heard, English writer now living in Southern California. His mystical philosophy greatly influenced Aldous Huxley.

Aldous Huxley See DRUGS.

D. T. Suzuki, the leading popularizer of Zen Buddhism in the United States.

Alan Watts See DRUGS.

First Zen Institute, founded in San Francisco. Now has a center in Big Sur near Esalen.

Arthur Dikeman, at the Austen Riggs Clinic, where he is engaged in meditation research sponsored by the National Institute of Mental Health.

The Beatles: George Harrison, Paul McCartney, Ringo Starr, and John Lennon; singing group in the vanguard of rock 'n roll, whose music has been influenced by Eastern music and who have been attracted by mystical thought.

Edward Maupin, a director of Esalen Institute, formerly on the staff of the Neuropsychiatric Institute at UCLA. His Ph.D. dissertation on meditation was probably the only one in America on that subject.

EVOLUTIONARY PHILOSOPHY

Julian Huxley, brother of Aldous Huxley; this English biologist related science to human social life and to religion.

Gerald Heard See above, MYSTICISM.

Pierre Teilhard de Chardin (1881-1955), French Jesuit paleontologist and thinker. He aimed at a metaphysic of evolution, holding that it was a process converging toward a final unity.

PSYCHOANALYSIS

Sigmund Freud (1856-1939), Austrian psychoanalyst and founder of psychoanalysis.

Otto Rank (1884-1939), Freud's pupil, who sought to modify Freud's theories to fit the needs of an industrial society.

Carl Jung (1875-1961), Swiss psychologist and psychiatrist, who founded analytic psychology. Former student of Freud.

Alfred Adler (1870-1937), Austrian psychoanalyst and student of Freud, who founded individual psychology.

David Rappaport, with Austen Riggs Clinic.

Robert Holt, George Klein: co-directors of Research Center for Mental Health, NYU, who are interested in the field of ego psychology.

Kurt Goldstein, psychiatrist and psychologist theorist, who invented the term "self-actualization."

Harry Harlow, professor of psychology at the University of Wisconsin and founder of the Primate Laboratory there.

Abraham Maslow, professor of psychology at Brandeis University. Noted for animal research and studies of human motivation; pioneering studies of psychological health.

Tony Suditch, editor of the *Journal of Humanistic Psychology.*

EXISTENTIALISM

Martin Buber, Jewish theologian and philosopher, who is the originator of the "I-Thou" concept.

Paul Tillich, Protestant theologian, who believed it was necessary to "demythicize" the Bible; author of *The Courage to Be* and *The Dynamics of Faith.*

Rollo May, psychotherapist and philosopher, who was a student of Alfred Adler. On the staff of both the William Alanson White Institute of Psychotherapy and New York University.

Victor Frankl, founder of logotherapy and author of *Man's Search for Meaning.*

Medard Boss, French psychiatrist.

Ludwig Binswanger, Swiss psychiatrist.

PSYCHOSIS

R. D. Laing, founder of the London Blowout Center at Tavistock Clinic.

Julius Silverman, connected with the National Institutes of Health, who is planning to work with the Esalen Blowout Center.

K. Dabrowski, Polish research psychiatrist and author of *Positive Disintegration.*

Mental Research Institute, Palo Alto, California.

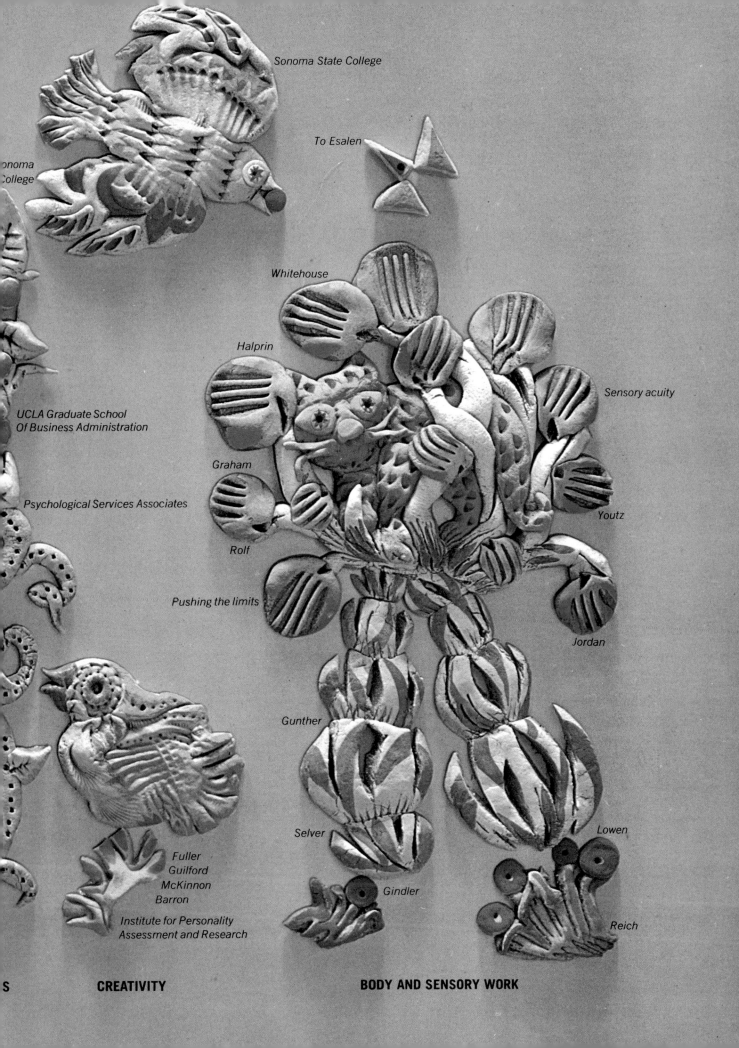

Sonoma State College

To Esalen

onoma
College

Whitehouse

Halprin

Sensory acuity

UCLA Graduate School
Of Business Administration

Graham

Psychological Services Associates

Youtz

Rolf

Pushing the limits

Jordan

Gunther

Selver

Lowen

Fuller
Guilford
McKinnon
Barron

Gindler

Institute for Personality
Assessment and Research

Reich

S   **CREATIVITY**   **BODY AND SENSORY WORK**

FRANK   GREER   HESS   HOFFMAN   LATANE   MC CONNELL   MILGRAM   MOWRER

JEROME D. FRANK ("The Face of the Enemy"), a professor of psychiatry at Johns Hopkins University School of Medicine, is a member of the National Board, National Committee for a Sane Nuclear Policy, and a member of the Board of Directors, Council for a Livable World. In 1966 he testified by invitation before the Senate Foreign Relations Committee on the psychological aspects of international conflict. In 1967 he published *Sanity and Survival* (Random House), on the psychological aspects of disarmament.

After completing his undergraduate work at Harvard, Frank studied with Kurt Lewin at the University of Berlin. He returned to Harvard for his Ph.D. in psychology, then spent a postdoctoral year at Cornell with Lewin. Study for his M.D. at Harvard was followed by psychiatric training at the Henry Phipps Psychiatric Clinic at Johns Hopkins. Dr. Frank is past president of both the Society for the Psychological Study of Social Issues and the American Psychopathological Association.

SCOTT GREER ("The Shaky Future of Local Government") received his B.A. in sociology and English literature from Baylor University and earned his Ph.D. at UCLA. He taught initially at Occidental College, where he was research director for the Laboratory for Urban Culture.

In 1956 he was chief sociologist with the Metropolitan St. Louis Survey. This study was published as part of the volume *Exploring the Metropolitan Community*, edited by John C. Bollens (University of California Press, 1961).

Dr. Greer's publications in the field of urban studies are numerous, the more recent having been *Metropolitics: A Study of Political Culture* (Wiley, 1963), and *Urban Renewal and American Cities* (Bobbs-Merrill, 1965). Dr. Greer is also a poet, and has published

two volumes, the last being *Via Urbana* (A. Swallow, 1963). Until recently he was director for Metropolitan Studies at Northwestern University, where he is a professor of sociology and political science.

ROBERT D. HESS ("Political Attitudes in Children") did his undergraduate work at the University of California, Berkeley, then spent almost 20 years at the University of Chicago. In 1966 he went to Stanford as a fellow at the Center for Advanced Study in the Behavioral Sciences and is now Lee Jacks Professor of Child Education and professor of psychology at Stanford.

Hess received his Ph.D. in human development from Chicago in 1950. He was chairman of the Committee on Human Development from 1959 to 1964, then professor of human development and education, and, during his last few years on the Chicago faculty, director of the Urban Child Center and the Early Education Research Center.

MARTIN HOFFMAN ("Homosexuality and Social Evil"), a University of Illinois M.D., has been a psychiatric resident at the State University of New York at Syracuse and at Mount Zion Hospital and Medical Center in San Francisco. Dr. Hoffman, the author of *The Gay World* (Basic Books, 1968), serves as consultant to the Gender Identity Research and Treatment Clinic at the UCLA School of Medicine. He is also staff psychiatrist at the San Francisco Health Department's Center for Special Problems.

BIBB LATANÉ (coauthor, "When Will People Help in a Crisis?") took his Ph.D. in psychology at the University of Minnesota and then taught for six years at the Department of Social Psychology at Columbia University. He is now associate professor of psychology at Ohio

State University. Dr. Latané's research efforts span the general area of social and emotional behavior. In the course of his research, he has worked with such diverse species as psychopathic criminals, albino rats, Navy enlisted men, gerbils, sky divers and college sophomores. In addition to his research and teaching responsibilities, Dr. Latané is consulting editor of *Sociometry*. He is also editing a series of introductory paperbacks in social psychology.

JAMES V. MCCONNELL, contributing editor, is professor of psychology at the University of Michigan; he is best known for his studies of memory transfer at the physiological level and for his abiding interest in the theory and composition of science fiction. With a Ph.D. under Dallenbach at the University of Texas, he has taught at Texas and Michigan. He also works as research psychologist with the Mental Health Research Institute at Michigan. He has consulted for the Smithsonian Institution, Department of Defense, and Department of Commerce on a variety of problems connected with his interests in motivation and learning. A frequent contributor to scientific journals, McConnell also edits *The Journal of Biological Psychology* and the popular, though serious, *Worm-Runners Digest*.

STANLEY MILGRAM ("The Small-World Problem") is professor of psychology at the Graduate Center of The City University of New York. In 1960 he received his Ph.D. in social psychology from Harvard. After spending three years at Yale University as assistant professor of psychology, Dr. Milgram returned to Harvard for four years of teaching and research and thence to his present position. His publications have been translated into French, German, Italian, Hebrew, and Spanish, and in 1964 the American Association for the Advance-

MURPHY   SIMON   STOLLER   TALBOT   THOMPSON   UHR   ZIMBARDO

ment of Science awarded him its socio-psychological prize for his research on obedience to authority.

O. HOBART MOWRER ("Civilization and Its Malcontents") is known for his work as the founder of integrity therapy. A president of the American Psychological Association from 1953 to 1954, Dr. Mowrer received his Ph.D. from Johns Hopkins University in 1932, and since 1948 has been research professor of psychology at the University of Illinois.

He has an active interest in the rehabilitation of drug addicts through programs like the one offered at Synanon House in California. A workshop at another rehabilitation center, Daytop Village in New York, provided Dr. Mowrer with some of the material for his present article.

MICHAEL MURPHY ("Esalen") did graduate work in philosophy, served in the Army, then went to an ashram in India and studied meditation for a year and a half. In 1961, he and his brother, Dennis (film writer and author of the novel *The Sergeant*), inherited 150 acres of coastal land just south of Carmel, California— a mile-long strip complete with hot springs, cypress trees, cabins, and a lodge, just perfect for seminars. In 1962, he and Dick Price, who was a classmate at Stanford, began programs at Esalen seeking to understand the limits of human potential.

WILLIAM SIMON ("Sex and American Society"), who received his Ph.D. from the University of Chicago, is a member of the American Sociological Association, the Society for the Study of Social Problems, and the American Civil Liberties Union. He is presently a program supervisor in sociology and anthropology at the Institute for Juvenile Research in Chicago. He and his wife, Marlene, have

in press a book entitled *Community*, to be published by Scott, Foresman.

FREDERICK H. STOLLER ("The Long Weekend"), after receiving his doctorate from UCLA, where he was trained in classical clinical psychology, served as a senior psychologist at Camarillo State Hospital. There he "obtained first-hand experience with people in trouble and learned not to be frightened of them— an important asset." He is now senior research associate at the Public Systems Research Institute and associate professor in the School of Public Administration, University of Southern California. The center is operated under the auspices of the School of Public Administration, and Dr. Stoller finds his contact with an interdisciplinary group studying broader social structures a valuable supplement to his primary work on research and training in group methods.

ALLAN TALBOT ("The Lessons of New Haven—the Erstwhile Model City"), as a member of Mayor Richard C. Lee's staff, was directly involved with New Haven's urban renewal—first as the mayor's administrative assistant, later as assistant director of the New Haven Redevelopment Agency, and in 1964–1965 as director of administration for Community Progress, Inc., the city's antipoverty program. Talbot's book, *The Mayor's Game* (Harper & Row, 1967), was a widely read account of those years of promise in New Haven. He is presently director of Program Development at the Urban Development Corporation. Mr. Talbot received his B.A. and M.A. in political science from Rutgers University.

WILBUR THOMPSON ("The City as a Distorted Price System") is a distin-

guished figure in a relatively neglected field, urban economics. He received his B.A. degree from what was then Wayne University in Detroit; his M.A. and Ph.D. in economics from the University of Michigan. Since 1949 he has been mostly at Wayne State University, where he is now a professor of economics. He is a prodigious writer, and his book *A Preface to Urban Economics* (Johns Hopkins, 1965) is a classic in its highly specialized field. For the past four years he has been a regular lecturer in the Urban Policy Conferences conducted in numerous U.S. cities by the Brookings Institution.

LEONARD AND ELIZABETH UHR ("The Quiet Revolution") are both prolific writers. Mrs. Uhr is a novelist, and her husband is the author of four books and more than 70 experimental and theoretical papers. Currently a professor in the Computer Sciences Department at the University of Wisconsin, Dr. Uhr is considered one of the most knowledgeable drug experts today. He graduated from Princeton and received his Ph.D. from the University of Michigan, where he remained until 1965 as research psychologist in the Mental Health Research Institute and an associate professor in the Department of Psychology. The objective behavioral measurement of the effects of psychoactive drugs has occupied much of his time.

PHILIP G. ZIMBARDO ("The Psychology of Police Confessions") received his Ph.D. in psychology from Yale University. He was an associate professor of psychology at New York University, where he received the Distinguished Teacher Award, and has been a visiting professor at Yale, Stanford, and Barnard. He is now a professor at Stanford University.

Bibliographies

I. Cities, Ghettos, and Politics

When Will People Help in a Crisis?

BYSTANDER INTERVENTION IN EMERGENCIES: DIFFUSION OF RESPONSIBILITY. J. M. Darley, B. Latané in *Journal of Personality and Social Psychology*, Vol. 8, pp. 377–383, 1968.

GROUP INHIBITION OF BYSTANDER INTERVENTION IN EMERGENCIES. B. Latané, J. M. Darley in *Journal of Personality and Social Psychology*, Vol. 10, No. 3, p. 215, 1968.

A LADY IN DISTRESS: INHIBITING EFFECTS OF FRIENDS AND STRANGERS ON BYSTANDER INTERVENTION. B. Latané, J. Rodin in *Journal of Experimental Social Psychology*, Vol. 5, No. 2, p. 189, 1969.

MURDER THEY HEARD. S. Milgram, P. Hollander in *The Nation*, Vol. 198, pp. 602–604, 1964.

RISK-TAKING AS A FUNCTION OF THE SITUATION, THE PERSON, AND THE GROUP. N. Kogan, M. Wallach in *New Directions in Psychology III.* Holt, Rinehart and Winston, 1967.

THIRTY-EIGHT WITNESSES. A. M. Rosenthal. McGraw-Hill, 1964.

THE THREAT OF IMPENDING DISASTER. G. H. Grosser, H. Wechsler, M. Greenblatt, eds. M. I. T. Press, 1964.

The Shaky Future of Local Government

COMMUNITAS: MEANS OF LIVELIHOOD AND WAYS OF LIFE. Paul and Percival Goodman. University of Chicago Press, 1947.

GOVERNING THE METROPOLIS. S. A. Greer. Wiley, 1962.

NEGRO POLITICS; THE SEARCH FOR LEADERSHIP. J. Q. Wilson. Free Press, 1960.

REVEILLE FOR RADICALS. S. Alinsky. University of Chicago Press, 1946.

URBAN RENEWAL AND AMERICAN CITIES. S. A. Greer. Bobbs-Merrill, 1965.

The Lessons of New Haven— the Erstwhile Model City

DIMENSIONS OF METROPOLITANISM. J. P. Picard. Research Monograph 14. Urban Land Institute, 1967.

THE FIFTEENTH WARD AND THE GREAT SOCIETY. W. L. Miller. Houghton Mifflin, 1966.

THE MAYOR'S GAME. A. R. Talbot. Harper & Row, 1967.

REPORT OF THE NATIONAL ADVISORY COMMISSION ON CIVIL DISORDERS. U.S. Government Printing Office, March, 1968.

URBAN AMERICA: GOALS AND PROBLEMS. Subcommittee on Urban Affairs, Joint Economic Committee, Congress of the United States, U.S. Government Printing Office, 1967.

WHO GOVERNS? R. A. Dahl. Yale University Press, 1961.

The City as a Distorted Price System

MICHIGAN IN THE 1970's. W. Haber, W. A. Spivey, M. R. Warshaw, eds. University of Michigan Bureau of Business Research, 1965.

PLANNING FOR A NATION OF CITIES. Sam B. Warner Jr., ed. M.I.T. Press, 1965.

A PREFACE TO URBAN ECONOMICS. W. R. Thompson. Johns Hopkins Press, 1965.

THE RATE AND DIRECTION OF INVENTIVE ACTIVITY: ECONOMIC AND SOCIAL FACTORS. A report of a Conference of the Universities—National Bureau Committee for Economic Research, Princeton University Press, 1962.

REGIONAL ACCOUNTS FOR POLICY DECISIONS. W. Hirsch, ed. Johns Hopkins Press, 1966.

TAMING MEGALOPOLIS. H. W. Eldredge, ed. Doubleday-Anchor, 1967.

URBAN RESEARCH AND POLICY PLANNING. L. F. Schnore, H. Fagin, eds. Sage Publications, 1967.

The Small-World Problem

MATHEMATICAL MODELS IN THE SOCIAL SCIENCES. J. G. Kemeny, J. L. Snell. Blaisdell, 1962.

MATHEMATICAL MODELS OF SOCIAL INTERACTION. A. Rapoport in *Handbook of Mathematical Psychology*, Vol. 2, Chap. 14. D. Luce, R. Bush, E. Galanter, eds. Wiley, 1963.

STRUCTURAL MODELS: AN INTRODUCTION TO THE THEORY OF DIRECTED GRAPHS. F. Harary, R. Z. Norman, D. Cartwright. Wiley, 1965.

Political Attitudes in Children

CHILDREN AND THE DEATH OF A PRESIDENT: MULTI-DISCIPLINARY STUDIES. M. Wolfenstein, G. Kliman. Doubleday, 1965.

CHILDREN AND POLITICS. F. Greenstein. Yale University Press, 1965.

DEVELOPMENT OF POLITICAL ATTITUDES IN CHILDREN. R. D. Hess, J. V. Torney. Aldine, 1967.

POLITICAL LIFE: WHY PEOPLE GET INVOLVED IN POLITICS. R. Lane. Free Press, 1959.

POLITICAL SOCIALIZATION: A STUDY IN THE PSYCHOLOGY OF POLITICAL BEHAVIOR. H. Hyman. Free Press, 1959.

II. Race and Race Relations

The Other Bodies in the River

THE AUTOBIOGRAPHY OF MALCOLM X. Grove Press, 1965.

DARK GHETTO. K. Clark. Harper & Row, 1965.

THE NEGRO AMERICAN. T. Parsons, K. Clark, eds. Houghton Mifflin, 1966.

THE SOULS OF BLACK FOLK. W. E. B. Du Bois. Peter Smith, 1966.

THE WRETCHED OF THE EARTH. F. Fanon. Grove Press, 1963.

Racism and Strategies for Change

BLACK PROTEST. J. Grant. Fawcett, 1967.

COLOR AND RACE. *Journal of the American Academy of Arts and Sciences*, Spring, 1967.

THE NEGRO IN AMERICA. WHAT MUST BE DONE. *Newsweek*, November 20, 1967.

THE NEGRO IN THE TWENTIETH CENTURY. J. H. Franklin, Isidore Star, eds. Vintage, 1967.

THE POLICE ON THE URBAN FRONTIER. G. Edwards. Institute of Human Relations Press, 1968.

RACE AND THE NEWS MEDIA. P. L. Fischer, R. L. Lowenstein, eds. Freedom of Information Center, University of Missouri, Anti-Defamation League, B'nai Brith, 1967.

REPORT OF THE NATIONAL ADVISORY COMMISSION ON CIVIL DISORDERS. Bantam, 1968.

SLAVE AND CITIZEN. F. Tannenbaum. Vintage, 1963.

SLAVERY. A PROBLEM IN AMERICAN INSTITUTIONAL AND INTELLECTUAL LIFE. S. M. Elkins. Grosset and Dunlap, 1963.

Civil Rights and the Vote for President

THE AMERICAN VOTER. A. Campbell, P. E. Converse, W. E. Miller, D. E. Stokes. Wiley, 1960.

BLACK AND WHITE. L. Harris, W. J. Brink. Simon and Schuster, 1967.

THE CASE OF THE MISSING DEMOCRAT. A. Campbell in *New Republic*, July 2, 1956.

THE NATIONAL ELECTION OF 1964. M. C. Cummings, Jr., ed. Brookings Institution, 1966.

THE SHIFTING ROLE OF CLASS IN POLITICAL ATTITUDES AND BEHAVIOR. P. E. Converse in *Readings in Social Psychology*. 3rd ed. E. E. Maccoby, T. M. Newcomb, E. L. Hartley, eds. Holt, Rinehart and Winston, 1958.

STRANGERS NEXT DOOR. R. M. Williams, Jr. Prentice-Hall, 1964.

TRENDS IN WHITE ATTITUDES TOWARD NEGROES. National Opinion Research Center, 1967.

Encounter in Color

CHILDREN OF CRISIS. R. Coles. Little, Brown, 1967.
EXPERIMENTAL EFFECTS IN BEHAVIORAL RESEARCH. R. Rosenthal. Appleton-Century-Crofts, 1966.
IDENTITY AND THE LIFE CYCLE. E. H. Erikson in *Psychological Issues*, Vol. 1, No. 1, 1959.
INTERPERSONAL STYLES AND GROUP DEVELOPMENT. R. Mann. Wiley, 1967.
MICROCOSM: STRUCTURAL, PSYCHOLOGICAL, AND RELIGIOUS EVALUATION IN GROUPS. P. E. Slater. Wiley, 1966.

III.   Aggression and Rebellion

Civilization and Its Malcontents

CIVILIZATION AND ITS DISCONTENTS. S. Freud. Hogarth Press, 1930.
THE CRIMINAL'S PROBLEM WITH PSYCHIATRY. S. L. Halleck in *Psychiatry: Journal for the Study of Interpersonal Processes*, Vol. 23, pp. 409–412, 1960.
THE INSECURE CHILD: OVER-SOCIALIZED OR UNDER-SOCIALIZED? D. R. Peterson in *Morality and Mental Health*. Rand McNally, 1967.
PSYCHIATRY AND THE DILEMMAS OF CRIME. S. L. Halleck. Harper & Row, 1967.
THE STRUCTURE OF HUMAN PERSONALITY. H. H. Eysenck. Macmillan, 1960.

Student Activists: Result, Not Revolt

ACTIVISM AND APATHY IN CONTEMPORARY ADOLESCENTS. J. H. Block, N. Haan, M. Smith in *Contributions to the Understanding of Adolescents*. J. F. Adams, ed. Allyn & Bacon, 1967.
FROM GENERATION TO GENERATION. S. N. Eisenstadt. Free Press, 1956.
THE LIBERATED GENERATION. R. Flacks in *Journal of Social Issues*, Vol. 23, pp. 52–75, July, 1967.
THE PORT HURON STATEMENT. Students for a Democratic Society, 1962.
A PROPHETIC MINORITY. J. Newfield. New American Library, 1967.
STUDENT POLITICS. S. M. Lipset, ed. 1967.
THE UNCOMMITTED. K. Keniston. Harcourt, Brace and World, 1965.

Impulse, Aggression, and the Gun

AGGRESSION AND DEFENSE. C. D. Clemente, D. B. Lindsley, eds. University of California Press, 1967.

AGGRESSION: A SOCIAL-PSYCHOLOGICAL ANALYSIS. L. Berkowitz. McGraw-Hill, 1962.
PSYCHOLOGY OF AGGRESSION. A. H. Buss. Wiley, 1961.
ROOTS OF AGGRESSION: A RE-EXAMINATION OF THE FRUSTRATION-AGGRESSION HYPOTHESIS. L. Berkowitz, ed. Atherton, 1968.
RIOTS, VIOLENCE, AND DISORDER. L. H. Masotti, ed. Sage, 1968.

The Face of the Enemy

AN ALTERNATIVE TO WAR OR SURRENDER. C. E. Osgood. University of Illinois Press, 1962.
THE HUMAN DIMENSION IN INTERNATIONAL RELATIONS. O. Klineberg. Holt, Rinehart and Winston, 1964.
IN COMMON PREDICAMENT: SOCIAL PSYCHOLOGY OF INTERGROUP CONFLICT AND COOPERATION. M. Sherif, C. Sherif. Houghton Mifflin, 1966.
INTERNATIONAL BEHAVIOR. H. Kelman, ed. Holt, Rinehart and Winston, 1965.
THE NATURE OF HUMAN CONFLICT. E. McNeil, ed. Prentice-Hall, 1965.
PSYCHIATRIC ASPECTS OF THE PREVENTION OF NUCLEAR WAR. Committee on Social Issues, Group for the Advancement of Psychiatry, 1964.
SANITY AND SURVIVAL: PSYCHOLOGICAL ASPECTS OF WAR AND PEACE. J. Frank. Random House, 1967.

The Psychology of Police Confessions

THE COMPULSION TO CONFESS. T. Reik. Farrar, Straus & Giroux, 1959.
COMMUNIST INTERROGATION AND INDOCTRINATION OF "ENEMIES OF THE STATE." L. E. Hinkle, H. C. Wolff in *Archives of Neurology and Psychiatry*, Vol. 76, pp. 115–174, August, 1956.
DISTINGUISHING CHARACTERISTICS OF COLLABORATORS AND RESISTERS AMONG AMERICAN PRISONERS OF WAR. E. H. Schein, W. E. Hill, H. L. Williams, A. Lubin in *Journal of Abnormal Social Psychology*, Vol. 55, pp. 197–201, 1957.
PSYCHOLINGUISTICS AND THE CONFESSION DILEMMA. R. Arens, A. Meadow in *Columbia Law Review*, Vol. 56, pp. 19–46, 1956.
THE PSYCHOLOGY OF CONFESSION. M. W. Horowitz in *Journal of Clinical and Experimental Psychopathology*, Vol. 18, pp. 381–382, 1957.
REACTION PATTERNS TO SEVERE, CHRONIC STRESS IN AMERICAN ARMY PRISONERS OF WAR OF THE CHINESE. E. H. Schein in *Journal of Social Issues*, Vol. 13, pp. 21–30, 1957.

SOURCES OF DISTORTION AND DECEPTION IN PRISON INTERVIEWING. N. Johnson in *Federal Probation*, Vol. 20, pp. 43–48, 1956.

IV.   Social Deviancy: Drugs and Sex

The Quiet Revolution

THE BEYOND WITHIN: THE LSD STORY. S. Cohen. Atheneum, 1964.
DRUGS AND PHANTASY: THE EFFECTS OF LSD, PSILOCYBIN, AND SERNYL ON COLLEGE STUDENTS. J. C. Pollard, L. Uhr, E. Stern. Little, Brown, 1966.
THE HALLUCINOGENIC DRUGS. F. Barron, M. E. Jarvik, S. Bunnell, Jr. in *Scientific American*, Vol. 210, No. 4, 1964.
THE HALLUCINOGENIC DRUGS: A PERSPECTIVE WITH SPECIAL REFERENCE TO PEYOTE AND CANNABIS. W. McGlothlin. RAND Corporation, 1964.
UTOPIATES. R. Blum. Atherton Press, 1964.

Daytop Village

DAYTOP LODGE—A NEW TREATMENT APPROACH FOR DRUG ADDICTS. J. A. Shelly, A. Bassin in *Corrective Psychiatry*, Vol. 11, No. 4, pp. 186–195, 1965.
THE NEW GROUP THERAPY. O. H. Mowrer. Van Nostrand, 1964.
REALITY THERAPY: A NEW APPROACH TO PSYCHIATRY. W. Glasser. Harper & Row, 1965.
SO FAIR A HOUSE: THE STORY OF SYNANON. D. Casriel. Prentice-Hall, 1963.

Questions for the Global Conscience

THE CHALLENGE OF MAN'S FUTURE. H. Brown. Viking, 1954.
DOCTRINES AND ATTITUDES OF MAJOR RELIGIONS IN REGARD TO FERTILITY. R. M. Fagley in *World Population Conference*, Vol. III, United Nations, 1967.
THE KHANNA STUDY. J. B. Wyon, J. E. Gordon in *Harvard Medical Alumni Bulletin*, No. 41, pp. 24–28, 1967.
POPULATION AND FOOD SUPPLIES: THE EDGE OF THE KNIFE. R. Revelle in *Proceedings of the National Academy of Science*, Vol. LVI, No. 2, pp. 328–351, 1966.
POPULATION PROCESSES IN SOCIAL SYSTEMS. J. M. Beshers. Free Press, 1967.
RELIGIOUS FACTORS IN THE POPULATION PROBLEM. A. J. Dyck in *The Religious Situation*. D. Cutler, ed. Beacon Press, 1968.

Tell us what you think

All over the country today students are taking an active role in the quality of their education. They're telling administrators what they like and what they don't like about their campus communities. They're telling teachers what they like and what they don't like about their courses.

This response card offers you a unique opportunity as a student to tell a publisher what you like and what you don't like about his book.

EVALUATION QUESTIONNAIRE

1. **Your school:** _____

   _____

2. **Your year:** ☐ Freshman ☐ Sophomore ☐ Junior ☐ Senior
   ☐ Graduate student

3. **Title of course in which READINGS was assigned:** _____

   _____

4. **Course level:** ☐ First year ☐ Second year ☐ Third year
   ☐ Fourth year ☐ Graduate

5. **Length of course:** ☐ Quarter ☐ Trimester ☐ Semester ☐ Year

6. **How many articles were you assigned to read?** _____

7. **How many articles did you read that weren't assigned?** _____

8. **Did you find the majority of the articles:**
   ☐ Very interesting ☐ Fairly interesting ☐ Not interesting

9. **If you think there's a gap between what you're studying and what's going on in the world today, did you find that the articles in READINGS helped bridge that gap?** ☐ Yes ☐ No

   If yes, how?
   ☐ Shed light on events in the news.
   ☐ Offered insight into personal problems and gave me ideas about solving them.
   ☐ Discussed the problems of individuals in ways that helped explain people I know.
   ☐ Offered insight into social problems and gave me ideas about solving them.
   ☐ Gave me information and arguments for attacking ideas I disagree with.
   ☐ Presented information and arguments that changed my own ideas.
   ☐ Other:_____

   _____

   _____

   If no, why?
   ☐ Seemed irrelevant to events in the news.
   ☐ Didn't identify personal problems important to me or suggest ways to solve them.
   ☐ Didn't make discussion of individual problems relevant to people I know.
   ☐ Didn't identify social problems important to me or suggest ways to solve them.
   ☐ Discussed individual and social problems but didn't make them important to me personally or show ways to deal with them.
   ☐ Didn't cause me to change my ideas about any important topic.
   ☐ Other:_____

10. **How interesting were the materials used in your course? How do you rate them?**
    Rating: 1 = Most interesting   7 = Least interesting
    Materials used:

	1	2	3	4	5	6	7
☐ **READINGS**	☐ 1	☐ 2	☐ 3	☐ 4	☐ 5	☐ 6	☐ 7
☐ Textbook	☐ 1	☐ 2	☐ 3	☐ 4	☐ 5	☐ 6	☐ 7
☐ Lectures	☐ 1	☐ 2	☐ 3	☐ 4	☐ 5	☐ 6	☐ 7
☐ Films	☐ 1	☐ 2	☐ 3	☐ 4	☐ 5	☐ 6	☐ 7
☐ Laboratory work	☐ 1	☐ 2	☐ 3	☐ 4	☐ 5	☐ 6	☐ 7
☐ Paperbacks	☐ 1	☐ 2	☐ 3	☐ 4	☐ 5	☐ 6	☐ 7
☐ Other_____	☐ 1	☐ 2	☐ 3	☐ 4	☐ 5	☐ 6	☐ 7

11. **How helpful were the introductions to each article?**
    ☐ Very helpful   ☐ Sometimes helpful
    ☐ Not helpful   ☐ Did not read them

12. **Would additional materials printed with each article have been helpful?** ☐ Yes ☐ No
    If yes, what kind?
    ☐ Marginal outlines of key points.
    ☐ Review questions.
    ☐ Glossaries of themes and concepts.
    ☐ Other: _____

13. **What textbook did you use?**
    Author(s):_____

    Title:_____

    How would you rate it?

    Content:
    ☐ Covered each area fully.
    ☐ Too much on some topics, not enough on others.
    ☐ Seemed up to date.
    ☐ Seemed out of date.

    ☐ Other: _____

    _____

    Level:
    ☐ Easy to read and generally interesting.
    ☐ Hard to read: explanations too complicated.
    ☐ Quality of writing not interesting.

    ☐ Other: _____

    _____

    Illustrations:
    ☐ Easy to understand, attractive, informative.
    ☐ Inadequate: hard to understand.
    ☐ Unclear, unattractive.
    ☐ Didn't help in understanding.

    ☐ Other: _____

    _____

14. **Are laboratory experiments part of your course work?**
    ☐ Yes   ☐ No
    If no, would you have liked to have had the equipment and opportunity to do psychological experiments as part of your course work? ☐ Yes ☐ No

15. **Comments on course, text materials, etc.:** _____

    _____

    _____

    _____

    _____

    _____

16. **What do you think of this questionnaire?** _____

    _____

    _____

    _____

    _____

    _____

Sex and American Society

CHANGING NATURE OF MAN. J. H. Van Den Berg. Dell, 1961.

HUMAN SEXUAL RESPONSE. W. Masters, V. Johnson. Little, Brown, 1966.

LOVE IN INFANT MONKEYS. H. Harlow in *Scientific American*, Vol. 200, pp. 68–74, 1959.

ON PSYCHOSEXUAL DEVELOPMENT. W. Simon, J. Gagnon in *Handbook of Socialization Theory and Research.* David Goslin, ed. McGraw-Hill (in press).

PATTERNS OF CHILD REARING. R. R. Sears, E. E. Maccoby, Harry Levin. Harper & Row, 1957.

THE PEDAGOGY OF SEX. W. Simon, J. Gagnon in *Saturday Review*, Vol. 91, pp. 74–76, 1967.

SEX AND BEHAVIOR. F. Beach, ed. Wiley, 1965.

SEXUAL BEHAVIOR IN THE HUMAN FEMALE. A. Kinsey, *et al.* Saunders, 1953.

SEXUAL BEHAVIOR IN THE HUMAN MALE. A. Kinsey, *et al.* Saunders, 1948.

SEXUALITY AND SEXUAL LEARNING IN THE CHILD. J. Gagnon in *Psychiatry*, Vol. 28, pp. 212–228, 1965.

Homosexuality and Social Evil

CITY OF NIGHT. J. Rechy. Grove Press, 1963.

THE GAY WORLD: MALE HOMOSEXUALITY AND THE SOCIAL CREATION OF EVIL. M. Hoffman. Basic Books, 1968.

GIOVANNI'S ROOM. J. Baldwin. Dial Press, 1956.

THE PROBLEM OF HOMOSEXUALITY IN MODERN SOCIETY. H. Ruitenbeek, ed. Dutton, 1963.

SEXUAL INVERSION: THE MULTIPLE ROOTS OF HOMOSEXUALITY. J. Marmor, ed. Basic Books, 1965.

The Long Weekend

FACE TO FACE WITH THE DRUG ADDICT: AN ACCOUNT OF AN INTENSIVE GROUP EXPERIENCE. D. Kruschke, F. H. Stoller in *Federal Probation*, Vol. 31, No. 2, pp. 47–52, 1967.

FOCUSED FEEDBACK: EXTENDING GROUP FUNCTIONS WITH VIDEO TAPE and MARATHON GROUP THERAPY. F. H. Stoller in *Innovations in Group Therapy.* G. M. Gazda, ed. Charles C Thomas, 1967.

GROUP PSYCHOTHERAPY ON TELEVISION: AN INNOVATION WITH HOSPITALIZED PATIENTS. F. H. Stoller in *American Psychologist*, Vol. 22, pp. 158–162, 1967.

THE LEMON EATERS. J. Sohl. Simon and Schuster, 1967.

THE MARATHON GROUP: INTENSIVE PRACTICE OF INTIMATE INTERACTION. G. R. Bach in *Psychological Reports*, Vol. 18, pp. 995–1002, 1966.

THE USE OF FOCUSED FEEDBACK VIA VIDEO TAPE IN SMALL GROUPS. F. H. Stoller in *Explorations in Human Relations Training and Research*, No. 1, National Training Laboratories, National Educational Association, 1966.

Esalen

CONJOINT FAMILY THERAPY. V. Satir. Science and Behavior Books, 1964.

EDUCATION AND ECSTASY. G. Leonard. Delacorte, 1968.

GESTALT THERAPY. F. Perls, R. Hefferline, P. Goodman. Delta, 1951.

JOY. W. Schutz. Grove Press, 1967.

TOWARD A PSYCHOLOGY OF BEING. A Maslow. Van Nostrand, 1962.

Index

Picture Credits

Cover photograph by Gordon Menzie

Photographs by
Raimondo R. Borea: pages 121, 122
Steve McCarroll: pages 2, 8, 14, 18, 20, 58, 66, 76, 82, 100, 112, 130, 142, 148
John Oldenkamp: pages 23, 24, 26, 28, 36, 52, 110 (photographic props by John De Marco), 124, 132, 133, 146
Steve Wells: page 94

Illustrations by
Pam Morehouse: pages 88, 91
Karl Nicholason: pages 4, 46, 48; painting page 63
George Price: pages 64, 138, 139, 140, 153–155
Don Wright: pages 30, 31, 32, 33, 34, 71; design page 88

Design by Tom Gould: pages 44, 94

Bread dough construction for Esalen foldout: Joyce Fitzgerald

David A. Dushkin, *President and Publisher*, CRM BOOKS

Richard L. Roe, *Vice-President, CRM BOOKS, and Director, College Department*
Sales Manager, College Department: Richard M. Connelly
Fulfillment Manager, College Department: Nancy Le Clere
College Department Staff: Elaine Kleiss, Carol Walnum, La Delle Willett

Jean Smith, *Vice-President and Managing Editor*, CRM BOOKS
Editors: Arlyne Lazerson, Gloria Joyce, Cecie Starr, Betsy H. Wyckoff
Editorial Assistants: Susan Ellenbogen, Jacquelyn Estrada, Ann Scales, Donna L. Taylor

Jo Ann Gilberg, *Vice-President, CRM BOOKS, and Director, Manufacturing and Production*
Production Manager: Eugene G. Schwartz
Production Supervisors: Barbara Blum, E. Cecile Mayer
Production Assistants: Georgene Martina, Patricia Perkins
Production Staff: Mona F. Drury, Margaret M. Mesec

Tom Suzuki, *Vice-President, CRM BOOKS, and Director of Design*

Art Director: Leon Bolognese
Designer: George Price
Associate Designers: Catherine Flanders, Reynold Hernandez
Assistant Designer: Robert Fountain
Art Staff: Jacqueline McLoughlin, Kurt Kolbe

Paul Lapolla, *Vice-President, CRM BOOKS, and Director, Psychology Today Book Club*

Assistant: Karen De Laria

Controller: Robert Geiserman
Assistant: Maryann Errichetti

Office Manager: Lynn D. Crosby
Assistant: Janie Fredericks

Officers of Communications/Research/Machines, Inc.
John J. Veronis, *President;* Nicolas H. Charney, *Chairman of the Board;*
David A. Dushkin, *Vice-President;* James B. Horton, *Vice-President*

This book was composed by
American Book–Stratford Press, Inc., New York, New York.
The book was printed and bound by
Kingsport Press, Inc., Kingsport, Tennessee.